The mega-city in Latin America

The mega-city in Latin America

Edited by Alan Gilbert

United Nations
University Press

TOKYO · NEW YORK · PARIS

BFW 7627-4/2

© The United Nations University, 1996

The views expressed in this publication are those of the authors and do not necessarily reflect the views of the United Nations University.

United Nations University Press
The United Nations University, 53-70, Jingumae 5-chome, Shibuya-ku, Tokyo 150, Japan
Tel: (03) 3499-2811   Fax: (03) 3406-7345
Telex: J25442   Cable: UNATUNIV TOKYO

UNU Office in North America
2 United Nations Plaza, Room DC2-1462-70, New York, NY 10017
Tel: (212) 963-6387   Fax: (212) 371-9454
Telex: 422311 UN UI

United Nations University Press is the publishing division of the United Nations University.

Typeset by Asco Trade Typesetting Limited, Hong Kong
Printed by Edwards Brothers, Ann Arbor, Michigan, USA
Cover design by Andrew Corbett

UNUP-935
ISBN 92-808-0935-0
03000 P

Contents

Contents

Tables

Figures

Foreword

With contributions from prominent urban planning scholars and experts in Latin America, *The Mega-city in Latin America* (edited by Alan Gilbert of University College London) represents the latest in a series of books and research outputs from the United Nations University Programme on Mega-cities and Urban Development.

Since Latin America was the first region to witness the rapid rise of mega-cities, the urban development issues addressed in *The Mega-city in Latin America* offer many important lessons to other regions in the world, particularly Pacific Asia. In addition to chapters on individual cities including Buenos Aires, Lima, Mexico City, and Rio de Janeiro, this book also explores important sectoral issues such as public administration, transportation, and housing in urban areas.

With the goal of examining the social, economic, and environmental aspects of large metropolitan centres, the UNU launched this research programme by organizing an international conference on Mega-city Growth and the Future in cooperation with the UN Population Division and the Tokyo Metropolitan Government in 1990. The UNU later initiated an ambitious study of evolving urban systems at the regional level, including Pacific Asia, Africa, and of course, Latin America. *Mega-city Growth and the Future*, the first volume in the series, and

Emerging World Cities in Pacific Asia have already been released, with the volume on Africa in the final editing stage.

As rector of the United Nations University, I am proud that the UNU has been involved in the research and dissemination of mega-city and urban development issues since the early 1990s and has made a valuable contribution to both related academic fields and to the preparatory work of the UN Habitat II Conference.

This work will continue well into the next century through the UNU Institute of Advanced Studies, a new research and training centre that started its activities in 1995 and is located next to the UNU head-quarters in Tokyo, Japan.

Heitor Gurgulino de Souza
UN Under-Secretary General and Rector
United Nations University

Preface

This book will appear during 1996, a significant year for the management of cities because the second United Nations Conference on Human Settlements (Habitat II) will be held in Istanbul in June. That meeting will focus on two themes: the sustainability of human settlement and the need to provide adequate shelter for all. A principal aim of the conference is to convince governments to take appropriate action to "overcome the growing, serious problems of social exclusion and the rapid degradation and disorganization of cities."

The need for such action in Latin America hardly needs emphasizing. By the year 2000, four out of five of the region's inhabitants will live in urban areas and 70 million people will live in the region's five largest cities alone. What is worrying about that fact is that life in those cities is already very difficult for far too many people. Life for the poor demonstrates many of the worst symptoms of the region's underdevelopment: vast areas of shanty towns, insufficient provision of infrastructure of services, and a lack of sufficient well-paid employment. Even the better-off suffer from urban problems, notably from serious traffic congestion, high concentrations of air and water pollution, and the lack of effective urban planning. In most Latin American cities, living conditions today are worse than they were in the middle 1970s; standards of living have deteriorated rather than improved. The only good thing to be said about this deterioration is that it has little to do with the cities' size or with the rate of population growth. Declining living standards have been much more the outcome of the debt crisis, economic recession, and rapid inflation. Bogotá, which escaped from the worst of all of these problems, is the one mega-city where living standards have improved, even though the city's population has been growing very quickly.

What is clearly needed in Latin America is both economic growth and better urban management. Fortunately, the prospects for growth in Argentina, Brazil, Colombia, and Peru are much better than they were in the 1980s; only Mexico continues to suffer badly from economic problems. What is more problematic is the ability of the urban authorities to manage the mega-cities. The aim of this book is to show how those mega-cities fit into their respective national economies and to examine the major problems facing urban management. Of course, the relevant national and local authorities are not unaware of the daunting task facing them; this volume aims to encourage them to face up to some of the problems that they have not always managed to confront in the past.

As editor, I should like to thank the contributors for responding to my frequent requests for changes and additional information, the staff at the United Nations University for their efforts at initiating and financing the study and for publishing this book, and the cartographic unit at University College London for preparing the figures so competently. As a contributor, I should like to thank the British Council, the Institute of Latin American Studies, the Nuffield Foundation, and University College London for funding visits to Latin America.

1

The Latin American mega-city: An introduction

Alan Gilbert

By the year 2000, the world will contain 28 mega-cities with more than eight million people each (UNDIESA and UNU, 1991: 6). Twenty-two of these giants will be in less developed countries and five in Latin America. In 1990, Latin America already contained four such cities (Mexico City, São Paulo, Buenos Aires and Rio de Janeiro) with a combined population of around 50 million (table 1.1, figure 1.1). Approximately one in nine of all Latin Americans lived in these four cities; one in six of the region's urban population. By the year 2000, the region may well contain the world's two largest cities, Mexico City and São Paulo.

The sheer number of people living in Latin America's mega-cities is not the only reason for looking at them carefully. Unfortunately, they also demonstrate many of the worst symptoms of the region's underdevelopment: vast areas of shanty towns, huge numbers of poor people, high concentrations of air and water pollution, and serious levels of traffic congestion. Many observers in Latin America have little confidence that such enormous conglomerations are manageable; many worry about the future. Not untypical are the fears expressed by Sánchez-León (1992: 201) about one of the aspirant mega-cities:

1

Table 1.1 **Latin America's giant cities, 1995**

City	Population (millions)
São Paulo	16.42
Mexico City	15.64
Buenos Aires	10.99
Rio de Janeiro	9.89
Lima	7.45
Bogotá	5.61
Santiago (Chile)	5.07
Belo Horizonte	3.90
Pôrto Alegre	3.35
Recife	3.17
Guadalajara	3.16
Caracas	2.96
Salvador	2.82
Monterrey	2.81
Fortaleza	2.66
Santo Domingo	2.58
Curitiba	2.27
Havana	2.24

Source: United Nations, Department of International Economic and Social Affairs, 1995: 132–9.

The Lima of today, with its population of five million, has changed Peru and these changes are also its problems – because Lima is a problem difficult to unravel. A large part of the population, particularly the children and young people, lives in poverty. These are the children of chaos, of poverty, and of urban violence. This vast population exists in a city that does not offer them any chance of personal and social growth, though it has allowed, and even encouraged, a number of creative, organized initiatives.

What is a mega-city?

Mega-cities are "cities that are expected to have populations of at least eight million inhabitants by the year 2000" (UNDIESA, 1986: iii). Like so many threshold figures used in the social sciences, this minimum size seems to have been plucked from the air. There is no theoretical basis for asserting that a city with eight million people is qualitatively different from one with rather fewer inhabitants. Perhaps for this reason different authorities use widely differing definitions of a mega-city. Although Richardson (1993) and UNDIESA and UNU (1991) use the eight million benchmark, UNCHS (1987: 29),

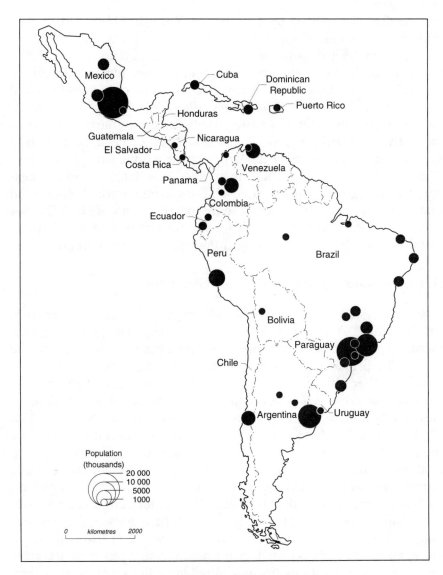

Figure 1.1 **Latin America's giant cities**

Ward (1990: xvii), and the World Bank (1991: 16) use ten million, while Dogan and Kasarda (1988: 18) implicitly use four million.

The term "mega-city" is frequently used as a synonym of words such as "super-city," "giant city," "conurbation," "megalopolis," "world city," and so on. Unfortunately, there is little agreement about what any of those terms means either. Entry to the world of giant cities or

3

metropolises is granted by Dogan and Kasarda (1988: 18) at four million, to the rank of super city by Lowder at five million (1987: 5), and the term "megalopolis" is attributed by Mayhew and Penny (1992) to "any continuous built up area of more than ten million inhabitants." Another term, "world city," seems to be only loosely linked to size at all (Hall, 1977; Friedmann, 1986). World city status, whatever that actually means, is more closely linked to function: "several modestly sized cities, e.g. Washington DC and Geneva, do fulfil true global roles whereas many far larger conurbations patently do not" (Simon, 1992: 185). That there is no adequate definition of a mega-city was recognized by a United Nations seminar which concluded that "there is a need to work out some sort of definition" (UNDIESA and UNU, 1991). While we wait for the formulation of an adequate definition, this book will work with the figure of eight million.

Are mega-cities different from smaller cities?

In what ways do cities with eight million people or more differ from smaller cities? A major difficulty in answering that question is that there is very little firm evidence to support the case one way or the other. The principal difficulty is to separate the effects of size from those of other variables (Richardson, 1973). Certainly, attempts to examine the relationship between size and the benefits and pathologies of urban growth have produced very little in the way of reliable results. There is seldom any clear relationship between size and any single variable of welfare or illfare. For example, while it is very easy to identify Los Angeles, New York, and Rio as giant cities which have terrible crime rates, other mega-cities such as Tokyo and Shanghai do not suffer from a great deal of crime. Nor is there any clear relationship within countries between city size and the quality of life. To continue with the example of crime, violence is worse in Rio than in the much larger São Paulo, in Detroit when compared with its giant neighbour New York, and in six Colombian cities much smaller than Bogotá (Richardson, 1973; *Coyuntura Social*, August 1993: 32).

Equally problematic is the fact that some large cities suffer from different problems than other cities of similar size. Most of the differences can be attributed to intervening variables. Air pollution is worst in cities with a great deal of manufacturing industry (Shanghai, Seoul, and São Paulo), in cities which use coal as a domestic and industrial fuel (Shanghai and Beijing), and in those which suffer regularly from temperature inversions (Los Angeles, Mexico City, and São Paulo).

4

Other large cities suffer much less seriously from air pollution (UNEP, 1992). Certainly the debate about optimum city size suggests that urban problems are not generally worse in giant cities, except possibly with respect to traffic congestion, land prices, and crime. Very large cities also have certain advantages particularly with respect to economic performance and service provision (Richardson, 1973).

Nevertheless, it is possible to argue that size of city does make a difference to certain kinds of problem (Gilbert, 1976; Johnston, 1976). Even if size effects are irregular and unsystematic, that does not mean that size makes no difference. Certainly UNDIESA and UNU (1991: 7) concluded that "there was general agreement that a mega-city is different from an ordinary city." White and Whitney (1992) also believe that city size affects environmental conditions; their argument is summarized in table 1.2.

White and Whitney argue that the poor living in mega-cities in less developed countries face worse problems than those living in smaller cities. The poor are particularly disadvantaged in terms of job opportunities, the cost of food, transportation, the environment, crime, and housing. By contrast, the rich in poor countries face additional

Table 1.2 **Pressure points in cities in less developed and more developed countries by size of centre**

	Less developed countries		More developed countries	
	Large[a]	Small/medium	Large[b]	Small/medium
Job opportunities	H	M	L	M
Food	H	M	L	L
Water	H (L)	M	L	L
Energy	H	H	L	L
Education	H	H	L	L
Transportation	H	M	L	L
Recreation	L	L	M	H
Health	H	H	L	M
Environment	H	L	H	M
Crime	H	L	H	L
Housing	H	L	H	L

Source: White and Whitney, 1992: 16.
H = High pressure point
M = Medium pressure point
L = Low pressure point
(L) = Different strength of pressure point for low-income and MDC populations
a. Plus low-income populations in more developed country cities.
b. Plus upper-income populations in less developed country cities.

difficulties in large cities – higher crime rates, worse housing, and environmental problems – but also benefit, notably through better job opportunities, education, and health facilities.

To what extent can we agree with this argument? A first response to the table is that it is far too generalized. Large cities in less developed countries vary dramatically in their socio-economic characteristics: Buenos Aires has little in common with Calcutta despite their similarity in size. A second response is to query the lack of dimensions. White and Whitney define neither less developed countries nor large cities. It is difficult to know therefore whether they are referring to cities with more than 100,000 people or to those with more than 10 million. How large is a large city? At what point does a country move from the less-developed to the more-developed category? A third response is to question whether the urban poor in developed countries really live lives like those in poor countries. Is inner-city life for the poor in Washington DC really like that of the poor in Calcutta?

To what extent does White and Whitney's estimate of the environmental effects of city size match the evidence from Latin America? Are Buenos Aires, Mexico City, Rio, and São Paulo different from smaller Latin American cities? Unfortunately, there is little in the way of reliable data with which we can compare the quality of life in cities of different sizes. Certainly, no study has calculated an overall indicator of the urban quality of life on which such a comparison could be based. Therefore, we are forced to use more qualitative information, even anecdotal material. On this basis it is possible to argue that the general quality of life in the largest cities is seldom worse than that in smaller cities. Indeed, in many respects it is frequently much better; that is precisely the reason why so many people have moved to Latin America's largest cities over the years. However, as White and Whitney suggest, size is likely to affect different variables and different income groups in different ways. Consequently, it is worth considering each of the variables on their list and to observe how size affects each indicator in Latin American cities.

Job opportunities

Until 1980, there is little doubt that there were more jobs, and more better-paid jobs, in the largest cities. While the situation undoubtedly changed during the economic crisis of the 1980s, particularly in Mexico, it is difficult to conclude that the employment situation is more difficult in large cities than in smaller ones. Table 1.3 certainly suggests that there is no clear pattern. In Brazil, unemployment rates are

Table 1.3 **Unemployment levels by city and country (percentages)**

	1992	1993
Argentina		
Urban areas	7.0	9.6
Buenos Aires	6.7	10.6
Brazil	4.8	n.a.
Main 6 cities	5.8	5.3
Rio de Janeiro	5.4	n.a.
São Paulo	3.4	n.a.
Chile	n.a.	4.6
Santiago	4.9	4.0
Colombia		
Main 4 cities	10.0	8.5
Bogotá	8.4	7.4
Mexico		
35 cities	2.8	3.3[a]
Mexico City	3.4	3.9[a]
Monterrey	3.2	4.9[a]
Tampico	5.0	5.4[a]
Peru	6.7	n.a.
Lima	9.4	9.9
Venezuela	8.0	6.6
Caracas	5.7	n.a.

Sources: ECLAC, 1994; *Revista del Banco de la República*, September 1993; Webb and Baca de Valdez, 1992; INEGI, 1993: table 2.2.
a. First six months of year.

lower in São Paulo and Rio de Janeiro than in the six largest metropolitan areas of the country combined. In Argentina, unemployment is higher in Buenos Aires than in the other urban areas combined, although it is currently higher in Córdoba and Rosario than in the capital. In Colombia, during the 1990s, Bogotá had consistently lower levels of unemployment than Barranquilla, Cali, and Medellín. In Peru, Lima has a higher level of unemployment than the rest of the country; in Venezuela, Caracas has a lower rate. In Mexico, unemployment is higher than average in the capital, but some smaller cities have higher rates of unemployment. In sum, there is no clear conclusion. Differences in occupational structures are clearly more important determinants of unemployment rates than size of city.

Nor do poverty levels seem to be higher in large cities. As Tolosa shows in chapter 9, Rio de Janeiro has a higher proportion of poor people than Belo Horizonte, but São Paulo has a much smaller proportion of poor than either Rio or Belo. Studies comparing living conditions in Buenos Aires and the rest of Argentina show that structural poverty is much less marked in the metropolitan area than in the country as a whole (CEPA, 1992 and 1993). In the cities of Colombia, the incidence of poverty among households in Bogotá in 1985 (18 per cent) was half the rate found in Medellín and was lower than the average of thirteen large Colombian cities combined (27 per cent) (Muñoz, 1991: 286). A United Nations study of poverty levels in the middle 1980s found that levels of poverty in Bogotá, San José, Panama City, Lima, Montevideo, and Caracas were all lower than those found in other urban areas of their respective countries (Fresneda, 1991: 164). Most large cities, therefore, compare very favourably on poverty indicators (Bolvinik, 1991).

Food
Unlike the situation in African cities, the urban poor in Latin America produce little food in their backyards. In this respect there is little difference between living in a small or a large city; there is too little spare land for a productive garden in most Latin American cities. Many people obtain food outside the market, but mainly by retaining links with kin in the countryside and returning frequently for visits. When they come back to the city, the buses are full of chickens, vegetables, fruit, and other kinds of produce. The cost of food in large cities is probably higher than in smaller cities, but much depends on where cities are located. Food costs are much higher in Ciudad Guayana or Brasília than in Caracas or São Paulo. In any case, urban subsidies reduce food costs – at least they did until 1980, when many subsidies were cut. If recent cuts to subsidies have made life more expensive for the poor in large cities, the same is true for the poor in every city. Evidence on malnutrition is scarce but there is little to suggest that it is more rampant in the largest cities; ironically it is usually higher in the rural areas. In the late 1970s, for example, 62 per cent of rural families were malnourished compared to 26 per cent of urban families (Wilkie and Perkal, 1984).

Water
As in most third world countries, water networks are better in most large Latin American cities than in most smaller cities (Richardson,

1993: 50). Chapter 4 shows that service conditions in large cities are generally superior to those in other urban areas of the same country. This is a consequence of huge investments in infrastructure provision during the 1960s and 1970s. The major cities have always received more resources from central government because of their political importance. They have also better organized servicing agencies both because of the pressure exerted by the large number of powerful companies located there and because of their higher per capita tax revenues.

Of course, there are exceptions to this general tendency. Buenos Aires has relatively poor water provision because of the extensive use of wells in large swathes of the city. Similarly, Caracas is served worse than the rest of urban Venezuela. In general, however, the largest cities have better water provision.

Energy
Electricity is available in most homes. There are few reliable data about provision by city but it is certain that most large cities and most industrial centres have the best services. The worst problems are to be found in small cities. In Colombia, indeed, there were numerous civic strikes during the 1980s as a result of such service deficiencies (Santana, 1989).

Education
Literacy rates often show marked differences between cities of different size, although the pattern is not always quite that expected. In Colombia, for example, there is remarkably little difference in the level of education of the population in different cities except at the university level, where Bogotá has far more graduates than most smaller cities (*Coyuntura Social*, May 1990: 43). Similarly, in Brazil, whereas 16 per cent cannot read or write in the intermediate cities of the State of São Paulo, the proportion in Greater São Paulo is 20 per cent (see chapter 10). In general, however, education provision is better in larger than in smaller cities.

Transportation
Figueroa argues in chapter 5 that large cities suffer from worse traffic congestion than smaller cities, that rush-hour flows into central areas are higher, and that average journey times tend to be much longer. Similarly, Richardson (1973: 29) recognizes that "increasing city size probably does generate higher traffic congestion costs." The reason is

that distances between home and workplace are usually longer. It is also because large cities are more prosperous and have higher levels of car ownership. However, even if traffic problems become more acute as cities grow in size, the level of traffic congestion is determined more by a city's shape and its land-use structure. Some small cities suffer badly from traffic congestion.

Recreation

There can be little doubt that the major cities have a much wider array of leisure facilities. There are more cinemas and theatres, more varied and higher-quality shopping facilities, and a wider range of clubs of all types. It is unlikely, of course, that the poor gain access to most of these facilities; even attending a football match is beyond the budget of many. Nevertheless, the range of recreation opportunities is still higher for the poor in the larger cities.

Health

Health care in any Latin American metropolitan areas is generally much better than in the rest of the country. There are more hospitals and doctors per head than in smaller cities because there is a much higher level of private health-care provision. In Brazil, the ratio of doctors, nurses, and hospital beds to inhabitants is superior in Rio and São Paulo compared to the situation in most other metropolitan areas (see chapters 9 and 10). However, health conditions are not better in São Paulo than in the medium-sized cities of the same state. In 1985, life expectancy was one year lower in Greater São Paulo and there was a vast difference in infant mortality rates: 31 babies out of every thousand died in the intermediate cities compared to 54 in the metropolitan area. Greater São Paulo only does better when compared with smaller cities in the north-east of the country, where health conditions are appalling (Wood and Carvalho, 1988).

Environment

Several major Latin American cities, notably Mexico City, Santiago, and São Paulo, suffer badly from air pollution. However, air pollution is not only a function of size. Mexico City suffers because it is an industrial city, has vast numbers of cars, is in a relatively dry part of the country, and suffers from temperature inversions in winter (see chapter 8). Rio de Janeiro suffers less from air pollution because it has sea breezes to clear the fumes. Despite their size, many small cities suffer very badly from air pollution; until action was taken in 1984, the city of Cubatão in Brazil was notorious for its noxious air, the consequence of uncontrolled emissions by heavy industries in a location prone to temperature inversions.

Crime
Pinheiro (1993: 3) argues that "it is clear that the rapid growth of large cities and the cramming of their increasingly impoverished inhabitants into restricted areas has undermined sociability and increased the level of violence occurring in conflicts." Richardson (1973: 102) agrees, although with an important proviso: "In conclusion, the evidence is clear that the incidence of crime is higher in big cities than in smaller towns, and in urban than in rural areas. The social and economic costs of crime are greater for big city residents than for others ... [nevertheless] it is much less convincing to argue that more crime is a direct result of city size." Evidence from Latin America shows that certain large cities have lower crime rates than some smaller cities. In Colombia, the murder rate in Medellín is much higher than that in Bogotá.

Housing
Chapter 4 shows that size of city influences residential tenure. While the evidence is hardly conclusive, La Paz, São Paulo, Bogotá, Mexico City, and Caracas all have distinctly lower rates of home ownership than their respective national urban averages. Of course, the relationship between size and ownership is not close because too many other variables influence the level of ownership (Gilbert and Varley, 1991). Nevertheless, there is a systematic tendency for larger cities to have higher levels of rental tenure. Richardson (1993: 39) attempts to explain this finding in terms of the cost of land and infrastructure: "Land values are an exponential function of city size ... For most households, accommodation costs in large cities are usually higher than in smaller cities."

Overall, therefore, the case that size of city makes a real difference to living standards in Latin America is unproven. Size probably causes additional problems in terms of transport, crime, and housing, but produces clear advantages in terms of work, infrastructure, and services. Poverty indicators also tend to be lower in large cities. Unfortunately, this kind of analysis does not take us very far, given that it takes no account of government policy. For many years, Latin American governments tended to pamper their largest cities. Not only did such cities contain a significant proportion of active voters, they also had most of the gossiping classes. In so far as the largest cities were also capital cities, governments were particularly sensitive to protest in their backyards. Mega-cities needed to be placated and, consequently, large cities did well in terms of government spending. Large-city bias meant that both rich and poor were treated rather better than their cousins elsewhere.

Despite this analytical problem I would suggest that mega-cities do face special problems in three important areas which have yet to be addressed. The first is in the area of public administration. Running a large city is complex and is made more difficult by the way so many giant cities have spread into neighbouring administrative areas. Of course, such problems are not peculiar to large cities. As Davey (1993: 3) points out: "Porto Alegre, a city of 1.4 million people, is only the largest of 22 municipalities in a metropolitan region of 2.5 million [and] Recife, with 1.3 million people, is one of 12 municipalities in a metropolitan region of 2.3 million." Nevertheless, the problems are bound to be more serious as cities grow and spread into neighbouring areas.

A second problem relates to the issue of local democracy. It is difficult for governments to consult their populations in smaller cities but it is particularly difficult in a city of, say, 15 million people. This is perhaps a contributory factor in explaining why so few capital cities have popularly elected local administrations (see chapter 3).

Finally, the issue of social equity is more complicated in large cities. Chapters 6 to 11 are consistent in deploring the high level of inequality in Latin America's largest cities and in arguing that the distribution of income has deteriorated in recent years. And, although there is little evidence that levels of income inequality are higher in large cities than in smaller cities, the poor are more likely to be segregated in distant ghettoes in the mega-cities. Because of the larger distances and the larger settlements in giant cities, rich and poor are almost bound to live further from one another (but see chapter 4). While this is hardly likely to affect their social lives – rich and poor would not mix anyway – many would argue that healthy cities should not be so starkly divided. People in different income groups should come into contact on a regular basis.

The rich certainly gain more from living in large cities than the poor. The rich are more likely to get jobs, the poor less likely; service provision for the rich is good, that for the poor problematic. Critically, the rich are able both to benefit from the advantages of large cities and to escape most of the diseconomies. Thus, even if average conditions are better in the mega-cities, the poor may gain little advantage. If the poor gain from superior infrastructure, such as education and water supply, other apparently superior facilities may not help them. Large cities may have excellent hospitals, clubs, restaurants, and universities, but most of these are open only to those with money. The poor may as well be living in a different city as far as these kinds of facility are concerned. Similarly, the range of better-quality jobs available in the largest cities benefits the poor only in so far as such jobs create more work in lower-paid activities. The poor, lacking university education and appropriate social skills, will not gain access to highly paid forms of employment. Many of the advantages of large cities, therefore, are not on offer to the masses.

The poor also reap more of the disadvantages. In so far as levels of car ownership are much higher in large cities, traffic congestion is worse. Of course the rich are also delayed by traffic jams, but the affluent can listen to their car stereos, whereas the poor are held up in crowded buses. Similarly, air and water pollution is likely to affect the poor much more than the rich. Indeed, those with enough money can buy accommodation in the least polluted areas. Pollution does reach the high-income suburbs in some Latin American cities, but the rich always live in the least affected areas. The rich can also escape more easily from noise and pollution. They belong to country clubs, and they can also get out of the city at weekends because they are more likely to own a car and even a second home. In sum, urban problems in large cities affect rich and poor in very different ways.

Should anything be done to slow down the growth of Latin America's big cities?

Whatever we conclude about the quality of life in giant cities, many observers argue that their growth should be slowed (see Gilbert and Gugler (1992: chap. 8) for a more detailed summary). First, they are draining resources from the rest of the country. As Sachs (1988: 340) puts it: "Large cities absorb above all the young and enterprising labor force. The distribution of costs and gains between the hinterland and the large city is thus once more biased in favor of the city: the countryside bears the social cost of bringing up this labor force. The benefit of their work accrues to the cities, except for the remittances of part of their meager pay to families left behind." Second, whether or not they are too large, the major cities are growing too rapidly. As Teune (1988: 373) puts it: "It may be that most patholo-

13

gies of large cities are short-term effects of growth rather than inherent in them as a particular form of human organization." Finally, "because of their complexity, the life-supporting systems of large cities are highly vulnerable" (Sachs, 1988: 345). The danger is that this vulnerability may be "transformed into catastrophic realities" (ibid.: 347).

To many writers, the answer to these problems is to stem the tide of growth. According to Max-Neef (1992: 97) "the sensible move would be to revitalize the small cities – victims of a mistaken idea of progress – that are struggling to survive." Similarly, Wilhelm (1992: 199) asserts that "Latin American countries should encourage stronger networks of cities in order to arrest the intense concentration of urban life in one or two megacities. This requires the growth and development of middle-sized cities."

This kind of view dominated thinking in Latin America for many years and was the basic premise on which many regional development programmes were built. The construction of new cities, such as Brasília and Ciudad Guayana, the establishment of regional development agencies and infrastructure programmes, as in Amazonia, and the popularity of industrial decentralization programmes throughout the region, all reflected both a real and a rhetorical desire to slow metropolitan expansion. Large cities were seemingly both inefficient and inequitable; they were draining the lifeblood of the nation; they were likely to lead to a social explosion; they demonstrated every conceivable form of social pathology. Their growth should be slowed.

Unfortunately, regional planning in Latin America has not been a huge success. With the exception of Cuba, government action has never managed to stem the tide of migrants to the major cities, to stimulate growth in most poor regions, or to help the poor, even in regions where economic growth occurred (Aguilar-Barajas, 1990; Auty, 1990; Boisier, 1987; Gilbert and Goodman, 1976; Goldsmith and Wilson, 1991). As de Mattos (1990: 26) puts it: "after three decades of effort ... the experience of regional planning ... has led to results which, in the best of cases, can only be called modest."

Perhaps the most damning indictment of regional planning and deliberate efforts to slow metropolitan expansion in Latin America is that the pace of metropolitan growth slowed during the 1980s, precisely the time when regional planning and deliberate government intervention was at its weakest (Gilbert, 1993). Chapter 2 shows that there was little growth in any of Latin America's mega-cities during the 1980s. Among the largest seven cities only Bogotá and Lima grew

14

by more than 2 per cent per annum and Buenos Aires, Rio de Janeiro, and Mexico City grew annually by only 1 per cent.

The pace of growth of the major cities slowed because of changes in the wider economic and social environment. As the basis for development changed during the 1980s, the major cities were disadvantaged. The manufacturing plants that were so favoured by the import-substituting industrialization model and which clustered in the major cities in the 1960s and 1970s suffered badly during the 1980s. Structural adjustment and the new export-oriented model of development decimated much of Latin America's domestic industry. Recession and the removal of urban subsidies hit producers and consumers hard. Trade liberalization allowed foreign manufacturers to compete in Latin America's previously protected markets. The result was sometimes terrible for the major cities. Mexico City lost one-quarter of its manufacturing jobs between 1980 and 1988, and, in Argentina, Córdoba and Rosario lost large numbers of manufacturing jobs during the early 1990s.

In the past, "many government policies [had] unintended spatial impacts distorting the spatial allocation of resources and in general unnecessarily increasing the degree of urban concentration" (Henderson, 1991: 223). Today, the situation has changed and many major cities find themselves in a far less favourable position as a result of international competition. Some Latin American mega-cities will prosper but others will not. Inefficient companies in the giant cities are in no position to sell goods abroad, and many have already gone out of business.

A second change that has slowed the growth of the major cities is the movement of industrial companies out of the metropolitan areas into smaller cities nearby. This process has been under way around Buenos Aires, São Paulo, and Mexico City for some years but the pace of change accelerated during the 1970s and 1980s (Rofman, 1974; Gilbert, 1974). There are now clear signs of an emerging polycentric urban form (Richardson, 1989). This process is very marked in the vicinity of São Paulo, where "many branch and assembly plants are locating in industrial towns within a 200-km radius of the city of São Paulo such as São José dos Campos, Piraciciba, Americana, Limeira, Rio Claro, and Campinas ... In other words, we are witnessing the extension of the localization economies of existing industrial complexes from a strictly 'urban' to a somewhat broader 'regional' scale" (Storper, 1991: 61–2).

The final change to have affected the mega-cities is the slowing of migration as a result of economic decline. During the 1980s, people stopped moving to Latin America's mega-cities in such massive numbers. Chapter 2 shows that, during the 1980s, more people moved out of Caracas, Santiago, and Mexico City than moved in. This change in the normal pattern may well continue.

Under these circumstances, the argument that Latin America's largest cities are too large is irrelevant. In any case, since government efforts to slow urban growth in the past were unsuccessful, the reintroduction of similar programmes is hardly to be recommended. Even if it were recommended, few governments would accept such advice. The world has changed and most Latin American governments seem determined to reduce the level of state intervention. They believe that the market should determine the location of economic activity, not the state. Even if some governments are still tempted to intervene, savage cuts in their budgets make that difficult. Decentralization was always conducted in a rather expensive way; incentives were always preferred to prohibition. Now that governments have fewer resources they cannot build new cities, industrial estates, or major infrastructural projects without major private-sector backing. As such, explicit spatial policies are no longer in favour. Few attempts will be made to build grandiose new capital cities in Latin America in the near future (Gilbert, 1989).

The future for Latin America's cities

World roles

Latin America's largest cities prospered during the era of import substitution. They gained because they attracted most of the new manufacturing plants. Capital cities also benefited from huge expansions in the government bureaucracy required to operate that developmental model. The 1980s saw a break in that approach and the onset of a regime more committed to free trade and market forces. Over the last twenty years, Latin America has become more integrated into the world economy. The conventional wisdom has been that Latin America should seek to develop more exports. To do this, governments should devalue the national currency, make their exports more competitive, and encourage local companies to seek out foreign markets. Most Latin American governments have encouraged this trend and have been strongly supported from Washington.

A second element in Latin America's integration into the world

Table 1.4 **Economic growth in selected Latin American countries, 1980–1993 (annual growth in GDP)**

Country	1980–84	1985–89	1990–93
Argentina	−3.0	−2.3	5.9
Brazil	−0.5	2.5	0.0
Chile	−0.1	4.8	6.0
Colombia	−1.5	3.0	3.5
Mexico	−0.6	−1.2	2.9
Peru	−2.4	−2.5	0.1
Venezuela	−3.5	−0.9	5.7

Source: ECLAC, 1992 and 1993.

economy is the opening of its markets to imports. Country after country has cut its previous levels of protection. With the signing of GATT, with the various integration schemes within the Americas (NAFTA, Mercosur and the Group of Three), and with reductions in import tariffs and constraints on overseas capital, Latin America's major cities are functioning in a very different economic environment. How they will cope cannot be answered simply because they vary so much. For a start, each of their national economies is very different. Some have undoubtedly recovered from the impact of the 1980s and have restructured their economies in ways which will make them more competitive internationally. Chile, Colombia, and Mexico have entered the new liberalization phase enthusiastically; Brazil and Peru much less whole-heartedly. Certainly recent records of economic growth show considerable differences. Table 1.4 reveals that some Latin American economies have been expanding, while others have stood still. Clearly, the prospects for each of the major cities depend critically on the state of their respective national economies.

Even where liberalization is leading to faster economic growth, it cannot be assumed that every urban area will benefit: the local impact of liberalization is likely to differ considerably between areas. Mexico already provides a good illustration of the variable impact of this process. From the late 1980s, Mexico shifted from being one of Latin America's most protected countries to one of its most open. It continues to follow this strategy because it has the advantage of sharing a three-thousand-kilometre border with the world's largest market. During the 1980s, integration led to a huge expansion in manufacturing employment along the northern frontier. The number of workers in the *maquiladoras* (export processing plants) increased from 75,000

17

in 1976 to 470,000 in 1993 (INEGI, 1993). At the same time, Mexico City and the other major industrial cities lost out as manufactured imports helped put uncompetitive plants out of business.

The future of the giant cities depends, therefore, upon their ability to adapt to the new competitive environment. They need to maintain their share of national production, competing successfully with foreign imports, and they need to participate more actively in export production. Some major cities in Latin America look well placed to do this. There is little doubt that São Paulo will thrive because it contains Brazil's most efficient industries and most of its research and information technology capacity. Similarly, Bogotá seems to be flourishing despite trade liberalization, whereas Colombia's traditional industrial centre, Medellín, is doing less well. But the futures of Caracas, Lima, and Rio de Janeiro seem much less assured. Rio might be able to take on some of the dimensions of a "world city," particularly in terms of media, communications, and tourist functions, but it is much less likely that Lima ever will (Friedmann, 1986; Chase-Dunn, 1985). The ability of each of the largest cities to prosper in the future is explored in some detail in chapters 6 to 11.

Coping with urban problems

Competent urban management is vital in mega-cities. However, it is extremely difficult to maintain even existing levels of competence in economies which are in decline. Any city which is suffering from an economic recession will have difficulty in providing enough jobs and decent housing for its inhabitants. It will also have problems in providing adequate infrastructure and services. Economic growth is a necessary, if hardly a sufficient, basis for raising the quality of urban life. As a result, many of the improvements that were made in Latin America during the 1970s were undone by the stringencies of the debt crisis.

In so far as good governance clearly requires both political stability and democratic participation, Latin America's potential has improved greatly in recent years. First, few countries in the region are suffering from political instability and, for good or ill, there is little possibility of a social revolution in most parts of the region. Second, there has been a strong trend towards democratic government in recent years. The military regimes that dominated in most countries in the 1970s gave way to civilian regimes during the 1980s. While there are hints of a shift backwards in a few places, it is a long time since democratic government was quite so well established in the region. Third, there are incipient signs of greater participation in government decision-making. More power is being given to local government, more ordinary people are being consulted about their needs and desires. Of course, there is little sign that sufficient financial resources are being allocated to these local governments. The danger is that responsibility is being given to local authorities without the means to resolve the serious difficulties that they face.

There are also signs that some Latin American governments are managing to rectify a few of the problems that have faced urban areas for decades. Mexico City, for example, is beginning to control its air pollution and to curb use of its excessive numbers of cars. Despite the recession, its government has managed to increase water and electricity provision.

Unfortunately, these examples of good urban government are still the exceptions. Competent administration is anything but obvious in most cities of Latin America. It is certainly lacking in Buenos Aires, where industrial and domestic waste is pouring into the River Plate (chapter 6). It is less than evident in São Paulo, where increasing levels of crime in the streets and a generalized lack of confidence in the justice and police systems lead Kowarick (1991) to call Brazil's largest city the "metropolis of industrial underdevelopment." It is far from obvious in Peru as the state of public services deteriorates in the nation's capital (Riofrío, 1991).

There is another respect in which we cannot be wholly optimistic. This concerns the distribution of income and social segregation. The recession made urban Latin America more unequal. The gap between the top 10 per cent of the population and the rest increased during the "lost" decade. Those who could put their money in dollars, or who could invest abroad, did very well from the recession. They were protected from devaluation, rapid inflation, and smaller government subsidies in ways unavailable to the ordinary citizen. The testimony given in the chapters on Buenos Aires, Rio de Janeiro, and São Paulo is particularly strong in this respect. During the 1980s, highly unequal cities became even more unequal.

In the near future, a resumption of economic growth will improve living conditions for the poor and the middle classes. However, the overall result of liberalization and the rolling back of the "welfare" state is likely to accentuate existing income inequalities. Unless social welfare policies are well targeted, the situation for the poor may well deteriorate even if there is economic growth. The jobs open to the

19

poor in an increasingly casualized labour force promise neither security nor decent incomes. In this sense, the future of the giant cities is problematic.

Structure of the book

Since I have argued that there is no consensus as to what a mega-city is, the choice of which cities to include in this book was not an easy one to make. Clearly, the real monsters had to be included, but it was less evident where the threshold into mega-city status should be drawn. Certainly, I believe that the threshold should be lower than eight or ten million people because the broad view of this volume is that although the largest cities do have special problems, they are clearly not very different from other major cities. Thus, the volume discusses all Latin American cities which have more than four million people, and many chapters also include major cities, such as Caracas, which have fewer than that. However, those cities with more than six million people have a chapter each. A case could clearly have been made for including chapters on the next largest cities, Santiago and Belo Horizonte (table 1.1), but in the end limited space led to their exclusion.

In addition to the six chapters on individual cities, there are four systematic chapters. The first discusses the demography of urban growth in the region and the other three focus on what are particularly sensitive issues in very large cities: public administration; transport; and land, housing, and infrastructure. Chapters on other major problems in mega-cities, such as employment and pollution, were not included because those variables are less susceptible to size than to other intervening variables; there is no apparent link between unemployment levels or levels of pollution and city size.

The brief that was given to every writer was to consider as many as possible of the following questions:

- Are mega-cities different from smaller cities?
- In so far as they are different how are they different?
- Are mega-cities worse or better places to live than smaller cities?
- Is the growth of mega-cities financially sustainable?
- Is the growth of mega-cities economically sustainable in a changing world economy?
- Can mega-cities be administered competently in a world of growing "democracy" and "decentralization"?

- Are the populations of mega-cities likely to continue to grow rapidly or will the current pattern of deceleration continue?
- Are mega-cities developing a form that is rather akin to a series of cities within a region: a polycentric pattern that is not a single city at all?
- If the growth of mega-cities is more problematic than that of smaller cities, what should be done to slow the former's growth and what should be done to slow the growth of smaller cities so as to prevent them becoming mega-cities?

Several clear conclusions emerge from these chapters. First, the largest cities of Latin America are highly variable both in terms of their present socio-economic characteristics and their future prospects. The individual authors in this volume differ considerably in their judgement of the future. This reflects both their own interpretation of the world and where they live in Latin America. It is far easier to be optimistic in Bogotá than in Lima. Second, whether urban problems improve or deteriorate has rather little to do with size of city and a great deal to do with trends in the wider economy and society. Increasingly, of course, those trends are determined not just by local decisions but by decisions made in the headquarters of transnational corporations and in Washington, London, Brussels, Paris, Berlin, and Tokyo. Third, Latin America's megacities are not going to grow to unmanageable proportions because their growth rates have generally slowed right down. There is no reason to believe that they will grow as rapidly as in the 1960s. Fourth, management is a critical issue for the future but it is difficult to know whether the quality of management will improve or deteriorate through time. Again, variation is more important than similarity; there are no simple answers to the question of urban management.

References

Aguilar-Barajas, I. (1990) "An evaluation of industrial estates in Mexico, 1970–1986." *Progress in Planning* 34: 95–187.

Auty, R.M. (1990) *Resource-based industrialization: Sowing the oil in eight developing countries.* Clarendon Press.

Boisier, S. (1987) "Decentralization and regional development in Latin America today." *CEPAL Review* 31: 133–44.

Bolvinik, J. (1991) "Conceptos y métodos de medición de la pobreza." In Fresneda et al. (eds.), 1–42.

CEPA [Comité Ejecutivo para el Estudio de la Pobreza en la Argentina] (1992)

Evolución reciente de la pobreza en el aglomerado del Gran Buenos Aires 1988–1992. Buenos Aires: MEOSP.

CEPA (1993) *Necesidades básicas insatisfechas. Evolución intercensal 1980–1991*. Buenos Aires: MEOSP.

Chase-Dunn, C. (1985) "The system of world cities, A.D. 800–1975." In M. Timberlake (ed.), *Urbanization in the world-economy*, Academic Press, 269–92.

Davey, K.J. (1993) *Elements of urban management*. Urban Management Program Discussion Paper no. 11.

de Mattos, C. (1990) "Paradigmas, modelos y estrategias en la práctica latinoamericana de planificación regional." *Revista Interamericana de Planificación* 23: 5–40.

Dogan, M., and J.D. Kasarda (eds.) (1988) *The metropolis era*. Vol. 1: *A world of giant cities*. Vol. 2: *Mega-cities*. Sage.

ECLAC [Economic Commission for Latin America and the Caribbean] (1992) "Preliminary overview of the Latin American and Caribbean economy 1992." *Notas sobre la economía y el desarrollo*, 537/538.

——— (1993) "Preliminary overview of the Latin American and Caribbean economy 1993." *Notas sobre la economía y el desarrollo*, 552/553.

——— (1994) "Preliminary overview of the Latin American and Caribbean economy 1993." *Notas sobre la economía y el desarrollo*, 556/557.

Fresneda, O. (1991) "Dimensión y características de la pobreza en Colombia." In Fresneda et al. (eds.), 45–138.

Fresneda, O., L. Sarmiento, and M. Muñoz (eds.) (1991) *Pobreza, violencia y desigualdad: Retos para la nueva Colombia*. United Nations Development Programme.

Friedmann, J. (1986) "The world city hypothesis." *Development and Change* 17: 69–83.

Gilbert, A.G. (1974) *Latin American development: A geographical perspective*. Penguin.

——— (1976) "The arguments for very large cities reconsidered." *Urban Studies* 13: 27–34.

——— (1989) "Moving the capital of Argentina: A further example of utopian planning." *Cities* 6: 234–42.

——— (1993) "Third World cities: The changing national settlement system." *Urban Studies* 30: 721–40.

——— (1994) *The Latin American city*. Latin America Bureau and Monthly Review Press.

Gilbert, A., and D.E. Goodman (1976) "Regional income disparities and economic development: A critique." In A. Gilbert (ed.), *Development planning and spatial structure*, Wiley, 113–42.

Gilbert, A.G., and J. Gugler (1992) *Cities, poverty and development: Urbanization in the Third World*. Oxford University Press (second edition).

Gilbert, A.G., and A. Varley (1991) *Landlord and tenant: Housing the poor in urban Mexico*. Routledge.

Goldsmith, W.W., and R. Wilson (1991) "Poverty and distorted industrialization in the Brazilian Northeast." *World Development* 19: 435–55.

Hall, P. (1977) *The world cities*. Weidenfeld and Nicolson (second edition).

Henderson, J.V. (1991) *Urban development: Theory, fact and illusion*. Oxford University Press.

INEGI [Instituto Nacional de Estadística, Geografía e Informática'] (1993) *Mexican Bulletin of Statistical Information*, no. 9.

Johnston, R.J. (1976) "Observations on accounting procedures and urban-size policies." *Environment and Planning A* 8: 327–39.

Kasarda, J.D., and A.M. Parnell (eds.) (1993) *Third world cities: Problems, policies, and prospects*. Sage.

Kowarick, L. (1991) "Ciudad y ciudadanía. Metrópolis del subdesarrollo industrializado." *Nueva Sociedad* 114: 84–93.

Kowarick, L., and M. Campanario (1986) "São Paulo: The price of world city status." *Development and Change* 17: 159–74.

Lowder, S. (1987) *Inside the Third World city*. Croom Helm.

Mayhew, S., and A. Penny (1992) *The concise Oxford dictionary of Geography*. Oxford University Press.

Max-Neef, M.A. (1992) "The city: Its size and rhythm." In Morse and Hardoy (eds.), 83–97.

Morse, R.M., and J.E. Hardoy (eds.) (1992) *Rethinking the Latin American city*. Woodrow Wilson Center Press and The Johns Hopkins University Press.

Muñoz, M. (1991) "La pobreza en 13 ciudades según lineas de pobreza e indigencia 1985." In Fresneda et al. (eds.), 273–92.

Pinheiro, P.S. (1993) "Reflections on urban violence." *Urban Age* 1: 4.

Richardson, H.W. (1973) *The economics of urban size*. Saxon House.

—— (1989) "The big, bad city: Mega-city myth?." *Third World Planning Review* 11: 355–72.

—— (1993) "Efficiency and welfare in LDC mega-cities." In Kasarda and Parnell (eds.), 32–57.

Riofrío, G. (1991) "Lima en los 90. Un acercamiento a la nueva dinámica urbana." *Nueva Sociedad* 114: 143–9.

Rofman, A.B. (1974) *Dependencia, estructura de poder y formación regional en América Latina*. Buenos Aires: Editorial Suramericana.

Sachs, I. (1988) "Vulnerability of giant cities and the life lottery." In Dogan and Kasarda (eds.), 337–50.

Sánchez-León, A. (1992) "Lima and the children of chaos." In Morse and Hardoy (eds.), 201–7.

Santana, P. (1989) *Los movimientos sociales en Colombia*. Ediciones Foro Nacional por Colombia.

Simon, D. (1992) *Cities, capital and development: African cities in the world economy*. Belhaven.

Storper, M. (1991) *Industrialization, economic development and the regional question in the Third World*. Pion.

Teune, H. (1988) "Growth and pathologies of giant cities." In Dogan and Kasarda (eds.), 351–76.

UNCHS [United Nations Centre for Human Settlements (HABITAT)] (1987) *Global report on human settlements 1986*. Oxford University Press.

UNDIESA [United Nations Department of International Economic and Social Affairs] (1986) *Population growth and policies in mega-cities: Seoul*. Population Policy Paper no. 4. New York: United Nations.

—— (1995) *World urbanization prospects: The 1994 revision*. New York: United Nations.

UNDIESA and UNU [United Nations University] (1991) *Summary report and recommendations of the symposium on the mega-city and the future: Population growth and policy responses*, 22–25 October 1990, Tokyo.

UNEP [United Nations Environment Programme] (1992) *Urban air pollution in megacities of the world*. Blackwell.

Ward, P.M. (1990) *Mexico City*. Belhaven.

Webb, R., and G. Baca de Valdez (1992) *Perú en números, 1992*. Lima: Cuánto.

White, R., and J. Whitney (1992) "Cities and environment: An overview." In R. Stren, R. White, and J. Whitney (eds.), *Sustainable cities: Urbanization and the environment in international perspective*, Westview Press, 8–51.

Wilhelm, J. (1992) "Urban modernity in the context of underdevelopment: The Brazilian case." In Morse and Hardoy (eds.), 193–200.

Wilkie, J.W., and A. Perkal (1984) *Statistical abstract of Latin America* 23. University of California, Los Angeles.

Wood, C.H., and J.A.M. de Carvalho (1988) *The demography of inequality in Brazil*. Cambridge University Press.

World Bank (1991) *Urban policy and economic development: An agenda for the 1990s*. Washington DC.

———— (1994) *World development report 1994*. Oxford University Press.

2

Demographic trends in Latin America's metropolises, 1950–1990

Miguel Villa and Jorge Rodríguez

This chapter describes the principal trends in the demographic evolution of Latin America's major cities between 1950 and 1990. It examines the pace of metropolitan growth, trends in migration and natural increase, the role played by the largest cities in their national urban systems, and changes in the pattern of growth within the wider metropolitan region. It also considers the extent to which these trends are likely to continue in the future.

The discussion focuses on cities with more than four million inhabitants in 1990 – Bogotá, Buenos Aires, Lima, Mexico City, Rio de Janeiro, Santiago, and São Paulo – although Caracas is also included because of its dominant role in the Venezuelan economy. In estimating the populations of these cities, we have immediately faced the problem of defining their boundaries. This has not been an easy task, given the huge doubts expressed in the literature about the meaning of the term "metropolis" (Aylwin, 1991). The task is not eased by the changing nature of metropolitan development in recent years, which we discuss in detail below. Nevertheless, we do not believe that many readers will find our delimitation of the major cities too problematic. Unlike the huge London, New York, and Tokyo agglomerations, most Latin American metropolises are still broadly recognizable as cities. Therefore, we have generally ended by accepting the latest definitions of the national census authorities; a list of the municipalities included in each metropolitan area appears as an appendix (pp. 43–4).

Changing patterns of metropolitan growth

Latin America's population has increased hugely during the twentieth century and particularly since 1950 (Chackiel and Villa, 1992; CELADE, 1993a). Between 1950 and 1990, it increased from 159 million to 430 million, growing annually at 2.5 per cent. Not only has the population expanded rapidly, it has also moved home: Latin America is now predominantly an urban region. The pace of urban development has been really startling. Between 1950 and 1990, the urban population increased from 59 million to 306 million: an annual growth rate of 4.2 per cent. In 1925, three-quarters of Latin Americans lived in the countryside, an average that placed the region halfway between the most urbanized continents, Europe and North America (with 50 per cent urban population), and the least urbanized, Africa and Asia (with less than 10 per cent). Since then, Latin America has become more and more like Europe and North America. In 1990, the region had 72 per cent of its population living in urban areas and the projections indicate that it will have caught up with the developed regions by the end of the century (UN, 1993a; Chackiel and Villa, 1992).

Having so far talked at the regional level, it is important to recognize the important differences that exist between Latin American countries. Both Argentina and Chile urbanized early and had an urban majority in the 1930s, whereas most other countries in the region did not achieve this position until the 1950s. Similarly, whereas the urban systems of Argentina, Chile, and Peru are dominated by the huge concentrations of people in their national capitals, Colombia has a very balanced urban system, and Brazil and Ecuador lack a "primate city."

In the early 1990s, three Latin American cities had more than 10 million inhabitants and another five had more than four million. These eight cities increased their combined population from around 16 million in the early 1950s to approximately 70 million in 1990 (table 2.1). The dramatic nature of their growth during this period is clearly demonstrated by the huge numbers of additional people joining their populations every year; 312,000 people in São Paulo,

Table 2.1 **Latin America's largest cities: Population, 1950–1990**

City	1950	1960	1970	1980	1990
Bogotá	647,429	1,682,667	2,892,668	4,122,978	4,851,000
Buenos Aires	4,622,959	6,739,045	8,314,341	9,723,966	10,886,163
Caracas	683,659	1,346,708	2,174,759	2,641,844	2,989,601
Lima	645,172	1,845,910	3,302,523	4,608,010	6,422,875[a]
Mexico City	3,145,351	5,173,549	8,900,513	13,811,946	15,047,685
Rio de Janeiro	2,885,165	4,392,067	6,685,703	8,619,559	9,600,528[a]
Santiago	1,509,169	2,133,252	2,871,060	3,937,277	4,676,174[a]
São Paulo	2,333,346	4,005,631	7,866,659	12,183,634	15,183,612[a]

Source: National census figures.
a. Preliminary figures.

300,000 in Mexico City, and 142,000 in Buenos Aires. At certain times, metropolitan expansion accounted for as much as 40 per cent of national population growth.

Of course, the region's giant cities have not expanded at the same rate. Between 1947 and 1990, Buenos Aires grew at only 2 per cent per annum, around half the rate of growth in Mexico City and São Paulo, and very slowly when compared to the growth rates of over 5 per cent in Bogotá and Lima. As a result of these different rates of metropolitan growth, there has been some reordering of the largest cities within Latin America (figure 2.1).

Between 1950 and 1970, the proportion of the national population living in the largest eight cities of the region increased markedly (table 2.2). Since 1970, however, the level of metropolitan dominance has begun to decline and in at least four countries the population share of the largest city has fallen. This trend has come as rather a surprise to most governments and was certainly not predicted by the experts (de Mattos, 1979). Only Lima among the eight cities is still clearly increasing its share of the national population.

Some authors have argued that the region is now demonstrating clear signs of what Richardson (1980) calls "polarization reversal," with the secondary cities now growing more rapidly than the giant cities. Certainly, seven of the eight largest cities have seen a decline in their shares of the national urban population (table 2.3). Even if the real significance and causes of "polarization reversal" are subject to dispute (de Mattos, 1992a; Gilbert, 1993), a major change is under way.

Not surprisingly, this shift has also affected the level of urban pri-

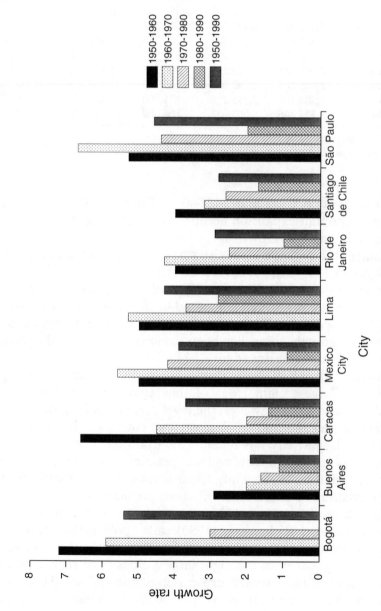

Figure 2.1 Annual growth rates of Latin America's largest cities, 1950–1990 (Source: Table 2.1)

Table 2.2 **Major Latin American cities: Population relative to the national total, 1950–1990**

City	Percentage (c. 1950)	Percentage (c. 1960)	Percentage (c. 1970)	Percentage (c. 1980)	Percentage (c. 1990)
Bogotá	5.4	9.6	14.0	14.8	16.4
Buenos Aires	29.1	33.7	35.6	34.8	33.4
Caracas	13.6	17.9	20.3	18.2	16.5
Lima	10.4	18.6	24.4	27.1	29.0[a]
Mexico City	12.2	14.8	18.5	20.7	18.5
Rio de Janeiro	5.6	6.2	7.2	7.2	6.6[a]
Santiago	25.4	28.9	32.3	34.8	35.0[a]
São Paulo	4.5	5.7	8.4	10.2	10.4[a]

Source: Table 2.1 and national census figures.
a. Preliminary figures.

Table 2.3 **Major Latin American cities: Share of national urban population, 1950–1990**

City	Percentage (c. 1950)	Percentage (c. 1960)	Percentage (c. 1970)	Percentage (c. 1980)	Percentage (c. 1990)
Bogotá	12.7	18.5	22.9	22.0	22.3
Buenos Aires	46.5	45.7	45.1	41.9	38.4
Caracas	25.2	26.5	26.3	21.6	19.6
Lima	29.4	39.3	41.0	41.5	41.3[a]
Mexico City	28.6	29.2	31.4	31.2	26.0
Rio de Janeiro	22.3	13.9	12.8	10.7	8.7[a]
Santiago de Chile	42.2	42.4	43.0	42.3	42.0[a]
São Paulo	18.0	12.8	15.1	15.1	13.8[a]

Source: Respective national census data.
a. Preliminary figures.

macy.[1] While the extent of urban primacy continues to be extreme by world standards, an outcome of the nature of the region's historical development, the degree of dominance has levelled off in Brazil, Chile, Colombia, and Peru, dropped slightly in Argentina and Mexico, and fallen markedly in Venezuela (table 2.4).

This slowing of metropolitan expansion represents a major secular change and will be highly welcome to governments that have for many years tried to reduce the dominance of the major cities. At the same time, the shift should not be allowed to obscure the fact that the proportion of the national population living in many of these giant cities is still very high and that in some cases large numbers of

Table 2.4 **Indices of urban primacy, 1950–1990**

Countries and cities	Index of primacy and populations (c. 1950)	Index of primacy and populations (c. 1960)	Index of primacy and populations (c. 1970)	Index of primacy and populations (c. 1980)	Index of primacy and populations (c. 1990)
Argentina (Buenos Aires)	**4.0**	**4.0**	**4.0**	**3.8**	**3.5**
Buenos Aires	4,622,959	6,739,045	8,314,341	9,723,966	10,886,163
Rosario	503,711	674,549	813,068	957,181	1,095,906
Cordoba	373,314	592,861	792,925	983,257	1,197,926
Mendoza	–	–	–	–	–
La Plata	273,220	404,129	485,939	605,623	773,559
Brazil (Rio and São Paulo)[a]	**0.8**	**0.7**	**0.8**	**0.9**	**0.9**
Rio de Janeiro	2,885,165	4,392,067	6,685,703	8,619,559	9,600,528
São Paulo	2,333,346	4,005,631	7,866,659	12,183,535	15,183,612
Recife	660,569	1,082,504	1,650,336	–	–
Porto Alegre	468,642	887,269	–	2,148,079	3,015,960
Belo Horizonte	–	–	1,501,629	2,460,012	3,416,905
Chile (Santiago)	**2.4**	**2.6**	**2.8**	**2.9**	**2.9**
Santiago	1,509,169	2,133,252	2,871,060	3,937,277	4,676,174
Valparaíso[b]	348,022	438,220	530,677	674,462	758,192
Concepción[c]	211,305	285,444	379,793	505,479	612,289
La Serena[d]	66,362	–	–	–	–
Antofagasta[d]	–	87,860	125,086	185,486	226,850
Colombia (Bogotá)	**0.7**	**0.8**	**0.9**	**0.9**	**1.2**
Bogotá	647,429	1,682,667	2,892,668	4,122,978	4,851,000
Medellín	397,738	948,025	1,475,740	1,963,873	1,585,000
Barranquilla	305,296	543,440	789,430	1,122,735	1,019,000
Cali	245,568	633,485	1,002,169	1,367,452	1,555,000

Mexico (Mexico City)	**3.0**	**2.8**	**2.7**	**2.8**	**2.0**
Mexico City	3,145,351	5,173,549	8,900,513	13,811,946	15,047,685
Guadalajara	440,528	851,155	1,491,085	2,192,557	3,012,728
Monterrey	375,040	708,399	1,213,479	1,913,075	2,593,434
Puebla	234,603	297,257	532,774	835,759	1,815,095
Peru (Lima)	**3.5**	**5.1**	**4.5**	**4.3**	**4.2**
Lima	645,172	1,845,910	3,302,523	4,608,010	6,422,875
Arequipa	102,657	163,693	306,125	446,942	620,471
Cusco	42,644	–	–	–	–
Trujillo	36,958	103,020	240,322	354,301	508,716
Chiclayo	–	95,667	187,809	279,527	410,468
Venezuela (Caracas)	**1.3**	**1.5**	**1.5**	**1.2**	**0.9**
Caracas	683,659	1,346,708	2,174,759	2,641,844	2,989,601
Maracaibo	270,087	461,304	681,718	962,014	1,358,266
Barquisimeto	125,893	225,479	371,270	–	–
Valencia	110,828	200,679	429,333	720,579	1,198,978
Maracay	–	–	–	599,238	810,413

Source: National population censuses and DEPUALC project.

Note: For Brazil, Chile, and Peru c. 1990 preliminary data are included.

a. Until 1960 the index was calculated on the population of Rio de Janeiro. For the later dates the population of São Paulo is used.

b. Includes the urban population of the communes of Valparaíso, Viña del Mar, Quilpué, and Villa Alemana.

c. Includes the urban population of the communes of Concepción, Talcahuano, and Penco.

d. Includes the urban population of the commune of Homónima.

people are still being added to the urban population. Despite a considerable slowing in the pace of its growth during the 1980s, some 125,000 people were still being added to Mexico City's population every year.

Causes of demographic change

Migration

Rapid rates of urban growth were caused initially by migration. In places, movement to the major cities has been long established, dating from as early as the end of the nineteenth century in the cases of Argentina and Uruguay. Even in the rest of the region, cityward migration is hardly a recent phenomenon, having become commonplace in the 1940s as rural people began to respond to new opportunities in the metropolitan areas (Alberts, 1977; CEPAL/CELADE, 1993; Herrera and Pecht, 1976). Between 1950 and 1960, newly arrived migrants added the equivalent of around 4 per cent of the metropolitan population every year to the populations of Bogotá, Caracas, and São Paulo. Elsewhere, the figures were less startling but still significant; 2.6 per cent to Rio de Janeiro and 2.0 per cent in Buenos Aires and Mexico City. During the 1960s, the relative weight of migration slowed but the absolute numbers of migrants moving to the major cities reached their peak (Herrera and Pecht, 1976).

The pace of migration continued to slow during the 1970s and fell markedly during the 1980s. Migration explained around half of Santiago's growth during the 1960s but only 15 per cent between 1982 and 1992. Indeed, during the 1980s, there were strong signs that as many people moved out of some metropolitan areas as moved in. Rodríguez (1993) estimates that net in-migration to Santiago fell from 10 per thousand people between 1977 and 1982 to two per thousand between 1987 and 1992. In Mexico City, CONAPO (1992) estimates that there was a net exodus of 300,000 people between 1985 and 1990.

Migration to metropolitan areas has always been affected by the nature of each nation's development path. In the southern cone, international migration was already stimulating metropolitan expansion during the last half of the nineteenth century. Elsewhere, it was only when import-substituting industrialization got under way, during the 1940s, that floods of migrants began to move towards the growing cities. It was hardly surprising that most industrial companies established factories in the major cities with their concentrations of high-income earners, their superior infrastructure, and their access to top decision-makers. Migrants followed the jobs to the cities.

Import-substituting industrialization also changed life in the countryside. By channelling investment into the cities it starved the countryside of resources. By distorting exchange rates, it discouraged agricultural production for export. By introducing modern methods of cultivation and agricultural finance into certain areas of the countryside, it led to the rapid disintegration of traditional forms of rural life. In a context of rapidly declining mortality, the expanding rural population was forced to look for work elsewhere (Castells, 1973; PREALC, 1990; de Oliveira and Roberts, 1989). Given the increasing economic opportunities available in the larger cities, many rural people moved to the metropolitan areas.

During the 1980s, of course, the pattern of development in Latin America changed. The region suffered its worst recession since the 1930s and, generally, it was the largest cities that bore the brunt of structural adjustment. Metropolitan living conditions deteriorated, real wages fell, and rates of unemployment rose. This deterioration in the quality of metropolitan life quickly became obvious to potential migrants, who began to stay at home.

With the introduction of a new model of development based on export production, freer trade and market liberalization, the balance between urban and rural living conditions changed. Some rural areas benefited from the new model as investors sought to exploit opportunities in agriculture, mining, or tourism, while most cities lost out (Daher, 1992; Gilbert, 1993; Soler and Rubio, 1992; de Mattos, 1992a; 1992b). Metropolitan populations felt the full force of liberalization and the rolling back of the state; they suffered from more pollution and traffic congestion, declines in subsidies and social welfare facilities, and a worsening in the distribution of income.

For the first time in several decades, metropolitan centres no longer attracted most investment; the economies of many smaller cities began to grow much more quickly. In Chile, cities such as Antofagasta, Coquimbo-La Serena, and Temuco experienced the fastest rates of growth. In Mexico, border cities such as Tijuana, Ciudad Juárez, and Mexicali, tourist centres such as Acapulco and Ensenada, and cities in agricultural export zones, such as Sinaloa, all grew faster than the major urban centres. In Brazil, Belém, Belo Horizonte, Curitiba, Fortaleza, Pôrto Alegre, and Salvador expanded more quickly during the 1980s than Rio and São Paulo, with the fastest growth of all

33

occurring in cities with between 100,000 and 500,000 inhabitants (IBGE, 1992).

Despite this shift in comparative advantage, there is little doubt that metropolitan centres have retained many of their privileges. Their economic structures have been damaged but are still very strong; their social infrastructure has been weakened but is still superior to that in most other cities. As a result, most have continued to attract migrants, even during the dark days of the 1980s (CEPAL, 1991a; 1991b; UNCRD, 1994).

Natural increase

Gradually, natural increase became the most important component of metropolitan growth; by the 1960s it had become much more significant than migration. Natural increase overtook migration because the majority of the migrants were so young. Within a few years of arrival in the city, most had produced children. The contribution of natural increase to urban growth was further magnified by the fact that death rates were far lower in urban areas than in the countryside, a tendency that became even more marked as mortality in the giant cities continued to fall.

Lower death rates in the metropolitan areas were a consequence of their superior living and health conditions. For example, Caracas has one doctor for every 600 people compared to the Venezuelan average of one per thousand. In Colombia, 90 per cent of births in Bogotá are attended by a doctor compared to only 70 per cent nationwide. In Peru, 77 per cent of the mothers who gave birth between 1986 and 1991 had received prenatal medical care compared to a national average of only 43 per cent. Of course, major variations in death rates are apparent between metropolitan areas; in Santiago infant mortality rates average only 14 per thousand live births, whereas in Rio de Janeiro they average 46 (table 2.5). Nevertheless, infant mortality rates in most parts of the countryside are much higher than in Rio.

If longer life expectancy and falling rates of infant mortality have raised the pace of natural increase, trends in fertility have had the opposite effect. For many years, rates of metropolitan fertility have been in decline. Fertility rates have fallen for several well-documented reasons (UN, 1987). A key factor has been the increasing availability of modern contraception in the large cities. Rates of use are very much higher than in non-metropolitan areas and the use of contraceptives in most metropolitan cities doubled between the 1950s

Table 2.5 **Death rates, life expectancy, and infant mortality in Latin America, 1950–1970, 1970–1979, and 1980–1990**

Country and city	Death rate (per thousand)			Life expectancy at birth (years)			Infant mortality (per thousand live births)		
	1950–1969	1970–1979	1980–1990	1950–1969	1970–1979	1980–1990	1950–1969	1970–1979	1980–1990
Argentina	13 (60)	9 (75)	7 (85)	66 (60)	68 (75)	70 (85)	58 (60)	45 (75)	27 (89)
Buenos Aires	11 (60)[a]	–	–	68 (60)	–	–	30 (60)[a]	–	20 (89)
Brazil	11 (55)	8 (79)	8 (85)	51 (52)	62 (79)	64 (85)	140 (50)	75 (79)	63 (87)
São Paulo	9 (55)	7 (79)	–	48 (40)	64 (79)	68 (85)	115 (50)	55 (79)	35 (88)
Rio de Janeiro	–	–	–	–	–	–	–	58 (78)	46 (84)
Chile	12 (60)	8 (75)	6 (90)	57 (60)	65 (75)	71 (85)	115 (60)	80 (70)	17 (89)
Santiago	10 (60)	6 (75)	5 (90)	–	–	–	–	49 (70)	14 (89)
Colombia	12 (55)	8 (75)	6 (87)	57 (60)	63 (75)	68 (85)	97 (60)	50 (79)	40 (87)
Bogotá	6 (55)	–	5 (87)	–	67 (75)	69 (85)	–	43 (79)	22 (87)
Mexico	13 (55)	8 (75)	6 (85)	51 (52)	61 (70)	66 (80)	114 (52)	74 (70)	41 (87)
Mexico City	11 (55)	7 (75)	–	51 (40)	63 (70)	69 (80)	132 (50)	75 (70)	30 (87)
Peru	25 (50)	18 (62)	9 (87)	49 (62)	56 (72)	61 (87)	136 (62)	105 (75)	64 (86)
Lima	13 (50)	–	–	–	–	–	–	61 (74)	30 (86)
Venezuela	13 (55)	6 (75)	5 (87)	60 (62)	67 (75)	70 (87)	80.5 (60)	45 (75)	36 (87)
Caracas	7 (55)	–	–	–	–	–	–	–	–

Sources: Cámara de Comercio de Bogotá, n.d.; CELADE, 1993b; Rodríguez, 1993; CEPAL/CELADE, 1993; United Nations, 1993c; Recchini de Lattes, 1971; *Demographic Health Survey* and *World Fertility Survey* series, various years.
a. Federal Capital.

and 1960s and the 1980s. By the 1980s, couples in Bogotá, Mexico City, and Rio de Janeiro were using contraception as frequently as couples in Buenos Aires had done in the early 1960s. At that time, fertility in Buenos Aires had fallen to levels which could barely maintain the population.

Of course, the availability of contraception does not mean that families will use it. However, there appears to be common agreement that urban, and particularly metropolitan, life reduces the desire to have children. A key factor is that the urban productive system reduces the economic value of children and increases the cost of bringing them up. Urban life also increases the chances of social mobility, providing that the birth of children is postponed. City life encourages rationality in family decision-making and raises the status of women by opening up new kinds of career beyond motherhood.[2]

Clearly, couples in most large Latin American cities now share similar attitudes towards the size of their family. For that reason, fertility rates across metropolitan areas have become more and more equal. Fertility rates in many erstwhile highly productive cities have fallen particularly rapidly. In Mexico City and Buenos Aires, gross fertility rates, which had been very different in 1962 at 5.8 and 2.1 respectively, had become quite similar – 3.0 and 2.7 – by the 1980s. Even if it is clear from Rosen and Simmons' (1967) classic study that fertility levels are determined less by the fact of metropolitan life than by the characteristics of particular cities, fertility levels in most urban areas are now remarkably similar (table 2.6).

Indeed, the decline in fertility rates has spread far beyond the major cities. Until the 1980s, fertility rates were much lower in the largest cities than in other areas. Over the last decade, however, national, urban, and metropolitan fertility rates have become much more equal (table 2.6). In several countries, some secondary cities now have lower fertility rates than the metropolitan centres. In Colombia, for example, Medellín and Cali have lower fertility rates than Bogotá (Cámara de Comercio, n.d.).

Age and sex structure

During the last thirty years, Latin America's giant cities have experienced a significant increase in the population of working age (20–60 years). This expansion has been a direct result of the tendency for young adults and their children to move to the city. At first, their arrival lowered the average age of the metropolitan population, but,

Table 2.6 **Fertility rates, number of children desired, and use of contraceptives in Latin America, 1950–1970, 1970–1979, and 1980–1990**

Country and city	Gross fertility rate[a]			Average number of children desired			Use of contraceptives[b]		
	1950–1970	1970–1979	1980–1990	1950–1970	1970–1979	1980–1990	1950–1970	1970–1979	1980–1990
Argentina	3.1 (62)	3.1 (72)	3.1 (80)	–	–	–	–	–	–
Buenos Aires	2.1 (62)	2.7 (72)	2.7 (80)	2.7 (62)	–	–	62 (62)	–	–
Brazil	6.2 (62)	4.5 (70)	3.5 (85)	–	–	2.8 (86)	–	–	57 (86)
São Paulo	5.0 (62)	3.6 (70)	2.9 (85)	–	–	2.7 (86)	–	–	63 (86)
Rio de Janeiro	3.6 (62)	–	2.6 (85)	2.8 (62)	–	2.3 (86)	32 (62)	–	63 (86)
Chile	5.3 (62)	3.3 (72)	2.6 (90)	–	–	–	–	–	–
Santiago	4.2 (60)	2.7 (72)	2.3 (90)	–	–	–	–	–	–
Colombia	6.8 (62)	4.4 (75)	2.9 (90)	–	4.1 (76)	2.6 (90)	–	30 (75)	55 (90)
Bogotá	5.7 (62)	2.8 (75)	2.4 (90)	3.4 (62)	3.5 (76)	2.4 (90)	27 (62)	57 (75)	62 (90)
Mexico	6.8 (62)	6.2 (75)	3.6 (86)	–	4.5 (76)	3.0 (87)	–	23 (75)	44 (86)
Mexico City	5.8 (62)	4.8 (75)	3.0 (86)	3.4 (62)	3.9 (76)	2.5 (87)	25 (62)	46 (75)	56 (86)
Peru	–	5.3 (76)	4.1 (86)	–	3.8 (77)	2.7 (87)	–	11 (76)	46 (86)
Lima	–	3.4 (76)	2.5 (86)	–	3.5 (77)	2.5 (87)	–	49 (76)	63 (86)
Venezuela	6.5 (62)	4.9 (76)	–	–	4.2 (77)	–	–	49 (76)	–
Caracas	5.2 (62)	3.3 (76)	–	3.4 (62)	3.5 (77)	–	42 (62)	60 (76)	–

Sources: CELADE, 1993b; Rodríguez, 1993; United Nations, 1993c and 1987; CELADE–CFSC, 1972. *Demographic Health Survey* and *World Fertility Survey* series, various years.

a. Refers to the number of women aged between 15 and 49 years in a state of union at the time of the survey.
b. Includes modern and traditional methods.

as both migration and fertility rates began to fall, the average age began to increase. In Mexico City, for example, 33 per cent of the population was under 15 in 1990 compared to 42 per cent twenty years earlier (CONAPO, 1992). In Bogotá, 33 per cent of the population was under 15 in 1985 compared to 45 per cent twelve years earlier (Cámara de Comercio, n.d.). As a result, the share of the population in the working age group has increased markedly.

Gradually, the proportion of older people has also begun to increase. In Santiago, the population aged 65 years or over increased from 4.1 per cent of the total in 1960 to 6.4 per cent in 1990 (Rodríguez, 1993). Currently, however, an ageing population is a significant issue only in the major cities of Argentina and Uruguay, where it is an outcome of the early experience of urban growth and the long-established slowing in the fertility rate. In Buenos Aires, 13 per cent of the population in 1980 was older than 60 (Recchini de Lattes, 1991).

Most metropolitan areas contain more women than men, a direct outcome of the higher incidence of women in migration flows (CEPAL/CELADE, 1993). Young women have long been attracted to the largest cities by the availability of work in commerce and domestic service (Alberts, 1977; Elton, 1979; Recchini de Lattes, 1991; Singelmann, 1993; Szasz, 1992). This tendency does not seem to have been affected by the recent slowing of migration.

The spatial pattern of metropolitan growth

Most urban planners in Latin America have long been concerned at the way metropolitan areas have spread outwards in apparently uncontrolled and explosive ways. The suburbs have spread like ink across blotting paper. In the process they have left enormous swathes of unused land within the urban perimeter and created vast low-income settlements with poor links to the rest of the metropolis (see chapter 4). This tendency has accentuated the problems of these cities, increasing transport problems, weakening infrastructure systems further, and putting impossible demands on local authorities with limited financial resources (Bähr and Mertins, 1993; CED, 1990; PREALC, 1990; Tulchin, 1993). Uncontrolled urban expansion has also led to the occupation of land quite unsuited to dense urban settlement. Major problems now face the settlers of low-income settlements located on land liable to flood, particularly in parts of Buenos Aires, Santiago, and São Paulo, and on steep hillsides subject to slippage, particularly in cities such as Caracas and Rio de Janeiro (Fadda, 1992; Ibarra et al. (eds.), 1986a; UNCRD, 1994).

Rapid metropolitan growth has caused additional problems when it has occupied fertile agricultural land. This has been a major headache in Bogotá, where the city is located at the edge of a large plain producing much of Colombia's wheat, potato, and barley and the bulk of its flower exports (Roda, 1992). In Lima, where the urban area increased thirty times between 1940 and 1993, the Province of Lima has lost three-quarters of its agricultural land (de Llona, 1991; Muñoz, 1991).

As the cities have expanded outwards, population growth in the central areas has slowed down. Few of the old administrative centres of the mega-cities have grown much in recent years, and in the case of the Federal District of Mexico, its population actually declined by 600,000 people between 1980 and 1990. This tendency has been particularly marked in the oldest parts of the cities since around 1970 (see chapter 4). The populations of central Buenos Aires, Caracas, Lima, and Mexico City are now in decline, and in Santiago there is public concern about the "depopulation of the historic core of the city" (CED, 1990; Rodríguez, 1993). Only the two Brazilian mega-cities seem to have escaped this trend: a result of new skyscraper developments and the development of increasing numbers of low-income tenements.

Since the 1970s, and in accentuated form during the 1980s, metropolitan expansion has taken a very different form from that in the past. Much of the growth is no longer within the urban perimeter. It has shifted to a number of towns and secondary cities within the wider metropolitan region but some distance from the main urban centre. This process has been one sign of the "polarization reversal" discussed earlier and is a first step in the creation of conurbations like those of Europe, the United States, and Japan.

As transport and communication networks have improved, and as infrastructural provision has been extended to secondary centres, companies have been able to operate successfully beyond the confines of the region's principal city. The process is not new in Latin America but it has recently intensified (Garza, 1978; Sabatini, 1991). The economic hinterland of Mexico City, which has gradually embraced Cuernavaca, Pachuca, and Toluca, now extends as far as Puebla and Querétaro, 128 and 224 km respectively by motorway from the capital (CONAPO, 1992) (see chapter 8). In Brazil, São Paulo's hinterland now embraces Campinas, Cubatão, Santos and São José

39

dos Campos. A discontinuous economic and urban complex now spreads hundreds of kilometres from the centre of São Paulo (Cano and Pacheco, 1991; de Mattos, 1992a; Kowarick and Jacobi, 1986; UN, 1993c; see also chapters 4 and 10). In Venezuela, a similar kind of process has been emerging for a number of years, with a chain of cities, including La Victoria, Maracay, and Valencia, spreading westwards from Caracas along the motorway to Puerto Cabello.

The tendency towards "concentrated deconcentration" has sometimes been encouraged by the state. In Argentina, the state has encouraged industrial companies to move to the outskirts of Greater Buenos Aires (Pesci and Ibañez, 1992). In Chile, there are plans to stimulate development in a wide area around Santiago, which include some population relocation and major improvements to the transportation system. The area concerned stretches 160 km to the west, 96 km to the north and 240 km to the south (Echeñique, 1992; Necochea, 1991; Sabatini, 1991).

Manufacturing industry has been the prime mover in this trend towards urban deconcentration and other sectors have lagged behind; indeed, tertiary activity has sometimes moved in the opposite direction, becoming more concentrated in the principal city. As manufacturing has moved out, however, the figures suggest that megacities have lost some of their national importance in this sector. Such figures are misleading in that, while the principal city often has a lower share of manufacturing employment and value added, its wider region has often strengthened its hold.

Only rarely has this trend been fully reflected in terms of the distribution of people. In Brazil, the area around São Paulo has grown more slowly than urban areas generally, the combined population share falling from 21 per cent of the state's population to 19 per cent between 1980 and 1991. Similarly, in Chile, the Santiago macroregion has grown more slowly than the nation's urban population. In the case of Mexico, the main metropolitan region has lost out even more dramatically, the combined urban population of the area between Mexico City, Puebla-Tlaxcala, Toluca, and Cuernavaca falling from 36 per cent in 1970 to 32 per cent in 1990 (Ruiz, 1993).

The future of the Latin American metropolis

Since 1980, most giant Latin American cities have experienced several common processes. First, there has been a slowing in the pace of population growth due to falling rates of fertility, a decline in the rate of in-migration, a fall in each mega-city's share of the national population, and a decline in the level of urban "primacy." Second, despite a slowing in their population growth rate, most cities have continued to spread outwards: a trend accentuated by the growth of car ownership and by increasing signs of contamination and congestion in the central city. Third, most cities have seen a decline in the proportion of their population living in the central area and a rise in the share living in the suburbs (see chapter 4).

At the same time, there have been some important differences between cities. Fertility rates have not fallen at the same rate in every major city; indeed, the gross reproduction rate in a few has risen. Net in-migration to some major cities has ceased but elsewhere metropolitan areas have continued to attract more people than they have lost.

All the signs are that, in the near future, the trends which have been slowing the pace of metropolitan expansion will continue to operate. Fertility rates will continue to decline in most cities, as will the pace of cityward migration. While the balance of natural increase relative to migration will continue to vary between cities, all will grow more slowly.

Despite the slowing pace of growth, none of the region's mega-cities will cease to expand and all will continue their rapid spread outwards. They will continue to be difficult to manage and will demand large investments in their infrastructure and services merely to prevent a decline in living standards. Finding work for their inhabitants will continue to be a major problem despite the slowing pace of population growth. With so many young people beginning to enter the labour force, with more women wanting paid work, and with young adults continuing to migrate to the cities, it is unlikely that un- and underemployment will be reduced. In addition, new state programmes will be needed to deal with emerging problems such as the rising number of old people.

It is likely that the metropolitan share of national economic activity will continue to decline as manufacturing companies continue to locate in secondary centres. As a result, patterns of migration may change, with fewer people moving to the largest cities and more moving to smaller centres such as Fortaleza in Brazil, Tijuana in Mexico, Córdoba in Argentina, Ibagué in Colombia, and Trujillo and Ayacucho in Peru. However, cities within the metropolitan region will continue to grow. Unfortunately, the quality of urban life is unlikely to improve in such centres, since they are following the model already taken by the major cities: low-density expansion in the periphery, limited infrastructural investment, and inadequate provision of public transport (CEPAL, 1993e).

It is difficult to predict whether the metropolitan centres will increase their share of the national population or not. On the one hand, the tendency towards deconcentration within the metropolitan region will reduce their national population share. On the other hand, given falling fertility rates in the countryside and small towns, much will depend on whether the metropolitan areas will continue to attract migrants. This will be determined in part by the economic performance of their respective nations. Cityward migration was slowed in the 1980s by economic recession. Economic revival is likely to encourage more people to move to the cities. A reactivation of investment in social infrastructure in the major cities, something that went by the board during the "lost decade," will attract migrants from the more deprived regions of the country. It seems likely that most cities will reach the "post-apocalyptic" state described by Pírez and Novaro (1993).

Clearly, the demographic forecasts prepared at the beginning of the 1980s were very wide of the mark. Latin America's major cities will not grow to the size once forecast. At the same time, a gradual recovery in the quality of urban life, even if it is still generally below the level reached before the onset of the economic crisis, promises to accelerate the pace of population expansion. There are also signs of better urban management which promise to reduce air pollution and traffic congestion and to improve the provision of basic services and infrastructure (Hardoy, 1993). There are even indications that some national governments are beginning to rethink how large cities should be administered, resuscitating the idea of metropolitan-wide government as a way of avoiding partial and improvised forms of administration (Aylwin, 1991; Carrión, 1992). In addition, the largest cities have recovered some of their economic advantages over most smaller centres. They have increasingly become centres of science and technology and of information management for their countries. In sum, even if the major cities of Latin America are likely to grow less quickly than was once predicted, they will survive and will continue to attract people and capital on a large scale.

Notes

1. In several respects, urbanization in Latin America is quite similar to that in other world regions. Urban primacy is certainly not a peculiarity of Latin America. There are many

countries around the globe, in both the developed and less developed worlds, which contain primate cities. Where Latin America does perhaps differ is that it contains a higher proportion of super-dominant cities, those with more than 25 per cent of the urban population (Gilbert and Gugler, 1992).

2. Data on other possible explanations of falling fertility, e.g. changing marriage patterns and the availability of abortion, are scarce and, so far, have shown no clear relationship with changing fertility levels (Berquó et al., 1985).

Appendix: Local authority areas included with each metropolitan area

Buenos Aires: Federal Capital, Almirante Brown, Avellaneda, Berazategui, Esteban Echeverría, Florencio Varela, General San Martín, General Sarmiento, La Matanza, Lanús, Lomas de Zamora, Merlo, Moreno, Morón, Quilmes, San Fernando, San Isidro, Tigre, Tres de Febrero, Vicente López.

Caracas: Department of Libertador, Baruta, Carrizal, Cecilio Acosta, Chacao, El Hatillo, El Junko (parish of Vargas), Guaicaipuro, José Manuel Alvarez, Leoncio Martínez, Los Salias, Petare, San Antonio, Sucre.

Lima: Lima, Ancón, Ate, Barranco, Bellavista, Breña, Callao, Carabayllo, Carmen de la Legua Reynosos, Chaclacayo, Chorrillos, Cieneguilla, Comas, El Agustino, Independencia, Jesús María, La Molina, La Perla, La Punta, La Victoria, Lince, Los Olivos, Lurigancho, Lurín, Los Olivos, Magdalena del Mar, Magdalena Vieja, Miraflores, Pachacamac, Pucusana, Pueblo Libre, Puente Piedra, Punta Hermosa, Punta Negra, Rimac, San Bartolo, San Borja, San Isidro, San Juan de Lurigancho, San Juan de Miraflores, San Luís, San Martín de Porres, San Miguel, Santa Anita, Santa María del Mar, Santa Rosa, Santiago de Surco, Surquillo, Ventanilla, Villa El Salvador, Villa María del Triunfo.

Mexico City: Federal District, Acolmán, Atenco, Atizapán de Zaragoza, Chalco, Chicoloapán, Chimalhuacán, Coacalco, Cuatitlán, Cuatitlán Izcalli, Ecatepec, Huixquilucán, Ixtapaluca, Jaltenco, La Paz, Melchor Ocampo, Naucalpán, Netzahualcóyotl, Nextlalpán, Nicolás Romero, Tecámac, Teoloyucán, Tepotzotlán, Texcoco, Tlalnepantla, Tultepec, Tultitlán, Zumpango.

Rio de Janeiro: Rio de Janeiro, Duque de Caxias, Itaborai, Itaguaí, Magé, Mangaratiba, Maricá, Nilópolis, Niterói, Nova Iguaçu, Paracambi, São Gonçalo, São João de Meriti.

Santa Fé de Bogotá: Capital District, Chia, Funza, Soacha.

Santiago: Santiago, Cerrillos, Cerro Navia, Conchalí, El Bosque, Estación Central, Huechuraba, Independencia, La Cisterna, La Florida, La Granja, La Pintana, La Reina, Las Condes, Lo Barnechea, Lo Espejo, Lo Prado, Macul, Maipú, Ñuñua, Pedro Aguirre Cerda, Peñalolén, Providencia, Pudahuel, Puente Alto, Quilicura, Quinta Normal, Recoleta, Renca, San Bernardo, San Joaquín, San Miguel, San Ramón, Vitacura.

São Paulo: São Paulo, Arujá, Barueri, Biritiba Mirim, Caieiras, Cajamar, Carapicuiba, Cotia, Diadema, Embu, Embu-Guaçu, Ferraz de Vasconcelos, Francisco

M. Villa and J. Rodríguez

Morato, Franco da Rocha, Guararema, Guarulhos, Itapecerica da Serra, Itapevi, Itaquaquecetuba, Jandira, Juquitiba, Mairipora, Mauá, Mogi das Cruzes, Osasco, Pirapora de Bom Jesus, Poa, Ribeirão Pires, Rio Grande da Serra, Salesópolis, Santa Isabel, Santana de Parnaiba, Santo André, São Bernardo do Campo, São Caetano do Sul, Susano, Taboão de Serra, Vargem Grande Paulista.

References

Ackel, L. et al. (1992) "Divisão territorial da cidade e diferentes cenarios populacionais: O caso de São Paulo." In Associação Brasileira de Estudos Populacionais (ABEP), *VII Encontro Nacional de Estudos Populacionais, Anais 1992*, 3, 231–69.
Aguilar, A. (1993) "Las ciudades medias en México. Hacia una diferenciación de sus atributos." *Revista Interamericana de Planificación* XXVI, 101/102: 129–53.
Ainstein, L. (1991) "El proceso de formación y administración territorial de Buenos Aires." *Ciudad y territorio* 86/87: 73–85.
Alberts, J. (1977) *Migración hacia áreas metropolitanas de América Latina. Un estudio comparativo.* CELADE, Serie E, no. 24.
Alberts, J., and M. Villa (1980) *Redistribución espacial de la población en América Latina.* CELADE, Serie E, no. 28.
Aldunate, A., et al. (1987) *Evaluación social de las erradicaciones: Resultados de una encuesta*, FLACSO (Facultad Latinoamericana de Ciencias Sociales), material de discusión.
Allou, S. (1989) *Lima en cifras.* Centro de Investigación, Documentación y Asesoría Poblacional (CIDAP) and Instituto Francés de Estudios Andinos (IFEA).
Arriagada, C. (1994) "Políticas sectoriales y población: El caso de Ciudad de México." Mimeo, Centro Latinoamericano de Demografía (CELADE).
Aylwin, A. (1991) "Interrogantes y planteamientos sobre un gobierno metropolitano para Santiago de Chile." *Revista EURE* 52/53, 143–56.
Baeninger, R. (1993) "Movimentos migratórios na transicão demográfica: Evidencias e reflexões sobre a esperiencia de São Paulo, Brasil." In ABEP–CELADE–IUSSP–PROLAP–SOMEDE, *IV Conferencia Latinoamericana de Población. La transición demográfica en América Latina y el Caribe.* INEGI–IISUNAM, II, 57–77.
Bähr, J., and G. Mertins (1993) "Urbanization in Latin America." *Applied Geography* 41: 89–109.
Banco Mundial (1992) *Informe sobre el Desarrollo Mundial 1992. Desarrollo y medio ambiente.* Oxford.
Berquó, E., et al. (1985) *São Paulo e sua fecundidade.* SEADE (Fundacão Sistema Estadual de Analise de Dados).
Bidegaín, G. (1989) *Desigualdad social y esperanza de vida en Venezuela.* Instituto de Investigaciones Económicas y Sociales de la Universidad Católica Andrés Bello, Documento de Trabajo no. 34.
Boisier, S. (1992) *La descentralización: El eslabón perdido de la cadena transformación productiva con equidad*, ILPES, LC/IP/G.62-P.
——— (1993) *Post modernismo territorial y globalización: Regiones pivotales y regiones virtuales.* Instituto Latinoamericano y del Caribe de Planificación Económica y Social (ILPES), Serie Ensayos, no. 29, LC/IP/G.73.

Borgegård, L., and R. Murdie (1993) "Socio-demographic impacts of economic restructuring on Stockholm's inner city." *Tijdschrift voor Economische en Sociale Geografie* 84: 269–80.

Borthagaray, J. (1992) *Provisión de vivienda en el área metropolitana de Buenos Aires*. CEPAL, LC/L.677.

Brahm, L. (1990) "Estructura espacial del desarrollo humano del Gran Santiago." *Revista EURE* 52/53, 87–105.

Brunstein, F. (ed.) (1988) *Crisis y servicios públicos: Agua y saneamiento en la región metropolitana de Buenos Aires*. Centro de Estudios Urbanos y Regionales (CEUR).

Brunstein, F., et al. (1989) "Crisis y condiciones de vida en el Gran Buenos Aires." In Lombardi and Veiga (eds.), 135–74.

Buchhofer, E., and A.G. Aguilar (1991) "La crisis reciente en la economía mexicana. ¿Respiro en el crecimiento de la Ciudad de México?" *Revista Interamericana de Planificación* 24: 176–207.

Calderón, F., et al. (1993) *Hacia una perspectiva crítica de la modernidad: Las dimensiones culturales de la transformación productiva con equidad*. CEPAL, Documento de Trabajo no. 21.

Cámara de Comercio de Bogotá (n.d.) *Bogotá: Prioridad social. Plan de desarrollo económico y social 1990–1994*. Bogotá.

Camargo, A. (1992) "A mortalidade infantil em São Paulo e a ocorrência das causas perinatais." In Associação Brasileira de Estudos Populacionais (ABEP), *VIII Encontro nacional de estudos populacionais*, 333–54.

Cano, W., and C. Pacheco (1991) "El proceso de urbanización del Estado de São Paulo y sus implicancias para la dinámica demográfica regional." *Revista EURE* 51: 43–7.

Carrión, F. (ed.) (1992) *Ciudades y políticas urbanas*. CODEL.

Castells, M. (1973) "La urbanización dependiente de América Latina." *Revista de Planificación* 8: 1–18.

———— (1989) *The information city: Information, technology, economic restructuring, and the urban-regional process*. Blackwell.

CED [Centro de Estudios del Desarrollo] (1990) *Santiago: Dos ciudades. Análisis de la estructura socio-económica-espacial del Gran Santiago*. CED.

CELADE [Centro Latinoamericano de Demografía] (1988) "Redistribución espacial de la población en América Latina y el Caribe. Una visión sumaria del período 1950–1985." Mimeo.

———— (1993a) *Población, equidad y transformación productiva*. CELADE–CEPAL–FNUAP, LC/G.1758 (Conf.83/3), LC/DEM/G.131.

———— (1993b) "América Latina. Proyecciones de población. 1950–2025." *Boletín Demográfico*, no. 51.

CELADE and CFSC [Community and Family Study Center of the University of Chicago] (1972) *Fertility and family planning in metropolitan Latin America*. University of Chicago.

CEP [Centro de Estudios Públicos] (1993) *Desafíos de la descentralización: Propuesta para consolidar la autonomía y el financiamiento local y regional*. CEP.

CEPAL [Comisión Económica para América Latina y el Caribe] (1989) *La crisis urbana en América Latina y el Caribe. Reflexiones sobre alternativas de solución*. CEPAL, LC/G.1571-P.

—— (1991a) *Panorama social de América Latina. Edición 1991.* CEPAL, LC/G.1688.

—— (1991b) *Magnitud de la pobreza en América Latina en los años ochenta.* CEPAL.

—— (1992a) *Latin America poverty profiles for the early 1990s.* CEPAL, LC/L.716(Conf.82/6).

—— (1992b) *Equidad y transformación productiva: Un enfoque integrado.* CEPAL, LC/G.1701/Rev.1-P.

—— (1992c) *La vivienda y la tierra en las grandes ciudades de América Latina.* CEPAL, LC/L.691.

—— (1992d) *El manejo del agua en las áreas metropolitanas de América Latina.* CEPAL, LC/R.1156.

—— (1993a) *La pobreza en Chile en 1992.* CEPAL, LC/R.1351.

—— (1993b) *Antecedentes estadísticos de la distribución del ingreso en los años ochenta. Chile y México.* CEPAL, LC/G.1772.

—— (1993c) *Antecedentes estadísticos de la distribución del ingreso en los años ochenta. Uruguay y Venezuela.* CEPAL, LC/G.1782.

—— (1993d) *Panorama social de América Latina. Edición 1993.* CEPAL, LC/G.1768.

—— (1993e) *Ciudades medianas y gestión urbana en América Latina.* CEPAL, LC/L.747

—— (1993f) *Antecedentes estadísticos de la distribución del ingreso en los años ochenta. Colombia.* CEPAL, LC/G.1763.

—— (1993g) *Antecedentes estadísticos de la distribución del ingreso en los años ochenta. Argentina, Bolivia y Brasil.* CEPAL, LC/G.1760.

—— (1994) *Estudio económico de América Latina y el Caribe.* CEPAL, II, LC/G.1774/Add.1-P.

CEPAL/CELADE, (1993) *Dinámica de la población de las grandes ciudades en América Latina y el Caribe.* CELADE, LC/DEM/R.198, Serie A, no. 282.

—— (1994) *Consenso Latinoamericano y del Caribe sobre Población y Desarrollo.* Declaración Oficial de la Conferencia Regional Latinoamericana y del Caribe sobre Población y Desarrollo, México, D.F., 29 de abril al 4 de mayo de 1993.

Chackiel, J., and M. Villa (1992) *América Latina y el Caribe: Dinámica de la población y desarrollo.* Documento de referencia DDR/1 para la reunión de expertos Gubernamentales sobre Población y Desarrollo en América Latina y el Caribe, Santa Lucía, 6–9 de octubre. CELADE.

Clichevsky, N. (1991) "Sobre la planificación urbana posible en los ochenta. El caso del área metropolitana de Buenos Aires." *Ciudad y territorio* 86/87: 87–98.

CONAPO [Consejo Nacional de Población] (1988) *Características principales de la migración en las grandes ciudades del país.* CONAPO.

—— (1991) *Sistema de ciudades y distribución espacial de la población en México.* Vol. 1. CONAPO.

—— (1992) *La Zona Metropolitana de la Ciudad de México: Problemática actual y perspectivas demográficas y urbanas.* CONAPO.

Collet, G., et al. (1992) *Gestão da terra metropolitana na America Latina: O caso de São Paulo.* CEPAL, LC/L.683.

Coraggio, J. (ed.) (1990) *La investigación urbana en América Latina: Caminos recorridos y por recorrer. Las ideas y su contexto, 3.* CIUDAD.

Daher, A. (1992) "Ajuste económico y ajuste territorial en Chile." *Revista EURE* 54: 5–13.

Daher, A., et al. (1990) "Territorios de exportación." *Revista EURE* 48: 25–36.

DANE [Departamento Administrativo Nacional de Estadística] (1988) *Boletín de estadística. Especial: La pobreza en 13 ciudades colombianas.* DANE.

———— (1989) *Boletín de estadística. Especial: La vivienda en Colombia 1973–1985. Principales resultados.* DANE.

Davis, K. (ed.) (1961) *Las áreas metropolitanas del mundo.* University of California Press.

de Llona, M. (1991) "Lima: una experiencia de gestión urbana alternativa." *Ciudad y territorio* 86/87: 145–63.

de Mattos, C. (1979) "Crecimiento y concentración espacial en América Latina: Algunas consecuencias." *Revista EURE* 16: 9–21.

———— (1992a) *El impacto de las políticas de distribución espacial de la población en el desarrollo, o ¿Afecta el desarrollo a la distribución de la población?* Documento presentado a la Reunión de Expertos sobre Distribución de la Población y Migración, Santa Cruz de la Sierra, Bolivia, 18–22 de enero, ESD/P/ICPD.1994/EG.VI/11.

———— (1992b) "Modernización neocapitalista y reestructuración productiva y territorial en Chile, 1973–90." *Revista EURE* 54: 15–30.

de Oliveira, O., and B. García (1984) "Urbanization, migration and the growth of large cities: Trends and implications in some developing countries." In United Nations, *Population distribution, migration and development*, United Nations, 210–246, ST/ESA/SER.A/89.

de Oliveira, O., and B. Roberts (1989) "Los antecedentes de la crisis urbana: Urbanización y transformación ocupacional en América Latina: 1940–1980." In Lombardi and Veiga (eds.), 23–80.

de Souza, C. (1985) *Urbanização brasileira: Uma análise dos anos setenta.* Fundação Getulio Vargas.

Delgado, J. (1991) "Valle de México: El crecimiento por conurbaciones." *Revista Interamericana de Planificación* XXIV, 94: 226–49.

Dogan, M., and J. Kasarda (eds.) (1988) *The metropolis era.* 2 vols., Sage.

Durán, H. (1992) *Políticas para la gestión ambiental adecuada de los residuos: El caso de los residuos sólidos urbanos e industriales en Chile a la luz de la experiencia internacional.* CEPAL, Documento de Trabajo no. 10.

Ebanks, E. (1991) *Socio-economic determinants of internal migration with special reference to Latin America and the Caribbean region.* CELADE, Serie A, no. 255.

Echeñique, M. (1992) "Ideas sobre el futuro de la ciudad de Santiago." *Estudios Públicos* 48: 5–16.

Elizaga, J. (1979) *Dinámica y economía de la población.* CELADE, Serie E, no. 27.

Elizaga, J., and J. Macisco (1975) *Migraciones internas. Teoría, método y factores sociológicos.* CELADE, Serie E, no. 19.

Elton, C. (1979) *Migración femenina en América Latina.* CELADE, Serie E, no. 26.

Fadda, G. (1992) *La vivienda en el área metropolitana de Caracas.* CEPAL, LC/L.680.

FAO [Food and Agriculture Organization of the United Nations] (1992) *Differentials in rural and urban development in selected countries of Latin America.* FAO.

Garza, G. (1978) "Estructura y dinámica industrial del área urbana de la Ciudad de México." *Demografía y Economía* 35: 139–181.

Gastal, A. (1992) "The environment and its effects on helth." In Pan-American Health Organization (PAHO), *International health. A north-south debate*, PAHO, Human Resource Development Series no. 95, 39–46.

Gatto, F. (1989) "Cambio tecnológico neofordista y reorganización productiva. Primeras reflexiones sobre sus implicaciones territoriales." *Revista EURE* 47: 7–34.

Geisse, G., and F. Sabatini (1988) "Latin American cities and their poor." In Dogan and Kasarda (eds.), 322–36.

Gilbert, A. (1993) "Ciudades del tercer mundo: la evolución del sistema nacional de asentamientos." *Revista EURE* 57: 41–58.

Gilbert, A., and J. Gugler (1992) *Cities, poverty and development: Urbanization in the Third World*, Oxford University Press (second edition).

Gilbert, A., et al. (eds.) (1982) *Urbanization in contemporary Latin America: Critical approaches to the analysis of urban issues*. Wiley.

Gross, P., et al. (1988) "Metropolización en América Latina y el Caribe: Calidad de vida y pobreza urbana." *Revista EURE* 43: 7–51.

Gross, P., and A. Rodríguez (1986) "Calidad ambiental urbana: El caso de Santiago de Chile." in Ibarra et al. (eds.), 231–74.

Gutman, P. (1988) "Cambio tecnológico y crecimiento urbano: Una agenda para la investigación en América Latina." *Revista EURE* 44: 7–15.

———— (1993) "La Habana y Seul: Ejemplos de metropolización." *Revista EURE* 57: 103–15.

Guzmán, J.M., and J. Rodríguez (1992) "La fecundidad pre-transicional en América Latina: Un capítulo olvidado," *Notas de Población* 57: 217–46.

Hardoy, J. (1990) "La investigación urbana en America Latina durante las dos últimas décadas." In Coraggio (ed.), 9–63.

———— (1991) "Antiguas y nuevas capitales nacionales de América Latina." *Revista EURE* 52/53: 7–26.

———— (1993) "El futuro de la ciudad latinoamericana." *Medio Ambiente y Urbanización* 43/44: 147–66.

Hardoy, J., and R. Schaedel (eds.) (1975) *Las ciudades de América Latina y sus áreas de influencia a través de la historia*. SIAP.

Hardoy, J., et al. (1992) *Environmental problems in third world cities*. Earthscan.

Hatt, P., and A. Reiss (eds.) (1961) *Cities and society. The revised reader in urban sociology*. Free Press of Glencoe.

Hauser, P., et al. (1982) *Population and the urban future*. State University of New York Press, New York.

Herrera, L., and W. Pecht (1976) *Crecimiento urbano de América Latina*. CELADE–Banco Interamericano de Desarrollo (BID).

Hinner, H. (1991) "Problemas ambientales en Santiago de Chile." Mimeo, informe para Carl Duisberg Arbeitskreis y Rheinland Pfalz/Alemania.

Hogan, D. (1992) "Migration dynamics, environmental degradation and health in São Paulo." In IUSSP–UIESP–ABEP–FCD–PAA–PROLAP–SOMEDE, *El poblamiento de las Américas. Actas*, International Union for the Scientific Study of Population (IUSSP), 2, 279–99.

Ibarra, V., et al. (eds.) (1986a) *La ciudad y el medio ambiente en América Latina*. Centro de Estudios Demográficos y de Desarrollo Urbano, El Colegio de México.

Ibarra, V., et al. (1986b) "La ciudad y el medio ambiente: el caso de la zona metropolitana de la ciudad de México." In Ibarra et al. (eds.) (1986a), 97–148.

IBGE [Fundação Instituto Brasileiro de Geografia e Estatística] (1992) *Censo Demográfico de 1991. Análises Preliminares*, 2 vols., IBGE.

IEAL [Instituto de Estudios de Administración Local] (1976) *Problemas de las áreas metropolitanas*. Instituto de Estudios de Administración Local.

Igarzabal, M. (1992) *Administración, control y gestión de la tierra urbana en el área metropolitana de Buenos Aires*. CEPAL, LC/L.678.

IPEA [Instituto de Planejamento Economico e Social] (1976) *Região Metropolitana do Grande Rio: Serviços de Interesse Comum*. IPEA.

Kowarick, L., and P. Jacobi (1986) "Crecimiento económico, urbanización y medio ambiente: La calidad de la vida en São Paulo, Brasil." In Ibarra et al. (eds.) (1986a), 197–228.

Labbé, F., and M. Llévenes (1986) "Proceso de erradicación de poblaciones en el Gran Santiago." *Estudios Públicos* 24: 197–242.

Lattes, A. (1984) "Algunas dimensiones demográficas de la urbanización reciente y futura de América Latina." In Universidad Nacional Autónoma de México [UNAM], El Colegio de México, and Programa de Investigaciones Sociales en Población de América Latina [PISPAL], *Memorias del Congreso Latinoamericano de Población y Desarrollo*, El Colegio de México, II, 893–930.

—— (1990) "La urbanización y el crecimiento urbano en América Latina, desde una perspectiva demográfica." In Coraggio (ed.), 257–315.

—— (1992) *Distribución de la población y desarrollo en América Latina*. Documento presentado a la Reunión de Expertos sobre Distribución de la Población y Migración, Santa Cruz de la Sierra, Bolivia, 18–22 de enero, ESD/P/ICPD.1994/EG.VI/9.

Legarraga, M. (1993) *Desarrollo frutícola en Chile*. Documento presentado al seminario sobre transformación de la producción agrícola en Paraguay, Asunción, 2–4 de noviembre, LC/R.1312 (Sem. 72/2).

León, F. (1991) "El empleo temporal en la agricultura chilena, 1976–1990. Síntesis y conclusiones." Mimeo.

Lombardi, M., and D. Veiga (eds.) (1989) *Las ciudades en conflicto. Una perspectiva latinoamericana*. Centro de Informaciones and Estudios del Uruguay (CIESU).

Lodder, C. (1976) *Distribução de renda nas areas metropolitanas*. IPEA.

Machado, L. (1993) "Processos migratorios e transição demográfica: O caso da metropole paulista." In ABEP–CELADE–IUSSP–PROLAP–SOMEDE, *IV Conferencia Latinoamericana de Población. La transición demográfica en América Latina y el Caribe*, INEGI–IISUNAM, II, 25–39.

Ministerio de Vivienda y Urbanismo (Chile) and Lincoln Institute of Land Policy, Urban Management Program (1993) *Strategic Urban Management Program*. Resumen de ponencias, Santiago, 16–17 de junio.

Montenegro, A. (1992) *La provisión de vivienda en Bogotá*. CEPAL, LC/L.687.

Morales, E. (1989) "Crisis urbana en el Cono Sur. Paradigma and enfoques. La ciudad de Santiago de Chile." In Lombardi and Veiga (eds.), 223–38.

Moreno, J. (1992) *Recuperación y repoblamiento de las áreas centrales deterioradas de las ciudades. La experiencia internacional*. Documento presentado a la Reunión Regional de Ministros y Autoridades Máximas del Sector de la Vivienda y Urbanismo de América Latina y el Caribe, CEPAL, LC/R.1124.

Morice, A. (1993) "Une légende à revoir: l'ouvrier du bâtiment brésilien sans feu ni lieu." *Cahiers des Sciences humaines*, 29, 2/3: 349–71.

Muñoz, H., et al. (1977) *Migración y desigualdad social en la Ciudad de México.* Instituto de Investigaciones Sociales de la Universidad Nacional Autónoma de México and El Colegio de México.

Muñoz, J. (1991) "Estructura urbana metropolitana de Lima." *Ciudad y territorio* 86/87: 115–24.

Naciones Unidas (1983) "La migración metropolitana y el crecimiento de la población en países en desarrollo seleccionados." *Boletín de Población de las Naciones Unidas* 15: 57–70.

Necochea, A. (1991) "Ideas-fuerza en torno al futuro de la región capital de Chile en una perspectiva de planificación territorial." *Revista EURE* 52/53: 53–73.

Negrón, M. (1991) "Realidad múltiple de la gran ciudad. Una visión desde Caracas." *Nueva Sociedad* 114: 76–83.

Negrón, M., and E. Niemtschik (1991) "Caracas: Una metrópolis en mutación." *Ciudad y territorio* 86/87: 99–106.

Oberai, A. (1989) *Problems of urbanization and growth of large cities in developing countries: A conceptual framework for policy analysis.* World Employment Programme, WEP 2-21/WP.169.

Ortiz, P. (1991) *La violencia en las regiones metropolitanas del Brasil.* Documento presentado al seminario "Causes and prevention of adult mortality in developing countries," Santiago, 7–11 de octubre, International Union for the Scientific Study of Population.

Ortiz de Zevallos, A. (1993) "Lima, crisis, plan y otros cuentos." *Medio Ambiente y Urbanización* 43/44: 15–22.

Ovalles, O., and K. Córdova (1986) "La calidad de vida en el área metropolitana de Caracas, Venezuela." In Ibarra et al. (eds.), (1986a) 61–95.

Palomino, N., et al. (1992) *Pobreza urbana: Mortalidad infantil y fecundidad en Lima Metropolitana 1991–1992.* Trabajo final presentado en el XV Curso regional intensivo de análisis demográfico para el desarrollo, impartido por CELADE, Costa Rica.

Peliano, A. (coordinator) (1993) *O mapa da Fome II: Informaçoes sobre a indigencia por municípios da Federação.* IPEA, documento de política no. 15.

Pesci, R., and A. Ibañez (1992) "Modernización y descentralización en las grandes ciudades: Reconversión y relocalización industrial en el Area Metropolitana de Buenos Aires." *Boletín Informativo Techint* 271: 3–47.

Pírez, P., and M. Novaro (1993) "El Gobierno de la ciudad latinoamericana." *Medio Ambiente y Urbanización* 43/44: 48–62.

Ponte, A., et al. (1992) "Aspectos de metropolizacão brasileira: Comentários sobre os resultados preliminares do censo demográfico de 1991." Mimeo, IBGE.

Population Crisis Comittee (1991) *Condiciones de vida en las 100 áreas metropolitanas más grandes del mundo.* Washington DC.

Portes, A. (1989) "La urbanización de América Latina en los años de crisis." In Lombardi and Veiga (eds.) (1986a), 81–134.

Prevot-Schapira, M. (1990) "Pauvreté, crise urbaine et émeutes de la faim dans le grand Buenos Aires." *Problèmes d'Amérique Latine* 95: 51–71.

PREALC [Programa Mundial del Empleo] (1987) *Pobreza y mercado de trabajo en el Gran Santiago.* Documento de trabajo no. 299. PREALC.

——— (1990) *Urbanización y sector informal en América Latina, 1960–1980.* PREALC.

Raczynski, D. (1988) "Costos y lecciones de las erradicaciones de pobladores." *Revista de CIEPLAN* 12: 23–8.

Rébora, A. (1993) "Los planificadores urbanos ante el cambio." *Revista EURE* 57: 31–40.

Reboratti, C. (ed.) (1987) *Población y ambiente en América Latina*. Programa Latinoamericano de Actividades en Población (PROLAP).

Recchini de Lattes, Z. (1971) *La población de Buenos Aires. Componentes demográficos del crecimiento entre 1855 y 1960*. Centro de Investigaciones Sociales, Instituto Torcuato Di Tella and CELADE.

——— (1989) "Women in internal and international migration, with special reference to Latin America." *Population Bulletin of the United Nations* 27: 95–107.

——— (1991) "Urbanization and demographic ageing: The case of a developing country, Argentina." In United Nations, *Ageing and urbanization*, United Nations, ST/ESA/SER.R/109.

Ribeiro R., et al. (1993) *Crise et réproduction sociale des familles dans la métropole de Rio de Janeiro – 1981/1990*. Document presented to 18th Session of 23rd General Congress of the International Union for the Scientific Study of Population, Montreal, 24 August – 1 September. IBGE.

Richardson, H.W. (1980) "Polarization reversal in developing countries." *Papers of the Regional Science Association* 45: 76–85.

Riveros, F. (1992) "Efectos regionales de las políticas económicas en Chile: 1974–1986." *Revista EURE* 54: 31–48.

Roda, P. (1992) *El suelo urbano en el área metropolitana de Santa Fe de Bogotá*. CEPAL, LC/L.679.

Rolnik, R. (1989) "El Brasil urbano de los años 80. Un retrato." In Lombardi and Veiga (eds.), 175–94.

Rodríguez, J. (1993) *La población del Gran Santiago: Tendencias, perspectivas y consecuencias*. CELADE, LC/DEM/R.200, Serie A, no. 283.

Rosen, B., and A.B. Simmons (1967) "Industrialization, family and fertility: A structural psychological analysis of the Brazilian case." *Demography* 8: 49–69.

Rufián, D., and E. Palma (1993) *La descentralización. Problema contemporáneo en América Latina*. ILPES, LC/IP/R.131.

Ruiz, C. (1993) "El desarrollo del México urbano: Cambio de protagonista." *Comercio exterior* 43, 8: 708–16.

Sabatini, F. (1991) "Santiago: Tendencias y posibilidades de desconcentración de la industria en la macro región central." *Revista EURE* 52/53: 75–86.

Sandbrook, R. (1986) "Crisis urbana en el tercer mundo." In Ibarra, et al. (eds.) (1986), 15–27.

Sarabia, M. (1992) *La administración de la tierra en el área metropolitana de Lima*. CEPAL, LC/L.682.

Satterthwaite, D. (1993) "Problemas sociales y medioambientales asociados a la urbanización acelerada," *Revista EURE* 57: 7–30.

Schteingart, M. (1987) "Mexico City." In Dogan and Kasarda (eds.), 268–93.

Sedlacek, G., et al. (1989) "Segmentação e mobilidades no mercado de trabalho brasileiro: Uma análise da área metropolitana de São Paulo." IPEA, Textos para discussão interna, no. 173.

Singelmannn, J. (1993) "Levels and trends of female internal migration in developing countries, 1960–1980." In United Nations Department for Economic and

Social Information and Policy Analysis, *Internal migration of women in developing countries*. United Nations.

Singer, P., et al. (1993) "San Pablo: crisis y transformación." *Medio Ambiente y Urbanización* 43/44: 23–31.

Sojo, A. (1993) *La singularidad de las políticas de población en América Latina y el Caribe en las postrimerías del siglo XX*. CELADE, LC/DEM/R.187, Serie A, no. 280.

Soler, F., and G. Rubio (1992) "Efectos espaciales de la actividad frutícola de exportación." *Revista EURE* 54: 65–78.

Szasz, I. (1992) *Mujeres inmigrantes en el mercado de trabajo de Santiago. El impacto de la reorientación económica*. CELADE.

Thomson, I. (1993) "Como mejorar el transporte de los pobres." *Revista de la CEPAL* 49: 137–53.

Trivelli, P. (1991) "Autoritarismo político y liberalismo urbano." *Ciudad y territorio* 86/87: 17–26.

Torres, A., and D. Pinheiro (organizers) (1990) *Seminário: Metropolização e rede urbana, perspectivas dos anos 90*. Instituto de Pesquisa e Planejamento Urbano e Regional (IPPUR) and Universidade Federal do Rio de Janeiro.

Tulchin, J. (1993) "Las fuerzas globales y el futuro de la ciudad latinoamericana." *Medio Ambiente y Urbanización* 43/44: 125–38.

UN [United Nations] (1987) *Fertility behaviour in the context of development: Evidence from the World Fertility Survey*. United Nations, ST/ESA/SER.A/100.

——— (1991) *Population growth and policies in mega-cities. Mexico City*. Department of International Economic and Social Affairs, ST/ESA/SER.R/105.

——— (1993a) *World urbanization prospects. The 1992 revision*. Department for Economic and Social Information and Policy Analysis, ST/ESA/SER.A/136.

——— (1993b) *World population prospects. The 1992 revision*. Department for Economic and Social Information and Policy Analysis, ST/ESA/SER.A/135.

——— (1993c) *Population growth and policies in mega-cities. São Paulo*. Department of International Economic and Social Affairs, ST/ESA/SER.R/122.

UNCRD [United Nations Centre for Regional Development] (1994) *Enhancing the management of metropolitan living environments in Latin America*. UNCRD.

Uribe-Echevarría, F. (1989) "Desarrollo regional en los años noventa. Tendencias y perspectivas en Latinoamérica." *Revista EURE* 47: 35–60.

Valladares, L. (1989) "Rio de Janeiro. La visión de los estudiosos de lo urbano." In Lombardi and Veiga (eds.), 195–222.

Villa, M. (1980) "Consideraciones en torno al proceso de metropolización en América Latina." *Notas de Población* 24: 57–105.

——— (1992) "Urbanización y transición demográfica en América Latina: Una reseña del período 1930–1990." In IUSSP–UIESP–ABEP–FCD–PAA–PROLAP–SOMEDE, *El poblamiento de las Américas. Actas*, IUSSP, 2, 339–56.

Villamizar, R., and R. Cardona (1986) "Bogotá y sus áreas de influencia: Bases de un diagnóstico." In Ibarra et al. (eds.) (1986a), 29–59.

Walton, J. (1993) *Urban poverty in Latin America*. Woodrow Wilson International Center for Scholars, Working Paper no. 202.

Webb, R., and G. Baca de Valdez (1992) *Perú en números. 1992*. Lima: Cuánto.

Yero, L. (1993) "Los estudios de futuro en América Latina." *Revista Internacional de Ciencias Sociales* 137: 413–23.

3

Contemporary issues in the government and administration of Latin American mega-cities

Peter Ward

Introduction

The purpose of this chapter is to go some way towards redressing an imbalance that exists in the current literature on mega-cities. The focus here is upon how mega-cities are administered and governed. All too often structures of city governance are taken as given or are ignored altogether. Scholars who have analysed mega-cities have usually done so through one or more of several optics. First, they have looked at the role of a mega-city within the global economy, usually from the point of view of its importance as a centre of production, control, or finance. Prime examples of this work are Friedmann and Wolff's (1982) originating hypothesis on "world cities" and, more recently, Sassen's (1991) work on New York, London, and Tokyo. A second approach has been to examine the restructuring of these cities, especially the development of so-called "control" functions to replace their earlier production role (O'Neill and Moss, 1991; Vogel, 1993). Some authors have also begun to look at the consequences of restructuring upon poverty and social organization within their urban areas (Sassen, 1991; Fainstein et al., 1992; Mollenkopf and Castells, 1991). A third focus has been to consider the extent to which these cities are becoming more or less similar over time. Particularly relevant here is whether cities in less developed countries, for example São Paulo and Mexico City, are changing physically and culturally in ways similar to their counterparts in advanced capitalist countries. Finally, the perspective adopted by most Latin American researchers during the past two decades has been more concerned with systematic aspects of a particular city's development (housing, health care, environmental problems, social movements, etc.), with little interest generally shown in the city's role in the global economy.

Whichever focus has been used to look at mega-cities, insufficient consideration has been given to the political-administrative structures through which such cities are governed and managed. In the rush to examine their economic bases and international roles, fundamental questions about their forms of administration and their governability have rarely been considered in a comparative perspective. How cities are governed tells us much about the nature of power relations and about the opportunities for citizen involvement in the management of the city.

Several important dimensions of city governance should be considered. First, what is the basis of legitimacy of the main government officers? Are they appointed or elected? If elected, is this according to partisan or non-partisan criteria? As I will demonstrate below, some Latin American city governments are constructed on the basis of political party allegiance, whereas others are based on loyalty to individual politicians. The United States has a strong tradition of non-partisanship in local government (Stanyer, 1976), particularly since the demise of traditional "machine politics" (Pohlmann, 1993). In the United Kingdom, most voters choose their councillors according to the political party each represents; they know or care little about the person they are electing. Thus, the legitimacy of government varies, as does the form of rationality which will govern an individual's behaviour once in office. Whether officers and councillors are appointed or elected, and how they are elected, may determine how they will perform, and will also affect the form of their expertise, their competence, and even their honesty or "softness" (Wade, 1989). The point here is that the structure of a city administration, and the terms under which it is expected to operate, help to shape the form of citizen involvement in city affairs.

A second issue relates to how activities and power are best organized when the urban area spreads into the jurisdiction of neighbouring authorities. This is almost uniformly the case for the mega-cities considered in this volume, and is a feature of most large cities throughout the region. Most metropolitan areas in Latin America embrace a number of different administrative units, each of which is vested with a different local authority. These may include areas with special federal jurisdictions (such as the Federal Capital of Buenos Aires and Mexico City's Federal District), states and counties (for example, the Provinces of Buenos Aires and Lima, or the State Government of São Paulo), urban authorities (usually municipalities or their equivalent), and so on. The legitimacy and rationale of each will vary, and careful ordering and clarification of the various "tiers" of authority is required if metropolitan development is to be coordinated in a meaningful way. Equally important is that the nature of intergovernmental relations between one level of authority and another needs to be properly understood.

Related to the issue of administrative organization is a third consideration: what functions should each tier of administration perform (land-use planning, infrastructural development, transportation, social services, service provision, security, cleansing, etc.)? Specifically, how can these functions be "nested" hierarchically so as to maximize efficiency, equity, access, or whatever local goals happen to be?

A final dimension of analysis is to identify the opportunities for local self-governance. To what extent do the citizens of Latin America's mega-cities mobilize politically and how far are they empowered to take genuine responsibility for local issues? What is the dominant ideology governing citizenship in each city and how has this ideology been "constructed"? There are two important considerations here. First, the institutional structures whereby citizens are represented – representational democracy; second, the structures and channels through which citizens participate in city governance – participational democracy.

These key features of city administration and governance have been neglected in the Latin American literature and have rarely been examined in comparative perspective. Too often government structures have been considered to have evolved independently, responding only to local circumstances. From the local perspective there seems to be little point to comparison. Yet these structures demand more systematic study, since they are at the heart of what determines whether large cities will be decent places in which to live. For Latin American governments this means coming to terms with new sets of responsibilities which, all too often, are alien to them. This is one reason why so many key concepts in the public administration field, for example "devolution," "empowerment," and "accountability," cannot easily be expressed in either Spanish or Portuguese.

Emerging imperatives for the 1990s

Recent political changes, both in Latin America and beyond, demand that we examine structures of urban governance and administration. First, the democratization process in Latin America has required that governments take a fresh look at the way in which cities are managed. Also, the growing disenchantment that many Latin American populations feel towards their political leaders has led to a resurgence of interest in popular participation. This feeling has encouraged new ways of thinking about urban government. As democracy has been extended to formerly authoritarian or one-party regimes, new institutional forms have had to be created. Traditional state–society relations, whether patrimonial, corporatist, or dominated by party political machines, have had to be recast. Representational democracy has also invoked a need to consider how civic structures of participation can be created that will change the political culture of dependency, encourage the involvement of heterogenous socio-economic groups in developing greater consensus in government, and, where partisan politics is an important determinant of who gets elected, achieve a balance in accommodating general citizen needs with a partisan agenda.

A second political shift is towards greater decentralization and devolution. This process appears to be emerging strongly in a number of less developed countries and has found growing support among international agencies such as the World Bank (Silverman, 1991; Jones and Ward, 1994). The willingness of national governments to embrace decentralization and administrative reorganization has been encouraged by the austerity measures introduced during the 1980s (Rodríguez and Ward, 1992, 1994; Rodríguez, 1996). Throughout Latin America, urban authorities have had to confront cuts in public expenditure and often growing pressure to privatize public utilities. Economic restructuring and political reform have required local authorities to do more with less. As a consequence, greater fiscal responsibility is being placed at the local level and municipal and state governments are required to raise more of their own revenues. Not surprisingly, people have become more concerned about how their local taxes are spent.

Third, many countries are introducing greater transparency to city budgeting and increasing the efficiency with which urban services are delivered. This involves more technocratic forms of management but also more devolution and empowerment; city administrators today recognize the political benefits of accounting more openly to those they serve. Local groups, often poorly organized and overtly radical in the past, now demonstrate greater realism and pragmatism. They are seeking fewer grandiose changes and a "qualitatively new effect in power relations" (Castells, 1977). They now want greater opportunities for self-government, so that they can defend their local rights and can participate in the improvement of their neighbourhoods (Castells, 1983; Assies, 1994). New social movements are better led and more adept at winning favours from the bureaucracy. Non-government organizations, too, have demonstrated greater pragmatism and efficacy in their relations with local authorities and in their support for social movements and local communities.

These changes in the political environment should encourage us to reflect analytically upon past experiences and to think imaginatively about which structures of city administration and governance within a democratic system appear to work best. They also require us to examine how existing structures might best be modified in order to take account of the new experiences and imperatives that have emerged during the early 1990s.

Structures of city government

Before turning to the analysis of mega-city government structures in Latin America, it is interesting to examine the structures of local government in the United States and in the United Kingdom. There are important differences between the two systems, particularly in the role party politics plays in electoral competition for office. In the United States, most city elections are non-partisan; people elect their councillors and mayors without consideration of whether they are Republican or Democrat. In the United Kingdom, the opposite is true; voters choose between candidates almost entirely on the basis of their declared party affiliation. This means that national political parties dominate local government much more in the United Kingdom than in the United States.

City government in the United States

In the United States, four clear premises underpin local government. First, the people elect their representatives. Second, there is a strong system of checks and balances which protects city government from excessive interference by federal and state administrations. Third, cities have considerable autonomy over many of their own affairs, administering their own taxes, setting their own utility charges, running primary and secondary education, policing themselves, and operating their own planning departments. Finally, most local authorities have relatively small populations and may cover only a part or a suburb of a larger urban tract. Most large urban areas contain a number of city governments.[1]

Within each city, the administrative structure normally fits one of the three basic models depicted in figure 3.1. In each case practices vary for the election of council members: in some cases council members represent individual districts of a city; elsewhere they may be elected from across the whole city. Some cities have a mixture of both, with key council positions (the mayor, for example) being elected by the whole city electorate.

Strong mayor – weak council: In cities such as Denver and Houston, the mayor has "strong" powers particularly over the selection of key officials (police chief, city attorney, treasurer, and department heads at city hall). These are important posts because they deal with sensitive areas such as personal security, civil rights, and financial management, which will determine whether the mayor is re-elected. The council is highly constrained in the extent to which it can overturn the mayor's decisions.

Weak mayor – strong council: In Atlanta, Los Angeles, and San Francisco, the mayor has much less power. The council hires and fires officials by majority vote and the mayor rarely has the right to veto a council decision. Sometimes, key officials are popularly elected, canvassing on the basis of their own mandate, independently of the council or mayor.

The city manager: Cities such as Austin or Dallas are run more like business enterprises. The elected council hires a city manager, who appoints the city's principal officers and carries full responsibility for running the city's affairs. The manager is accountable to the council and can be dismissed only by majority (or, in some places, by a two-thirds majority) vote. The city has a mayor, who often presides over council meetings, but day-to-day decisions are made by the manager. This structure is becoming increasingly common in the United States,

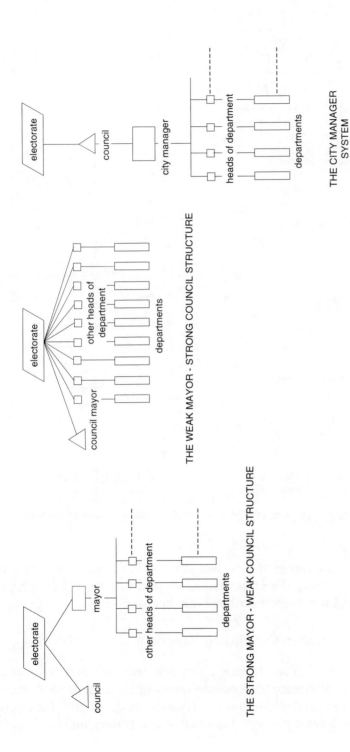

Figure 3.1 **Forms of city administration in the United States (Source: Stanyer, 1976)**

59

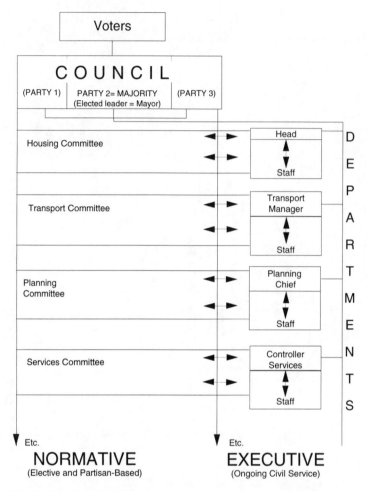

Figure 3.2 **The United Kingdom "parliamentary" council structure**

particularly in cities with less than 250,000 inhabitants, where it predominates. Among the larger cities, around half have managers and of the largest ten cities, four have managers.

City government in the United Kingdom

Figure 3.2 shows that British cities are administered by councils. Councillors are elected as representatives of political parties, the vast majority from the Conservative, Labour, and Liberal Democratic parties. The largest party in the council determines policy; if there is no outright majority a coalition between parties is necessary. This "parliamentary" system is serviced by a hierarchy of civil service officers whose role it is to implement policy. Professional, non-partisan officials are appointed by the council and continue in post even when the council changes. These officials service all council committees and run the city on a daily basis. The key power broker is not the mayor, who presides over the council and whose duties are largely ceremonial, but the council leader. The latter is elected from among the councillors of the majority party. Councils exercise a range of powers at the borough or city level, but are bound by the national laws laid down by Parliament.

Until the 1980s, metropolitan councils existed in London and six other conurbations to manage city-wide issues such as strategic planning and public transport.[2] They were abolished by the Thatcher government, which wished to break the Labour Party's hold over most of these councils. At that time most metropolitan government policies were almost diametrically opposed to those of the national government.

The principal weakness of local government in Britain is that it is so dependent on central government for its finance. Approximately 70 per cent of local government funding comes from central grants. In addition, the government currently places a series of controls over spending by local authorities. With councils being elected on the basis of political party affiliation, local policy hardly differs from area to area. When local priorities differ from national policy, local government is likely to come under attack.

This description of local government in the United States and Britain offers six basic principles by which metropolitan areas in Latin America might be administered. First, urban governments should be democratic. Whatever the administrative and management structure adopted, those serving in a policy-making capacity should be elected. There is no need for the officers in charge of implementing policy to be elected, provided that they are responsible and accountable to the council. Second, city government procedures and decisions should be transparent and all officers and councillors should be publicly accountable. Third, one authority should exist with responsibility for the whole of the city. Such a body should have power over certain metropolitan-wide concerns such as strategic planning, land-use zoning, transport policy, and responsibility for major infrastructure programmes and services. Fourth, all other responsibilities should be decentralized to lower-level bodies. Fifth, public participation should

61

be maximized and, wherever possible, power should be devolved to local communities and neighbourhoods. Finally, metropolitan authorities should have considerable fiscal autonomy. This is important if mandated authorities are to act without interference from higher levels of government.

Structures of government in Latin America's major cities

The following discussion examines the principal features of government structure and administrative practice in Latin America's major cities and judges them against the above-mentioned criteria. The discussion focuses on the four existing mega-cities, as well as drawing upon the experience of smaller capital cities such as Lima, Caracas, Bogotá, and Santiago.

1 The lack of a metropolitan authority

No major city in Latin America has a single authority which administers the whole urban area. Most cities are divided between a number of political-administrative units, and, although one municipality may be dominant, none has much wish or incentive to collaborate. This pattern is particularly marked in the metropolitan area of São Paulo, which consists of 39 separate municipalities, and in Greater Santiago, which is made up of 34 separate communes. Whereas São Paulo developed this structure by chance, failing to reform the administrative structure as the metropolitan area grew and absorbed one contiguous municipality after another, Santiago made a conscious decision to adopt it. An administrative reform in 1982 "balkanized" administration in Santiago, giving considerable responsibility to local government over a wide range of municipal matters.

If these two cities represent the extreme in terms of the number of municipal units, several other cities have similar structures. Rio de Janeiro consists of 13 separate municipalities, Buenos Aires has 20 local government units, and Mexico City falls under the jurisdiction both of the 16 delegated areas of the Federal District and of 27 municipalities. The exception is Lima, which does have the equivalent of a metropolitan government because the Province of Lima corresponds broadly with the mega-city's built-up area and is located within the a single state, the Department of Lima.

What makes administration particularly complicated is that many of these municipalities are themselves managed by separate higher-level administrative units. Mexico City is divided administratively between the Federal District and the State of Mexico. Administration in Buenos Aires is split between the Federal Capital and the surrounding State of Buenos Aires, the latter having its capital based in La Plata. Administration in Bogotá is split between the Federal Capital and the Department of Cundinamarca, and local government in Caracas between the Federal District and the State of Miranda. Indeed, among the largest eight cities of the region, only Lima, Rio de Janeiro, and São Paulo fall within a single second-tier authority (i.e. a state or a province).[3]

The division of authority between different second-tier authorities often causes conflict. In Mexico City, for example, the governor of the State of Mexico may be drawn from a different political party, or from a different faction of the same party, from the presidential nominee who runs the Federal District. As a result, there is minimal integration between agencies in the State of Mexico (responsible to the governor) and those of the Federal District (responsible to the *regente* or mayor). For example, until recently the metro system operated only in the Federal District; transportation in the State of Mexico was someone else's problem! In Buenos Aires, the national government provides electricity, water, and gas in the Federal Capital but the Province of Buenos Aires is responsible for infrastructure in the rest of the city (Pírez, 1993; see also chapter 6).

The multiplicity of municipal governments combined with different second-tier authorities makes coordinated action across the metropolitan area very difficult. In so far as there is any form of coordination it comes from three sources. The first is that one form of authority in most of these cities is much more powerful than the rest. For example, in Buenos Aires the administration of the Federal Capital (which contains 27 per cent of the total city population) has far greater influence with central government than the individual municipalities of the Province of Buenos Aires. The *intendente* of the Federal Capital holds a national cabinet post and formally runs the "municipality" on behalf of the central government. Similarly, in Mexico, the mayor of the Federal District holds a cabinet position and has much more political clout than the governor of the State of Mexico, let alone the mayors of the individual municipalities within the State.

A second source of coordination, at least in theory, comes from the consultative bodies which have been established in all four mega-cities to improve communication between the different administrative units. In practice, however, these bodies achieve little because they threaten existing power structures within each administrative area. As a result, they are little more than "letterhead" bodies with little in the way of effective power.

Finally, specific functions are occasionally managed at a metropolitan level because they are administered by larger-scale government agencies, although, as will be described below, these are often undergoing privatization. Thus, electricity provision for the whole of Mexico City is run by a federal agency. In Lima, the whole metropolitan area is supplied with water and electricity by two public companies (SEDAPAL and ElectroLima respectively). In Bogotá, a different mechanism operates: water services in some neighbouring municipalities are run under contract by the Bogotá water and sewerage company; elsewhere the company sells water in bulk to the municipality. Sometimes, too, utilities may be provided by a single private company, as is the case with CHILECTRA, which provides electricity to the whole of Santiago. In Buenos Aires, two private telephone companies compete for business across the metropolitan area.

2 Strong mayors and weak councils

A common feature of local government in most large Latin American cities is the power of the executive relative to the legislature. Much of the problem relates to the weakness of the councils. Unlike some of the mayors, who sometimes hold national cabinet office and often have considerable personal influence, the councils are very weak.

Frequently, councils have only nominal powers. In the Federal District of Mexico, although recent reforms have increased the role of the *Asamblea de Representantes* (Representative Assembly) from a consultative to that of a legislative body it remains relatively weak. In the Federal Capital of Argentina, the *Consejo Deliberante* (Deliberating Council) performs a similarly restricted role. In both cities, the mayor is the dominant actor and is appointed by the national president. Elsewhere councils have more responsibility but have few real controls over the power of the mayor. The mayor appoints the key department heads, and if the council has committees to monitor their actions, they do little more than act as public "watchdogs." Whether it is a municipal president in relation to the *cabildo* in Mexican municipalities in the State of Mexico, the *prefeito* in relation to the *Câmara de Vereadores* in São Paulo and Rio de Janeiro, or the mayor before the Deliberating Councils in the municipalities of the Province of Buenos Aires, it is the mayor who holds most of the reins of power.

Only in Santiago de Chile do the municipal councils wield real power. Administration in the city is decentralized and each of the 34 communes directly elects a council for four years. A member of the council is elected as mayor, unless a single councillor has managed to obtain more than 35 per cent of the electoral vote, in which case he or she is appointed automatically. The mayor presides over the council but has limited powers to appoint executive officers. Local officials are civil servants, and even department heads continue from one administration to the next. This structure weakens the power of the mayor relative to the council and to the executive.

3   The dominant role of partisanship

Unlike the United States, where it is the individual rather than any allegiance to a political group that matters, in Latin America party membership is critical. It is certainly much more important than a candidate's individual qualities or his or her ability to do the job. This is clearly the case where higher political authorities appoint the chief executive, as in the Federal District of Mexico.

Of course, nomination by the party is not inevitable. In Brazil, recent elections seem to have reduced the power of the political parties. Indeed, while some candidates have won power through their allegiance to a particular party (the case in 1988 of Luiza Erundina's election for the Workers'' Party in São Paulo being a good example), individual qualities appear to count more. Generally, indeed, party allegiance seems to be fickle and electors are not surprised to find candidates switching parties between elections, or forming splinter groups in loose coalitions. Leonel Brizola is perhaps the classic case of such behaviour. He has twice been elected mayor of Rio de Janeiro and once governor of the State, on each occasion representing a small minority party in coalition with other small parties.

Moreover, as local democracy spreads and electorates become more discerning, political bosses will need to select candidates for office who have some personal credibility and capacity to carry out the job. Also, the growing sense of citizenship and demands for transparency and accountability in Latin American cities are likely to intensify the emerging tension between party-based policy-making and the need to develop sound administrative practices that are less coloured by partisan considerations.[4] An individual's qualities, together with a proven capacity to govern effectively and to develop some level of consensus among hetereogenous social, economic, and political groups, will be crucial in getting that individual or party re-elected to power. While political parties may be expected increasingly to develop specific urban policy platforms and manifestos at election time, and while party affiliation is likely to continue to be an important determinant in elections and appointment to public office throughout Latin America, overt partisanship in the actual practice of city governance is likely to be eschewed, and is certainly in decline.

4 Overlapping, not interlocking bureaucracies

One of the principal impediments to effective administration in Latin American cities is the lack of an overall planning authority to coordinate the functions of different sector agencies (Londoño de la Cuesta, 1992; Ward, 1990). This is particularly important in so far as there is sometimes a multiplicity of agencies with competing or parallel responsibilities. This problem is aggravated by the way that the individual agencies ignore one another's needs and programmes and, at worst, actually compete with one another. At times, strong rivalries emerge between departments which seek to develop their programmes in maverick fashion. Where decentralized organizations form an important element of national and municipal government, they tend to act independently and make little effort to collaborate (Londoño de la Cuesta, 1992). In Bogotá, ICT, the now-defunct national housing agency, frequently built homes in areas that the local planning and servicing agencies did not want developed. The housing agency was forced to develop cheap land in the periphery of the city even though the public utilities did not want to provide infrastructure in such areas. In one notorious instance, a housing estate went without water for three years when the municipal company refused to supply it (Gilbert and Ward, 1985).

5 Privatization or municipalization?

One way of cutting through public inefficiency is to privatize state agencies. Privatization also has other virtues. It releases the public sector from the responsibility of investing in expensive infrastructure and of replacing and maintaining deteriorating service networks. It also offers governments a means of cutting their budget deficits by bringing in windfall revenues. For these reasons, privatization is flavour of the decade in Latin America and among the international development banks (Roth, 1987; World Bank, 1994). Privatization may be achieved in degrees, ranging from contracting out, through private supplements, to full privatization (Pohlmann, 1993: 284–5).

Several mega-cities have privatized or are in the process of privatizing public utilities. In Buenos Aires, the gas company has been sold off, electricity provision and telephones are in private hands, water and sanitation have been privatized through concessions, and even the metro and the suburban railways are candidates for sale. In Lima, the telephone company has been sold off and steps are being taken to reprivatize the water and electricity companies (supported by a US$300 million loan from the World Bank). In Caracas, the electricity and telephone companies are privately run. And in Santiago, the provision of electricity, telephones, and cleaning is now in private hands, although water and the metro are still the responsibility of public companies.

Progress towards the privatization of public services has been much slower in Mexico City, Rio de Janeiro, and São Paulo; indeed, the tendency is almost in the other direction. In Rio de Janeiro, the electricity and telephone companies have recently reverted to public ownership. In Mexico City, despite active privatization at the national level, there has been little divestment of public services. Garbage collection and street cleaning are being opened up to private competition and the telephone system has been privatized. To date, however, no moves have been made to sell off the major public utilities or the metro. One of the city's largest and most important municipalities privatized garbage collection in 1993, only to revoke the concession four months later owing to public dissatisfaction with the private service. One of the few major successes of the Workers' Party administration in São Paulo was its takeover of the private transport system in 1991 (Jacobi, 1995: 158). Governments in these three cities are subcontracting some activities to the private sector, but they are reluctant to embrace full privatization.

6 Fiscal responsibility: Doing more with less

All mega-cities depend heavily upon transfers of funds from central government and/or from state government. Sometimes, these transfers constitute the lion's share of recurrent expenditure. In addition, urban administrations may seek federal government assistance for special projects, particularly capital investment programmes for urban infrastructure. A common feature of Latin American local finance, therefore, is its heavy dependence upon central government.

67

In addition, urban governments seek major loans from institutions such as the World Bank, although this may dramatically raise their indebtedness and can sometimes undermine the city budget. In Bogotá, for example, major infrastructural improvements undertaken during the 1980s raised the proportion of recurrent expenditure allocated to debt servicing from 14 per cent to 41 per cent between 1980 and 1990 (Londoño de la Cuesta, 1992). In 1990, the city was running a deficit almost half of its annual recurrent expenditure. The incoming administration to São Paulo in 1988 found that it faced a billion-dollar external debt requiring a total overhaul of the city's finances.

Cities have different sources of independent local revenues: fees, taxes on production, fines and surcharges, consumption charges, property and title transfer taxes, and so on. Usually the most important source of local revenue is taxation of local property. Of course, revenues depend upon the quality, coverage, and regular updating of the property cadaster and most major cities are busy improving their cadasters. Often, indeed, they are privatizing or subcontracting property registration and assessment levies, one way of depoliticizing the collection process.

Faced by recurrent deficits and mounting debts, many governments have made a concerted effort to increase their revenues. While locally generated income still represents a small proportion of total income, many local authorities have managed to increase their local tax yield. They have raised local property taxes, transfers and sales taxes, taxes or charges on regulatory permissions authorized, and other taxes. For the first time in many years there are signs of a political will to introduce realistic levels of taxation and an improving capacity to administer tax collection.

Every government in Latin America now recognizes the need to cut expenditure and to reduce subsidies. Most governments are reducing subsidies on public transport, infrastructure, and services. Private bus companies are receiving fewer subsidies and even public transport companies are being forced to raise fares. In Mexico, the cost of travelling on the metro and the city-run bus system has risen progressively in recent years, although both still remain heavily subsidized. Throughout Latin America charges for water and electricity are increasingly set to cover the full cost of the service. In Santiago, charges for electricity are so high that disconnection for non-payment is common in low-income settlements. Elsewhere, poorer households are protected through subsidies, the income being recovered either through imposing higher charges on the rich (as in Bogotá) or through general taxation.

7   Marginalization of the public from mega-city governance

Public participation in government is very limited in Latin America. The extreme is reached in Mexico City, where the population of the Federal District is effectively disenfranchised (Ward, 1990). As noted above, the mayor (*regente*) of Mexico City is appointed by the national president and in turn selects the local mayors who head the sixteen *delegaciones*. Only recently have the citizens of the Federal District been given the right to elect any representatives; they now vote for the Representative Assembly, formerly a consultative body which now has some legislative powers, and which will in effect become a local congress in 1997. At least the Mexican government has announced reforms in the Federal District; the next mayor will be appointed by the president from among the members of the majority party in the elected Representative Assembly.

Fortunately, in most other major cities, both the principal executive and the legislature are elected. Even here, however, participational democracy is severely constrained by the limited effective powers of the local authority. Several cities have some sort of arrangement for local sub-councils but these are weakly linked to the centre. Residents' associations are weak and have little impact on decision-making. There is little clear understanding about how to move from a structure of active social movements and non-government organizations to one of citizen participation in the process of government. To date, there has been a distinct reluctance to empower citizens in Latin America's mega-cities.

Conclusion

None of the six principles of good administration listed earlier (pp. 61–2) is met in any of the Latin American cases analysed here. The city which comes nearest to matching these principles is Santiago de Chile, which has developed democratic, decentralized, and autonomous municipal authorities. It lacks a metropolitan tier of authority, but this is less problematic given that so many basic services are run privately. Its main problem is the lack of resources available to the communes containing large numbers of poor people.

Nevertheless, most mega-cities are wrestling positively with the issues of more effective public administration and more democratic and open government. Today, there is greater transparency and accountability, and more governments are beginning to balance their books. Invariably, however, they remain saddled with cumbersome bureaucracies, which lack any real coordination between the different administrative levels and jurisdictions. Most large Latin American cities clearly need greater financial and political autonomy. They need greater freedom from interference by higher levels of government so that they can get on with doing the job of running the city. If the party and executive do not comply with their electoral mandate, then they should lose office. There is also a need to create a metropolitan-level authority with responsibility for strategic functions such as physical and economic planning, transportation, and primary service provision. Such a body would resemble the former metropolitan councils in Britain. The Thatcher government abolished these councils because they were too independent. The existence of an elected authority exercising autonomy and implementing policy not of its liking was anathema to Conservative central government. However, in my view, it is precisely that level of vision and control that is required if Latin American cities are to develop in a more ordered and democratic way.

Clearly, metropolitan governments should be under the control of political parties. The non-partisan city-manager arrangement, so common in the United States, would not work in Latin America. City governments in Latin America will do best if they embrace party politics, rather than be excluded from them. Once elected, however, party representatives must demonstrate even-handedness in the disbursement of resources and eschew blatant partisanship. A clear separation must be maintained between party and government if cities are to be governed successfully.

Finally, the question of city size as an independent variable is questioned. This chapter has dealt exclusively with seven city cases, only four of which reach the size threshold of "mega-cities." It is necessary to ask whether these mega-cities confront challenges and issues that are fundamentally different from those faced by smaller metropolitan areas or even middle-sized cities. The short answer is no. Although mega-cities are more complex and invariably transcend several jurisdictions, the challenge is in essence the same: how to administer urban space in a way that is efficient, participatory, accountable, and democratic. For the reasons outlined at the beginning of this essay, cities of all sizes are beginning to confront these challenges. Overcoming these problems is a major problem everywhere, not just in the giant cities.

Acknowledgements

I am grateful to Luis Ainstein, Henry Dietz, Oscar Figueroa, Alan Gilbert, Milton Santos, Martim Smolka, Hamilton Tolosa, and Vilma Faria for their help in preparing the case study materials upon which this discussion is based. Each was asked to complete a template about "their" mega-city covering: political-administrative organization; bases of governmental legitimacy; government structure; principal activities undertaken by various levels of government; trends towards privatization; city financial arrangements and revenue-sharing; and so on. Maria Elena Ducci and Manuel Perló are also thanked for kindly providing additional information about Santiago and Mexico City respectively, and Terrell Blodgett for his insights on the operation of city governments in the United States.

Notes

1. This gives residents in those sub-areas (also called "cities") considerable local autonomy. Its weakness is that it favours the creation and maintenance of affluent sub-units and discriminates against those that are poor. It may lead to a "balkanization" of the larger unban area, dividing the population into homogeneous areas according to income.
2. London, Birmingham, Glasgow, Leeds, Manchester, Sheffield, and Tyneside.
3. Even Rio used to be divided into two separate states, Guanabara and Rio de Janeiro (see chapter 9).
4. As was clearly demonstrated in São Paulo by the Workers' Party's attempts to influence the direction of the Luiza Erundina administration (Jacobi, 1995).

References

Assies, W. (1994) "Reconstructing the meaning of urban land in Brazil: the case of Recife." In Jones and Ward (eds.), 102–7.

Castells, M. (1977) *The urban question.* Edward Arnold.

—— (1983) *The city and the grassroots.* Edward Arnold.

Fainstein, S., I. Gordon, and M. Harloe (eds.) (1992) *Divided cities: New York and London in comparative perspective.* Blackwell.

Friedmann, J. and Wolff, G. (1982) "World city formation: An agenda for research and action." *International Journal for Urban and Regional Research* 6: 309–43.

Gilbert, A.G., and P.M. Ward (1985) *Housing, the state and the poor: Policy and practice in three Latin American Cities.* Cambridge University Press.

Jacobi, P. (1995) "Alcances y límites de los gobiernos locales progresistas en Brasil. Las alcaldías petistas." *Revista Mexicana de Sociología* 95: 143–62.

Jones, G., and P. Ward (eds.) (1994) *Methodology for land and housing market analysis.* University College London Press.

Lombardi, M. and D. Veiga (eds.) (1989) *Las ciudades en conflicto: Una perspectiva latinoamericana.* Ediciones de la Banda Oriental, Montevideo.

Londoño de la Cuesta, J. (1992) "Problemas, instituciones y finanzas para el desarrollo de Bogotá: Algunos interrogantes." In Colombia, Departamento de Planeación, *Bogotá: Problemas y soluciones*, 13–38.

Mollenkopf, J., and M. Castells (eds.) (1991) *Dual city: The restructuring of New York*. New York: Russell Sage.

O'Donnell, G, (1989) "Transitions to democracy: some navigation instruments." In R. Pastor (ed.), *Democracy in the Americas: Stopping the pendulum*, Holmes and Meier, 62–75.

O'Neill, H., and M. Moss (1991) *Reinventing New York: Competing in the next century's global economy*. Urban Research Center, New York.

Pinch, S. (1985) *Cities and services: The geography of collective consumption*. Routledge & Kegan Paul.

Pírez, P. (1989) "El municipio y la organización del estado en Argentina." *Medio Ambiente y Urbanización* 28: 5–13.

——— (1993) "Politiquería, necesidades y gestión urbana en Buenos Aires, Capital Federal y/o Ciudad Metropolitana." Paper presented at the International Seminar, Gobiernos Locales y Demandas Ciudadanas en Grandes Ciudades. Instituto Mora, Mexico City, 1–3 July.

Pohlmann, M. (1993) *Governing the postindustrial city*. Longman.

Rodríguez, V. (1996) "Opening the political space in Mexico: local elections and electoral reform." In H. Dietz and G. Shidlo (eds.), *Urban elections in democratic Latin America*, Wilmington, Delaware, Scholarly Resources.

Rodríguez, V., and P. Ward (1992) *Policymaking, politics, and urban governance in Chihuahua*. LBJ School of Public Affairs, University of Texas.

——— (1994) *Political change in Baja California: Democracy in the making?* Center for US–Mexican Studies, University of California, San Diego.

Roth, G. (1987) *The private provision of public services*. Oxford University Press.

Sassen, S. (1991) *The global city: New York, London, Tokyo*. Princeton University Press.

Silverman, J. (1991) *Public sector decentralization: Economic policy and sector investment programs*. World Bank Technical Paper no. 188, Washington DC.

Stanyer, J. (1976) *Understanding local government*. Fontana.

Vogel, D. (1993) "New York City as a national and global financial center." In M. Shefter (ed.), *Capital of the American century: The national and international influences of New York City*, New York, Russell Sage Foundation, 49–70.

Wade, R. (1989) "Politics and graft: Recruitment, appointment, and promotions to public office in India." In P. Ward (ed.), *Corruption, development and inequality*, Routledge, 73–109.

Ward, P.M. (1990) *Mexico City: The production and reproduction of an urban environment*. Belhaven.

World Bank (1994) *World development report 1994*. Washington DC.

4

Land, housing, and infrastructure in Latin America's major cities

Alan Gilbert

Since 1950, Latin America's major cities have grown dramatically. The combined population of today's four mega-cities (Mexico City, São Paulo, Buenos Aires, and Rio de Janeiro) increased from some 13 million in 1950 to around 60 million in 1990 (UNDIESA, 1991). If we also include the three cities which have more than four million people (Bogotá, Lima, and Santiago), nearly 60 million additional people were added to Latin America's metropolitan population in forty years. This chapter is concerned with the effects of this massive population expansion on housing, servicing, and land use.

My general argument is that Latin America's major cities have coped with the pressures of rapid population growth extremely well. Housing and servicing provision has generally, if not universally, kept up with the pace of urban expansion. This does not mean that people live well, or that most people are well housed or serviced, or that the major cities are free of severe problems; it does mean that there is little sign of deterioration. Only in a couple of cities can a case really be made that living conditions are getting worse.

The problems facing Latin America's major cities are hardly peculiar to them. Indeed, they have begun to look more and more like the cities of the developed world. In many respects, "developed" and

Table 4.1 The growth of self-help housing in selected Latin American cities

City	Year	City population (000s)	Population in squatter settlements (000s)	Percentage
Rio de Janeiro	1947	2,050	400	20
	1957	2,940	650	22
	1961	3,326	900	27
	1970	4,252	1,276	30
	1991[a]	9,696	921	10
Mexico City	1952	2,372	330	14
	1966	3,287	1,500	46
	1970	7,314	3,438	47
	1976	11,312	5,656	50
	1990	15,783	9,470	60
Lima	1956	1,397	112	8
	1961	1,846	347	17
	1972	3,303	805	24
	1981	4,608	1,455	32
	1989	6,234	2,338	38
Buenos Aires	1956	6,054	109	2
	1970	8,353	434	5
	1980	9,766	957	10
	1991[b]	10,911	659	5

Caracas	1961	1,330	280	21
	1964	1,590	556	35
	1971	2,200	867	39
	1985	2,742	1,673	61
	1991	2,966	1,238	42
São Paulo	1973	6,561	72	1
	1980	8,493	321	5
	1985	8,929	440	6
	1987	9,109	813	8
	1991	9,483	1,050	9
	1989[c]	10,436	3,238	31
Bogotá	1955	917	367	40[d]
	1965	1,782	766	43[d]
	1975	3,069	921	30[d]
	1985	4,123	1,278	31[d]
	1991	4,824	1,254	26[e]

Sources: Gilbert, 1994: 82, which was based on a variety of primary and secondary sources, supplemented by Jacobi, 1990: 37; Kross, 1992: 154; IBGE, 1991; Molina et al., 1993: 153; UNCRD, 1994; and Villanueva and Baldó, 1994.

a. The figure for 1991 is based on the *favela* population. It therefore excludes consolidated self-help housing.
b. Changed basis of calculation.
c. Except for the 1989 figure, the figures for São Paulo record the proportion of the population living in *favelas*. They therefore underestimate the total population living in self-help housing. The 1989 figure records the proportion living in *favelas* and in "precarious housing." Figures are for the municipality of São Paulo.
d. Estimates based on the area of land developed by decade since 1935. Population figures estimated by author.
e. Changed basis of calculation.

75

"less developed" cities have been converging in form. Many cities in Europe and North America now contain stereotypical features of the Latin American metropolis: homelessness, unemployment, and a burgeoning "informal sector." Similarly, Latin American cities have begun to look much more like "developed" cities, sprouting sky-scrapers and adopting the car-based, privatized culture of the North American and Western European city. Latin America's major cities increasingly share the same urban problems as major cities in most developed countries. Such problems are the result of economic reces-sion combined with the unfettered workings of capitalist land and housing markets, the rolling back of the state, and the unlimited use of the private car. Latin American cities are different only in so far as they are generally poorer than cities in the developed world and also because they suffered much more seriously from economic decline during the 1980s.

This chapter deals with a number of related issues. First, it dis-cusses how effectively the huge growth in Latin America's metropoli-tan population has been accommodated: the way in which such vast numbers of people have been housed and the extent to which servic-ing has managed to keep up with demand. Second, it considers trends in residential structure: has segregation been increasing or decreasing and how has its form changed? Third, the chapter examines urban form: to what extent have Latin American cities developed poly-nuclear urban forms, a tendency that has been widespread among urban agglomerations in the developed world? What is happening to the inner city; is this expanding or contracting, commercializing or gentrifying?

The chapter includes discussion of four cities which have not so far achieved mega-city status: Bogotá, Caracas, Lima, and Santiago. Their inclusion has the advantage of showing how extreme size affects, and fails to affect, the process of urban growth. It also allows a wider breadth of experience to be addressed. Perhaps surprisingly, it also improves the data set, since some of these smaller cities have better information than some of the mega-cities.

Housing conditions

The nature of the housing problem

Housing conditions in Latin America's largest cities are clearly far from good. Too many people lack services and infrastructure, too

Table 4.2 **Service delivery in major Latin American cities, around 1990**

City	Homes with water 1985	Homes with water 1990	Homes with sewerage 1990	Homes with electricity 1990
Buenos Aires	100[a]	66[b]	55[b]	n.a.
Caracas	n.a.	78[b]	68[b]	n.a.
Rio de Janeiro	n.a.	69[f]	72[f]	n.a.
São Paulo	92[a]	99[c]	80[c]	99[c]
Bogotá	96[a]	99[e]	84[b] (75[e])	94[e]
Mexico City	99[a]	97[b]	82[b]	n.a.
Lima	80[a]	60[b] (89[d])	85[b]	96[d]
Santiago	n.a.	98[b]	92[b]	n.a.

Sources:
a. Gavidia, 1994: 21.
b. Lee, 1994: 31.
c. Taschner and Bruna, 1994: 100.
d. Webb and Fernández, 1991: 254.
e. Hataya et al., 1993: 65.
f. Special tabulation of National Household survey provided by Hamilton Tolosa.

many live in homes built of flimsy materials, too many live in over-crowded accommodation, too few have full security of tenure. During the lost decade of the 1980s, conditions may well have deteriorated. At the same time, the situation should be put into context. Latin America's largest cities have relatively few homeless, certainly when compared to the situation in the major cities of the developed world (World Bank, 1992: 14). And, despite the grave problems, most families live in adequate accommodation.

Of course, large numbers of people live in self-help housing and, because the number of self-help houses has increased dramatically over time, many would argue that the shelter problem is out of control. Indeed, concern that the Latin American city might be overwhelmed by shanty housing and its revolutionary inhabitants has long been one of the great fears of many observers (Germani, 1973; ECLAC, 1973). Table 4.1 seems to demonstrate that the fear was real; millions of people in Latin America's largest cities now live in self-help housing. In Lima, two families in five live in *barriadas* and *pueblos jóvenes*, some 1.8 million people in total. In Caracas, the total number of *barrio* dwellers is similar but accounts for three *caraqueños* out of five. In every city, the proportion of the population living in some kind of self-help accommodation has increased through time.[1]

The figures remind us of the problems facing the poor in Latin

American cities, but they actually tell us little about either political attitudes or housing conditions in self-help settlements. The increase in self-help housing has not led to a social revolution; indeed all the evidence points to the fact that home ownership in self-help settlements has had a politically conservative effect (Castells, 1983; Cornelius, 1975; Eckstein, 1977; Perlman, 1976; Portes, 1972; Ray, 1969). Self-help housing has also helped to improve the housing stock. What begins as a shanty soon becomes a consolidated house (Mangin, 1967; Turner, 1967). Gradually, electricity and water are installed in the neighbourhood, the roads are paved, bus services begin operating, and schools are built (Gilbert and Ward, 1985). On the basis of changes in electricity, water, and drainage provision, past experience can be interpreted very positively. Service improvements have permitted vast areas of shanty towns to be transformed into proper suburbs.

Indeed, table 4.2 shows that housing conditions are generally far better than the figures in the previous table suggest. The vast majority of households in the largest cities now have access to potable water and electricity, and most are connected to the sewerage system. Few cities have more than 5 per cent of their population living in housing built of flimsy materials.

Three decades of improvement

Housing conditions in the largest cities improved consistently between 1950 and 1980, a period of rapid population growth. By 1980, the provision of infrastructure had never been better (Dixon, 1987). While the quality of services varied considerably from city to city, table 4.3 shows that water, sewerage, and electricity delivery generally improved.

Figures for individual cities strongly support that conclusion. In Bogotá, the proportion of homes without water fell from 14 per cent in 1951 to 4 per cent in 1985 and those without electricity from 20 per cent to 4 per cent (Molina et al., 1993: 39). In the municipality of São Paulo, the proportion of dwellings with piped water increased from 58 per cent in 1950 to 64 per cent in 1970; those with electricity increased from 85 per cent to 96 per cent (Batley, 1983: 118).

If service levels generally improved, so did the tenure situation. In so far as most Latin American families claim that they wish to live in their own home, the dramatic jump in home ownership in Latin American cities is a sign of housing improvement (Gilbert, 1993;

Table 4.3 **Urban service delivery in selected Latin American countries, 1960–1990 (percentage without service)**

Country	Water		Sewerage		Electricity	
	1960	1990	1960	1990	1960	1990
Argentina	65	73	42	100	85	95
Brazil	55	95	55[b]	84	73	88
Chile	74	100	60	100	86	95
Colombia	79	87	61	87	83	n.a.
Mexico	68	94	70[b]	85	n.a.	n.a.
Peru	47	68	30	76	51	72
Venezuela	60[a]	89[c]	43[b]	90[c]	n.a.	84

Sources: United Nations, 1987: tables 42–4; World Bank, 1994: table A2.
a. 1964.
b. 1964.
c. 1980.

Table 4.4 **The development of owner-occupation in selected cities since 1950 (percentage of households owning their home)**

City	1947–52	1960–64	1970–73	1980–85
Mexico City	27	23	43	64
Guadalajara	29	28	43	52
Puebla	36	16	39	48
Caracas (DF)	47	45	52	64
Lima	n.a.	17	42	48
Santiago	26	37	57	64
Rio de Janeiro	33	n.a.	54	56
São Paulo	38	n.a.	54	56
Buenos Aires	27	58	61	73
Bogotá	43	46	42	57

Sources: Gilbert, 1993; Riofrío, 1978: 58; INE, 1986a; Jaramillo, 1992: 25; Valladares, 1984: 146; Yujnovsky, 1984: 345; and some national census and household survey figures.

Gilbert and Varley, 1991). Since 1950, the trend in every large Latin American city has been for more and more people to own their homes (table 4.4). The causes of this trend are clear. First, there has been a massive increase in the size of the middle class. Second, the development of mortgage systems has allowed more people to buy formal-sector homes. Third, Latin American governments have strongly encouraged the trend towards home ownership. Fourth, transport and infrastructure improvements have permitted the spread of suburbia. Finally, the massive growth of self-help suburbs and government programmes to service and legalize these areas has increased home ownership among the poor.

Obviously, Latin America's major cities continue to face huge shelter problems. The improvements have not been universal; indeed, a major problem in drawing conclusions about social conditions in Latin American cities is that they vary so much between different areas of the city. If service provision has improved remarkably in the more consolidated areas of every city, the authorities have never managed to keep up with the constantly increasing demand for services. The key problem in every city is to cover the newer areas. Figure 4.1 shows the changing pattern of water provision in Mexico City between 1950 and 1980. While provision in the metropolitan area improved consistently through time, there were always areas on the edge of the city which lacked services. If some governments have kept up reasonably well with the population explosion (Bogotá, Mexico City, and Santiago), others have done rather badly (Lima and São Paulo).

In addition to the obvious spatial variations there are vast differences in the quality of services between different income groups. Table 4.5 shows how dramatically the quality of servicing differs between income groups in Lima. A similar picture can be drawn for every other major Latin American city.

Housing during economic recession

If the quality of housing improved in most cities between 1950 and 1980, the trend since 1980 is much less certain. Although we still lack data for many cities for the 1990 round of census figures, it is likely that deterioration set in during the "lost decade" (Iglesias, 1992).[2]

We know that the incidence of poverty increased greatly in Latin America during the 1980s, particularly in the cities. The proportion of families living in poverty in urban Latin America rose from 25 per cent to 32 per cent between 1970 and 1985, an increase of almost 50 million people (UN, 1989: 39). The combined impact of inflation, rising unemployment, and cuts in social expenditure reduced living standards in most cities by years – in places by decades.

Housing conditions were clearly hurt by this rise in poverty. First, formal-sector construction slowed in most cities. Declines in private-sector construction were accompanied by cut-backs in state construction. During the 1980s, governments in Brazil and Venezuela cut back on their massive building programmes (Gilbert, 1989; Shidlo, 1990;

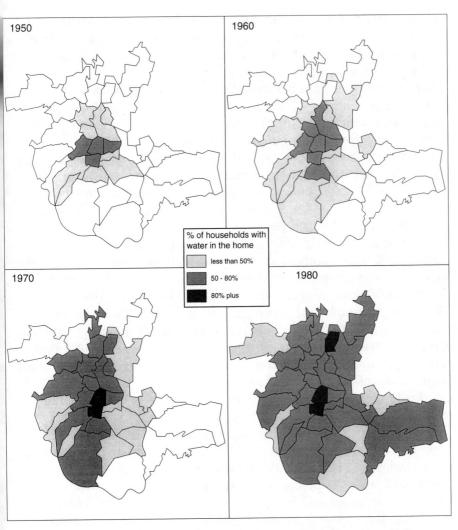

Figure 4.1 **Growth of piped water provision in Mexico City, 1950–1980**

Table 4.5 **Service delivery by income group in Lima, 1990 (percentage with service)**

Service	Bottom 10%	Top 10%	All Lima
Water in home	57.3	91.3	70.0
Water truck	20.0	4.4	8.6
13 hours or more of water	19.0	23.5	18.6
Sewerage	63.5	93.2	71.5
Electric light	87.5	98.6	90.5
Cook with kerosene	87.8	12.8	55.7

Source: Glewwe and Hall, 1992: 30.

81

Valença, 1992). Current doctrine in Argentina, Brazil, Mexico, and Peru is to maintain that position. In booming Chile and Colombia, the approach is offer subsidies to families to buy homes constructed by the private sector (Persaud, 1992).

Second, the self-help consolidation process was slowed by falling real incomes (Gilbert, 1989). Households had smaller disposable incomes with which to buy the materials needed to improve their homes. They were forced to spend more of their income on food (Cordera and González, 1991; Gutiérrez, 1990). Cuts in social spending by the state forced more households to consume private education and health. Longer working hours sliced into the time available to consolidate the house. The prospects for improving the self-help home deteriorated in consequence.

Third, most self-help settlements received fewer services because many public utility companies were badly affected by the debt crisis. Indeed, it was often the seriousness of their external commitments that accentuated national debt problems (Connolly, 1985; Gilbert, 1990). Major loans were contracted during the 1970s to expand service capacity. With the rise in real interest rates in the late 1970s, and rapid devaluation of local currencies occurring against the dollar, servicing external debts became a major burden. One result was a cut in government investment programmes. Another was that tariffs to customers rose. Local customers were increasingly charged commercial prices, sometimes as a result of privatization, but usually because state agencies were attempting to improve their budgets and to raise their revenues in order to repay the foreign loans. In Bogotá, electricity tariffs soared in the 1980s (see chapter 11). In Santiago, electricity and water supplies to many families were cut when tariffs began to rise faster than household earnings (Rodríguez, 1989).

Fourth, local governments sought to increase their revenues by raising taxes. Land taxes rose in many cities (Ward, 1990). The only benefit for self-help settlers was that governments were more disposed to give out land titles. Large numbers of land titles were distributed to self-help settlers in Caracas, Lima, Mexico City, Rio de Janeiro, and Santiago (Azuela, 1989; Coulomb and Sánchez, 1991; Gilbert, 1993; Persaud, 1992).

Fifth, although the recession slowed the pace of self-help consolidation, it also forced more families to contemplate the self-help option. Faced by cuts in their real wages, many households have been forced to move out of rental accommodation. Some had little option but to attempt to move into a squatter settlement. Fortunately, their

Table 4.6 **Tenure by income group in Bogotá and Lima**

Income group	% in group	Ownership	Renting	Other
BOGOTÁ				
Very low	3.8	34.9	48.8	16.3
Low	21.8	47.3	46.6	6.1
Medium-low	51.3	40.5	53.7	5.8
Medium	15.6	51.7	42.7	5.6
Medium-high	6.1	68.6	25.7	5.8
High	1.5	82.3	11.8	5.9
Total	45.9	45.9	47.9	6.2
LIMA				
Low	n.a.	60.5	28.3	11.2
Medium	n.a.	71.5	20.3	8.2
High	n.a.	74.2	18.0	8.0

Sources: Jaramillo, 1990: 82; Webb and Fernández, 1991: 251.

chances of occupying land free or very cheaply increased as a result of the wave of democratization that swept through the region during the 1980s. Many newly elected democratic governments were unwilling to repress land invasions; indeed, in Caracas, Lima, Rio de Janeiro, and São Paulo some actually encouraged informal processes of land alienation. With the debt crisis cutting their ability to supply urban populations with either housing or services, governments looked for less expensive ways of tackling the housing question. The poor had to be housed, but, if proper accommodation could not be provided, then the poor had to be allowed to do it themselves. Impoverished governments simply intervened less. That may not have been a satisfactory response, but at least it was less unpopular than repressing land invasions or insisting on unrealistically high levels of service provision. Democratic governments would not be reelected if they reacted otherwise. In cities, where the invasion of land was permitted, or where land could be acquired very cheaply through illegal processes such as the alienation of *ejidos*,[3] the result was a proliferation of new flimsy accommodation.

Sixth, in cities where land invasions were seldom permitted (for example, in Bogotá, Buenos Aires, and Mexico City), the cost of self-help plots proved too expensive for many households. Here the quality of accommodation deteriorated in the sense that more families were obliged either to rent or to share accommodation. In cities where renting had long been a common refuge for poor families (table 4.6), many newly formed households rented rooms in the neighbourhood. In Santiago, where renting is expensive, sharing increased markedly after 1973 and, in 1984, possibly as many as one family in five occupied an improvised shack in someone's back garden or used a room in their house (Ogrodnik, 1984). Most of these *allegados* were young, many were poor, and a high proportion of families were headed by single women (Gilbert, 1993: 86; Necochea, 1987; Trivelli, 1987). Whether the local response was for more families to share accommodation or for renting to become more common, the overall result was for room densities to rise.

In sum, recession damaged the prospects of upward residential mobility for many families, even if the precise impact in different cities varied. In some cities there was a huge expansion in the amount of flimsy self-help housing; elsewhere, the incidence of renting and sharing increased with little expansion in the squatter population. Local variations in housing markets, state policies, economic health, and political dynamics will have determined the final outcome (Gilbert, 1993).

Unfortunately, we have too little data to document the exact impact of the recession on housing conditions in Latin America's largest cities. However, evidence from Lima, the city worst hit by the recession of the 1980s, broadly supports the idea of deteriorating housing conditions. Table 4.7 shows that among the poorest 10 per cent and 30 per cent of households in Lima, the incidence of invasions increased markedly. For the city as a whole, the proportion of the population living in invasion settlements rose from 2 per cent to 10 per cent. Access to piped water also deteriorated among the very poor. In other respects, the signs of deteriorating conditions are less obvious; access to electricity clearly improved and the incidence of renting remained more or less constant.

Size of city as an influence on housing conditions

There is little empirical support for the belief that housing conditions in the giant cities are worse than in Latin America's other cities. Indeed, given the huge variation between countries, it would be surprising if there were any close correlation between city size and housing conditions. Even within countries, local housing and employment conditions vary so much that there is little relation between size of city and housing conditions. Table 4.8 illustrates this point by showing how the proportion of households living in *favelas* in Brazil's

Table 4.7 **Housing conditions during economic recession, Lima, 1985–1990**

	1985		1990	
Characteristic	10% poorest	30% poorest	10% poorest	30% poorest
Home in *vecindad*	11.1	9.9	5.3	9.5
Improvised housing	2.2	1.5	5.3	3.5
Invasion settlement	7.4	4.2	18.1	16.3
Rented home	10.5	16.4	10.6	18.0
Water from standpipe, tanker or well	27.0	19.5	32.9	21.1
Electricity provision	86.3	92.0	94.7	95.4

Source: Webb and Fernández, 1991: 253.

largest 15 cities varies independently of city size. Indeed, while the proportion of *favelados* in São Paulo is lower than the average for all 15 cities, that for Rio de Janeiro is higher. When the higher figures for the northern and north-eastern cities are removed, São Paulo still has a lower average than the revised national figure. The incidence of self-help housing is not linked to the size of the city.

It is also important to recognize that the ranking of cities in terms of housing quality varies with the indicator used. Some cities do well on one indicator but badly on another. Table 4.9 shows that the quality of housing between cities in Latin America and the Caribbean varies according to the nature of the land market, local employment characteristics, governmental ability to provide services, climate, and relief. The principal problems facing one city may be of minor importance in another. In one city, homes may have poor infrastructure and services but offer families plenty of space. In another city, families may suffer from severe overcrowding but have plenty of services. It is difficult to tell from table 4.9 whether the housing problems of Bogotá are better or worse than those of Kingston, Jamaica. Conditions in the former are more crowded and there is a much longer journey to work. However, households in Kingston have less access to drinking water and are much less likely to own their home. This table suggests that there is no simple explanation of bad housing conditions and city size certainly explains very little.

If there are two reasonably consistent differences between larger and smaller cities, the first is that the former tend to be better serviced and to have more tenants. Table 4.10 shows that conditions in large cities are generally better than in the rest of the urban area of the

85

Table 4.8 *Favela* **households by size of city in Brazil, 1990**

City	Number of homes (000s)	*Favelas* as percentage of total homes
São Paulo	3,668	5.8
Rio de Janeiro	2,409	9.8
Belo Horizonte	517	10.0
Salvador	470	3.7
Brasília	422	0.1
Pôrto Alegre	386	6.5
Fortaleza	384	13.3
Curitiba	328	6.7
Recife	311	42.2
Belém	257	15.1
Goiania	251	1.6
Campinas	221	17.8
Manaus	218	4.7
Santos	159	7.1
São Luis	151	3.9
Average of 15 cities		9.9
Average of 7 southern cities		7.2

Source: IBGE, 1991: table 5.2.

same country. The major cities tend to receive more resources from central governments because of their political importance, to have developed better-organized servicing agencies because of the pressure exerted by the large number of powerful national and foreign companies located in the major cities, and to have a higher tax base with which to contract foreign loans.

The other major difference between larger and smaller cities is in the incidence of renting and sharing. Table 4.11 suggests that owning a home is more difficult in large metropolitan areas than in smaller cities. While the evidence is hardly conclusive, La Paz, São Paulo, Bogotá, Mexico City, and Caracas all have distinctly lower rates of ownership than their respective national averages. Of course, there is hardly a close relationship between size and ownership; too many other variables influence the level of ownership. This is demonstrated by evidence from Mexico which shows that several cities, including Guadalajara and Puebla, have lower levels of ownership than Mexico City.

Ownership tends to be lower in larger cities because travel times

Table 4.9 **Housing indicators for selected Latin American cities, around 1990**

City	Floor area (m²)	Persons/ room	Water/ plot (%)	Illegality (%)	Journey to work (minutes)	Ownership (%)
Bogotá	8.8	1.7	99	8	90	62
Caracas	16.0	2.0	70	54	39	65
Kingston	15.3	1.5	87	33	60	41
Monterrey	8.6	1.2	91	4	25	83
Quito	8.6	1.8	76	40	56	79
Rio de Janeiro	19.4	1.0	97	16	107	62
Santiago	15.9	1.2	99	0	51	80

Source: World Bank, 1992.

Table 4.10 **Water and sewerage provision by urban area and major city, 1990**

Country	Water	Sewerage	City	Water	Sewerage
Argentina	80	70	Buenos Aires	66	55
Brazil	90	45	São Paulo	99	80
Chile	98	83	Santiago	98	92
Colombia	66	57	Bogotá	99	84
Mexico	78	61	Mexico City	97	82
Peru	42	39	Lima	89	85
Venezuela	90	81	Caracas	78	68

Sources: Pan-American Health Office; table 4.2.

Table 4.11 **Housing tenure by major city and in total urban area, around 1980**

Country	Owners	Tenants	City	Owners	Tenants
Argentina	68	15	Buenos Aires	73	16
Bolivia	69	15	La Paz	49	20
Brazil	63	22	São Paulo	56	35
Chile	63	19	Santiago	64	20
Colombia	68	24	Bogotá	57	40
Mexico	68	23	Mexico City	64	36
Peru	59	29	Lima	61	30
Uruguay	56	23			
Venezuela	75	18	Caracas	63	31

Sources: Table 4.4 and Gavidia, 1994: 23.

from the periphery to the urban centre are much longer. As such, many tenants living in central areas choose not to move out to the self-help periphery (Gilbert and Varley, 1991). The choice between central and peripheral accommodation in a smaller city is much less stark. Rates of ownership are also lower because access to land is generally more difficult. Governments tend to control state lands better in capital cities than elsewhere and land-price/earnings ratios tend to be higher in the largest cities.

The price of land

Trends in land prices

Most commentaries on Latin American cities sooner or later aver that land prices are excessively high. Many blame this problem on the process of land speculation and it is certainly true that far too many plots are being held out of the market in anticipation of a rise in price (Kowarick, 1988; Trivelli, 1987).[4] They also emphasize how spectacularly land values are rising. For example, Allen (1989: 8), citing IBASE (1982), claims that "the average price of land in São Paulo quadrupled between 1964–1978, and in Rio rose by three and three-quarter times its value." In Bogotá, FEDELONJAS (1988) claims that real land prices increased roughly six times between 1959 and 1988, and Villamizar (1982) that they increased annually by 4 per cent per annum between 1955 and 1978.

Until recently, the idea that land prices always rose rapidly in third world cities was conventional wisdom. Such a trend made sense. As Payne (1989: 45) puts it: "Under conditions of sustained high urban growth, urban land has enjoyed a level of demand well in excess of formally sanctioned supply, guaranteeing a good rate of return on investment." However, recent evidence has begun to detect signs of falling real land values in Santiago and in several Mexican cities (CED, 1990; Coulomb and Sánchez, 1991; Gilbert, 1989; Jones, 1991). Limited data from Guadalajara suggests that the Mexican recession had a strong impact on land prices. Between 1975 and 1980, the average price of peripheral plots rose in real terms by 14 per cent; between 1980 and 1985 it fell by 3 per cent (Gilbert and Varley, 1991: 93).[5] In Puebla, real land prices fell spectacularly after the crisis broke in 1982 (Jones, 1991) and a similar pattern also occurred in Querétaro, Toluca, and Mexico City (Jones, Jiménez, and Ward, 1993; Coulomb and Sánchez, 1991). In Santiago, land prices in high-income areas of the city rose spectacularly between 1979 and 1982, only to plummet in the next few years (CED, 1990).

If land values have fallen the reasons are fairly clear. As Durand-Lasserve (1990: 49) points out: "The contradiction between rapid land price increases and stagnant or declining urban incomes at least during the first phase of the crisis led to the erosion of the formal land market. This erosion is reflected in ... the outflow of capital from the land sector to either other economic sectors or to the up-market real estate business."

Whether changes in land prices matter depends in part on what is being measured. What precisely do average land values measure? Detailed work on an excellent data set of land prices in Bogotá demonstrate the problem perfectly: land prices between 1955 and 1988 rise during one longish period and fall during another; they shoot up one moment and fall the next. As such, the choice of time period is critical to analysis. Even more important is how to interpret the meaning of the average: what does an average land price rise measure when land prices rise rapidly at the periphery and slowly near the centre? Still more troubling is the fact that trends are very sensitive to changes in the way that the annual average is calculated. Dowall and Treffeisen's (1990: 118) reworking of the Bogotá data set turns an annual 4.4 per cent increase into "an annual decline in real terms of 1.4 per cent." Without going into a long technical discussion of the reasons why, my feeling is that few of the figures on trends in land prices are really to be trusted.

Do rising land prices matter?

Mohan and Villamizar (1982: 248) argue that a rise in land values only matters if it "widens the already high levels of inequality that exist in many poor countries." If the poor buy land and benefit from rising land values, then is there any reason to worry? If the poor sell land to the rich, won't incomes have been redistributed? Even if the poor buy from the rich, might they not benefit from later price increases?

Unfortunately, although Mohan and Villamizar's point is important, it is less than clear that the working of the land market in Latin America's cities is helping to redistribute income. Much agricultural land is owned by affluent families, so the sale of that land worsens the distribution of income. Even where agricultural land is owned by the poor, it is uncertain whether they ever receive the full market value.

And, if they buy plots which subsequently rise in value, it is uncertain whether they will be able to capitalize on the increase. Evidence from several cities is beginning to suggest that it is very difficult to sell plots of land once they have consolidated houses on them (Gilbert, 1993). Land is normally sold only when it contains little more than a shack (Gilbert and Ward, 1985); it is difficult to sell a proper house because banks are reluctant to offer mortgages on property in low-income settlements and sometimes there is no legal title. Better-off families prefer to buy empty plots on which to build houses to their own design. As such, it is difficult for a poor owner to reap the benefits of any rise in land values.[6]

But, even if the poor benefit from rising land values, this hardly helps those trying to buy a plot for the first time. It is the relationship between land prices and wages that is the key to housing affordability. The problem is demonstrated by evidence from São Paulo, where Kowarick and Campanário (1988: 39) report that the cost of land rose 3.6 times as quickly as the minimum salary between 1959 and 1986. New households without property were increasingly frozen out of the formal land market.[7]

New entrants to the housing market also suffer in so far as plot sizes tend to decline when land costs rise faster than incomes. In Bogotá, plot sizes fell quite dramatically during the 1970s and 1980s both for formal and informal construction sites. Between 1973 and 1975 formal construction sites averaged 155 square metres; ten years later the average had fallen to 73 (Molina et al., 1993: 59).[8] A similar trend was apparent for Bogotá for informal-sector housing plots, which fell from 157 square metres during the 1960s to 131 square metres in the later 1970s (Gilbert and Ward, 1985: 118). By the mid-1980s, plot sizes had fallen to 75 square metres (Molina, 1990: 304). Under such circumstances, population densities are almost bound to rise as families economize on their use of land.

The increasing price of land, therefore, is clearly a major problem in a city such as Bogotá and is even more of a problem in cities like Santiago, where a poor family does not have the same option of buying land without a full range of services. In certain Mexican cities, however, poor-quality peripheral land is not particularly expensive; in the middle and late 1980s a plot of land cost between two months' and five months' earnings at the minimum salary (Colomb and Sánchez, 1991; Gilbert and Varley, 1991). The land may be of poor quality, it may be distant from the main centres of employment, it may be lacking services, but it is cheap. In Caracas or Lima, where the poor generally obtain land through invasion, plots are virtually free.

The key point to recognize is that there is a great deal of variation between Latin American cities in the way that the poor acquire land. These different methods have a pronounced impact on the afford-ability of land in each city (Gilbert and Varley, 1991). What we need to know is not what is happening to some mythical average land price but what is happening to the cost of plots on the periphery relative to incomes. Unfortunately, it is just this kind of data that is rarely available. Until we have such a data set, we will be unable to judge whether the cost of low-income plots of land is increasing or decreas-ing over time relative to what the ordinary family earns.

Residential segregation

In the nineteenth-century city, most people lived close together. In the absence of motorized transport, the city had spread little and population densities were high. By the turn of the century, the rich had begun to move out of the city centre into detached suburban homes. As transport facilities improved, the pace of suburbanization accelerated and a wider range of social groups began to participate. Even the poor began to move out of central rental accommodation into the self-help suburbs. Of course, the process of suburbanization was very different for the poor: the rich moved one way, the poor another. By the 1950s, a definite pattern had been established in most cities, in which the rich lived in the most environmentally attractive areas of the city and the poor somewhere else. In São Paulo in 1970, "over three quarters of families in the top income bracket ... lived in seven districts within a radius of approximately 7 kilometres to the south and west of the city" (Batley, 1983: 102).

Latin American cities remain highly segregated and few locals will have any difficulty in reciting the names of the richest and the poorest settlements in the city. In Lima, everyone knows that San Isidro and Miraflores are rich while Comas and Villa El Salvador are poor; in Santiago, the extremes are found in affluent Providencia and Vitacura in the north-east and poor La Pintana and La Granja in the south. In Rio de Janeiro, the rich live in Leblon and Ipanema and the poor in the Baixada Fluminense. However, the pattern of segregation today is much more complicated than in the past. Figure 4.2 shows that it is no longer possible to state quite so categorically that the rich live in the north of Bogotá and the poor in the south. In Caracas, rich and

91

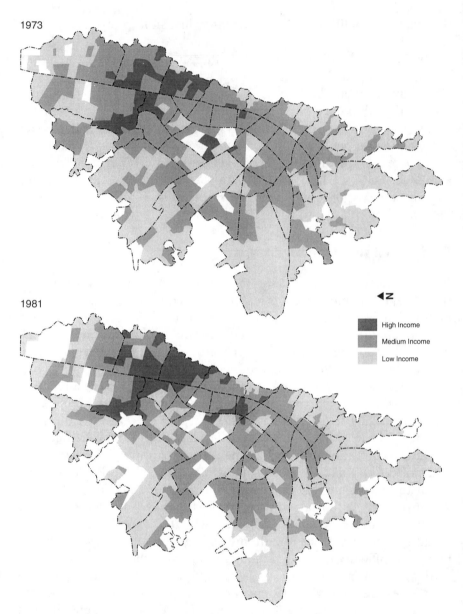

Figure 4.2 **Bogotá: Residential segregation, 1973 and 1981**

poor live in most zones of the city, albeit in clearly demarcated areas.

The pattern of segregation has become more complicated for a number of reasons. First, as urban areas have expanded in population and area, affluent areas have come into contact with lower-income areas. Sometimes, the expansion of these élite suburbs collides with working-class areas that were once some distance away. In Bogotá, for example, the affluent north has reached the low-income settlements of the periphery, clustered around the quarries of Usaquén (figure 4.2). Since the authorities could not be persuaded to move such well-consolidated areas, the rich had little choice but to live close to the poor.

Second, the growth of the middle class has complicated the pattern of residential segregation. The middle classes have increasingly taken over land close to low-income areas because they cannot afford land elsewhere. During the 1960s, several large construction companies bought land in the west and south-west of Bogotá which they developed into middle-class suburbs during the 1970s (Gilbert and Ward, 1985: 116). Today, such suburbs occupy land that would have been inconceivable some years ago.

Third, variegated topography has also helped to blur the neat pattern of segregation; indeed hilly cities are arguably less clearly polarized than flat cities. This is obvious in Caracas and in Rio de Janeiro, where many steep slopes have long been considered unsuitable for formal-sector construction. Since the land had little commercial value it was allowed to remain in the hands of the municipal authorities and during periods of rapid urban growth came under pressure from low-income groups; *barrios* and *favelas* often developed in close proximity to high-income and middle-income areas. Indeed, in Caracas, this process has continued in the highly accentuated terrain that is now being developed in the south and south-east of the city. Here, every exclusive residential development appears to have its low-income neighbour next door. A functional symbiosis has developed; the *urbanización* provides work for maids, shoe menders, laundresses, and the like, and the *barrio* provides the cheap labour.

At the same time, there is little sign of residential segregation disappearing. Indeed, in some respects there is greater polarization. As crime rates rise, the fear of burglary, kidnapping, and other crimes has encouraged many rich families to move into protected areas. Some move into blocks of luxury apartments located in the élite suburbs, offering, in São Paulo, "security in a city where violence is an acute problem" (Taschner and Bruna, 1994: 100). Other rich families move into what are effectively armed camps: residential developments surrounded by high walls with entry controlled by security guards. It is increasingly likely that rich Latin American children will grow up without having any contact with the urban poor. They attend exclusive private schools and universities, they play in luxury clubs, they shop in exclusive commercial centres, and they are never allowed out on their own. Even their traditional form of contact with the poor, through the live-in maid, has changed; most domestic servants now prefer to live with their own families and commute to work.

Urban planning has contributed little to the process of segregation, even if it is sometimes argued that zoning regulations were introduced in Latin American cities primarily to help keep poor people out of the élite suburbs (Amato, 1969). The most likely explanation of residential segregation has always been market forces; élite suburbs have long been protected by high land values and the costs of installing full services before housing is constructed. If governments have accentuated residential segregation, it is through their response to market pressures. Governments have given priority to the servicing of areas that could afford to pay for them. The water, telephone, and electricity companies have not ignored low-income areas because they were full of social lepers but because installing services in poorer areas is more complicated. It is more difficult to install infrastructure in settlements where the houses have already been built, especially when so many of their inhabitants have difficulty paying the bill.

Of course, some governments have gone out of their way to increase the level of residential segregation. Over the years, several military regimes have attempted to remove poor people from "slums" in high-income residential areas to "proper homes" in peripheral areas of the city. Orgies of squatter relocation occurred in Caracas in the 1950s, Rio de Janeiro between 1967 and 1973, and Buenos Aires between 1976 and 1981 (Valladares, 1978; Portes, 1979; Dwyer, 1975; Pajoni, 1982).

The most recent example of such "social cleansing" was practised by the Pinochet regime in Santiago between 1979 and 1985. In those six years, some 28,700 families were moved from *campamentos* located on private land (CED, 1990). Most of those families were moved from the central areas and from the affluent eastern suburbs into the communes of the far south and the north-west of the city. An administrative reorganization, in 1982, aggravated the effects of the removal programme. New municipal authorities were established with much greater powers. Unfortunately, the revenues available to each municipality differed considerably; the authorities facing the greatest social problems had only a fraction of the resources available to affluent districts such as Providencia and Vitacura. Portes (1990: 24) claims that "it is now difficult to talk about Santiago as a single city because groups thus segregated lead widely divergent lives and remain confined – by choice or force – to their distinct spatial locations."

If the Pinochet regime went out of its way to cleanse the city of its slums, are the poor and rich are any more segregated in Santiago than in any other major Latin American city? Is Santiago really any different from São Paulo, where "the poor are removed to the periphery, ever further and less well-serviced, while the rich live in central neighbourhoods well provided with infrastructure in housing of good quality, even of great luxury" (Sachs, 1990: 36)? Are any of the other major cities any different?

Population density

Population densities in most major Latin American cities today average between 100 and 130 persons per hectare. There are, of course, substantial variations between cities. As table 4.12 shows, the poorer cities, Bogotá, Lima, and Mexico City, have particularly high population densities, although Caracas, confined to its narrow valleys, is also densely populated. More affluent Santiago and São Paulo have lower densities.

Ingram and Carroll (1981: 265) claim that Latin American cities "do not appear to be significantly more dense than older central cities in the US. The peripheral densities of Latin American cities are similar to those found in North American cities."[9] This rather surprising finding is explained by the fact that North American cities have much more high-rise building. Indeed, what is worrying about population densities in Latin America is not the overall average but where the figures reach their peak. Most of the highest figures are found not in areas containing high-rise apartments but in consolidated low-rise, self-help areas. Thus, although areas of high-rise middle-class housing in Rio de Janeiro, such as Copacabana, have densities of over 300 persons per hectare, these densities pale in comparison with the high values of some of the *favelas* (Allen, 1989). Similarly, in Santiago, the highest values of between 200 and 250 persons per hectare are found in the low-rise suburbs (Bähr and Mertins, 1985; INE, 1986b). In Bogotá, the peak densities are also found in the poorer suburbs (Pineda and Jiménez, 1990), where poor families have attempted to economize on the high cost of land.

But, if this is the current pattern, what are the dynamics of change? Are Latin America's cities becoming less densely packed through time? Mills and Tan (1980: 317) suggest that this is almost inevita-

Table 4.12 **Population density and growth of urban area**

City	Year	Population (000s)	Area (hectares)	Density (persons/ha)
Bogotá	1900	100	909	110
	1928	235	1,958	120
	1938	330	2,514	131
	1964	1,730	14,615	118
	1985	4,177	32,866	127
	1991	4,960	30,300	164
Caracas	1936	235	542	430
	1950	694	4,586	151
	1971	2,184	15,000	145
	1981	2,583	19,750	131
	1990	2,989	23,300	128
Lima	1940	618	2,100	294
	1952	1,105	5,540	199
	1959	1,603	8,500	189
	1972	3,303	13,054	253
	1990	5,826	54,000	108
Mexico City	1930	1,049	8,609	122
	1940	1,560	11,750	133
	1950	2,872	24,059	119
	1960	4,910	47,070	104
	1970	8,455	68,260	122
	1980	12,140	91,211	133
São Paulo	1930	878	15,000	59
	1980	12,184	125,800	97
	1980	12,184	137,000	89
Santiago	1940	952	11,017	87
	1952	1,350	15,351	88
	1960	1,893	21,165	90
	1970	2,861	31,841	90
	1982	4,318	42,800	101

Sources: Coulomb and Sánchez, 1991; Dietz, 1978; Dowall and Treffeisen, 1990: 17; Gilbert, 1978; Gilbert, 1993; IBGE, 1984; INE, 1986a; Kross, 1992; UNCRD, 1994.

ble, given that international evidence shows that "large urban areas are more decentralised than small urban areas,... high income urban areas are more decentralised than low income urban areas (and) ... transportation improvements almost certainly lead to decentralisation."

Since Latin American cities have become both more affluent and more decentralized over recent decades, there should have been a clear reduction in overall densities. They have also improved their transportation systems, which, Echeñique (1982: 256) argues, should lead to an increase in the supply of land and therefore to declining densities. In fact, the figures in table 4.13 show anything but a clear trend. If there are signs that densities have fallen in Caracas and Lima, the opposite appears to have occurred in Bogotá, Santiago, and São Paulo. In Mexico City, densities first fell and then began to rise.[10]

I would argue that the reason why densities have not fallen universally is closely linked to the dynamics of land prices and local patterns of housing development. First, because land prices have remained high in most cities, and possibly even risen in some, it has been difficult for population densities to fall. Indeed, as the last section showed, the average size of building plots has been declining in several cities over time. Second, although extensive self-help development has brought lower densities in cities such as Lima, such accommodation does not guarantee low densities. Indeed, as I have already shown, some of the most densely packed suburbs are not high-rise residental areas but low-rise consolidated self-help areas. Third, many Latin American governments have tried, admittedly with varying success, to restrict the expansion of the urban area. This has been particularly common in cities where urban functions compete with agriculture for land. In so far as official attempts to restrict suburban growth have met with success, they have pushed up population densities.

Latin America's major cities, therefore, have been subject to different processes, some raising densities and some reducing them. The combination of processes has clearly affected different cities in differing ways. To understand what has happened, it is essential to recognize that although Latin America's major cities share many similarities, there are vital differences between them. For example, while all have large areas of self-help housing, the contribution that self-help accommodation makes to the housing stock differs considerably. The form of self-help also differs. In Lima, invasions have occupied vast areas of land in ways that have not been permitted in Bogotá or Mexico City. Arguably, the proliferation of self-help settlement on invaded land in Lima in recent years (see table 4.1) has reduced population densities in that city, whereas the land alienation processes characteristic of Bogotá and Santiago have encouraged denser forms of residential occupation. In short, Latin America's cities show diversity within similarity.

Table 4.13 **Population decline in the central city**

Bogotá	1964–73	1973–85	
Central area[1]	−2.2	−1.3	
Inner ring[2]	0.0	−1.1	
Lima	1961–72	1972–81	1981–92
Central area[3]	0.6	0.4	−0.9
Inner ring[4]		0.2	−1.6
Mexico City	1960–70	1970–80	1980–90
Cuauhtémoc	−1.4	−2.0	−2.2
Inner ring[5]	0.2	−1.4	−2.0
Second ring[6]	2.5	−0.1	−1.6
Santiago	1960–70	1970–82	1982–92
Commune of Santiago[7]	−2.2	−1.8	−1.4
Inner ring[8]	n.a.	0.0	−0.7
São Paulo	1960–70	1970–80	1980–87
Historic centre[9]	−1.4	0.0	n.a.
Inner city[10]	0.7	2.2	0.9
Inner ring	0.1	1.3	3.6
Intermediate ring	2.8	1.3	3.6

Sources: INE, 1986b; Kowarick and Jacobi, 1986: 200; Mohan and Villamizar, 1982; Pineda and Jiménez, 1990; UNCRD, 1994: 96; national censuses.

Notes:
1. Comuna 31: an area of 411 hectares.
2. Comunas 32, 41, 61, 71 and 81: an area of 1,406 hectares.
3. Lima and Breña.
4. Pueblo Libre (Magdalena Vieja), Jesús María, Lince, and La Victoria.
5. Cuauhtémoc, Miguel Hidalgo, Benito Juárez and Venustiano Carranza.
6. Acapolzaclo, Gustavo Madero and Iztacalpo.
7. The area of the commune of Santiago as recorded for 1960–70 was much larger than that covered in the later periods. In 1982 it was 22.3 square kilometres.
8. Communes of Estación Central, Independencia, Ñuñua, Pedro Aguirre Cerda, Providencia, Quinta Normal, Recoleta, San Joaquín and San Miguel; a total area of 108.2 square kilometres. The administrative areas of Santiago were changed in 1982 and calculation of comparable areas for the period before 1970 is not possible.
9. Seven innermost sub-districts of central ring.
10. Thirteen surrounding sub-districts.

The changing shape of the city

The polynuclear city

As they have grown, most large Latin American cities have incorporated nearby villages and towns. Caracas grew along the Guaire valley, gradually absorbing Sabana Grande, Chacao, Catia, Los Chorros, and Petare (Morris, 1978: 306). Bogotá grew northwards, absorbing Chapinero; Lima swallowed small centres such as Miraflores, Magdalena Vieja, Barranco, Chorrillos, and eventually Callao (Kross, 1992: 116). Mexico City took in Coyoacán, Mixcoac, and Tacacuya (Ward, 1990). Only Santiago seems to have grown without absorbing many neighbouring villages and towns.

In the process, each city developed sub-centres whose functions complemented those of the central city. Nevertheless, until recently, most cities were still highly focused on the original central area. Indeed, a high proportion of urban employment still remains in the central business district.

During the past twenty or thirty years, however, the dominance of the central area has declined sharply. In Bogotá, employment in the city as a whole increased by 46 per cent between 1972 and 1978 but only by 19 per cent in the central six *comunas* (Pineda and Jiménez, 1990). In the traditional centre, employment actually declined by 17 per cent. Employment of various kinds has moved out. Industrial activity has shifted to more peripheral locations, a move strongly encouraged by government planners. Tertiary activities have also decentralized as governments have built new office complexes, professionals have decamped to the more affluent suburbs, and shopping precincts have emerged throughout the city. Shops in the central area now compete with rivals in the suburbs.

Decline in the central area

Decentralization has now reached such a point that the central city is arguably in decline. Fewer businesses are prepared to locate in the traditional centre. Increasing pollution and congestion in the central areas have convinced many companies to locate elsewhere. There has been little recent sign either of gentrification or commercialization of the central area. Indeed, as Ward (1993: 1148–9) points out, huge empty areas remain undeveloped close to the central districts of most cities. The La Merced area in Mexico City, Brás in São Paulo, and the docklands in Rio de Janeiro all appear ripe for redevelopment, but little or nothing has actually happened.

The trend is reflected clearly in current patterns of land prices in Bogotá (figure 4.3), where values in the traditional downtown have "slipped to sixth place among the key office and retail areas of the city" (Dowall and Treffeisen, 1990: 73). Land values at the inter-

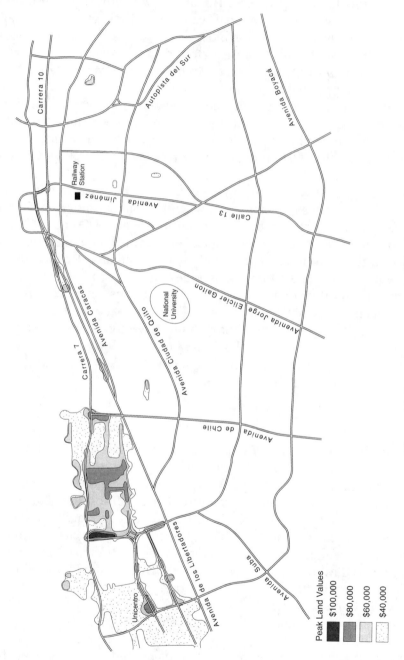

Figure 4.3 **Bogotá: Areas of peak land value**

section of Carrera Séptima and Avenida Jiménez, the real centre of the city in the 1950s and even the 1970s, "are in real terms at only one-sixth the level of twenty years ago" (ibid.).

Population densities in most central areas are also in decline (table 4.13). During the 1980s, central populations declined in each of the four cities for which there are data. In Lima, this was a new development, but in the other cities the process had been under way for some time. The centre of Mexico City has been in decline since 1950, those of Bogotá and Santiago since at least 1960. Large numbers of people have moved their homes out of the central city. In Lima, six central city districts together lost 150,000 people between 1981 and 1993, approximately 14 per cent of the original population. The population living in the district of Cuauhtémoc in central Mexico City fell by about half in forty years, declining from 1,049,000 inhabitants in 1950 to only 596,000 in 1990.

Table 4.13 also shows that the areas losing people have increased in areal extent. In the 1960s, only the innermost parts of the central area were in decline but, during the 1970s, much wider areas of Bogotá and Mexico City were affected, and in the 1980s extensive zones in Lima and Santiago also lost people.

Depopulation was caused initially by the expansion of commercial activity in the central area. Indeed, it was the arrival of new commercial and business activities which led to major declines in the housing stock, a tendency accentuated by "physical decay, urban redevelopment, and occasionally because of slum-eradication programs" (Ward, 1993: 1145). In places, urban renewal projects decimated low-income rental accommodation. In Mexico City, several major road schemes destroyed some 48,000 housing units during the 1960s, and construction of the major public housing complex in Tlatelolco destroyed a lot more (Coulomb and Sánchez, 1991). During the 1970s, 50,000 homes were destroyed by official efforts to remove the "lost cities" and decaying *vecindades* (rental tenements), and through the *ejes viales* road-widening programme of the Echeverría administration (Ward, 1990). In Caracas, urban renewal began in the 1940s with the El Silencio project and accelerated in the 1950s with the construction of the Centro Simón Bolívar, the Helicoide, the Avenida Bolívar, and the infamous superblocks. During the late 1960s, the Parque Central complex began, followed by construction of the metro in the 1970s. There has been so much urban renewal in central Caracas that very little of the original housing is left. In São Paulo, there has been less destruction of homes in the central area (Violich

101

and Daughters, 1987), but certain public works schemes, such as construction of the metro, have certainly affected areas such as Brás (Batley, 1982).

In places, too, earthquakes have hastened the process of urban renewal. The central areas of both Mexico City and Santiago were badly hit by serious tremors in 1985. Although the authorities replaced much of the damaged housing in Mexico City, a lot of housing was lost.

What is the future of the central city?

Central city areas are not likely to prosper in the next few years, but neither are they likely to change markedly. They will continue to lose people and jobs to the suburbs. However, they are unlikely to deteriorate as totally as the typical inner city of the United States (Dowall and Treffeisen, 1990: 25).

Neither is there much possibility that central city areas will be redeveloped even in those cities where economic recession is a problem of the past. There is too little interest from the private sector in investing in central city redevelopment, and, with conventional wisdom dictating that governments should intervene much less (Gilbert, 1992; World Bank, 1993), few governments will be inclined to launch massive programmes in the urban centre. Consequently there will be few grandiose schemes to transform central areas, either the construction of metros or major housing renewal projects. As Ward (1993: 1155) puts it: "one can identify circumstances where the private sector may be disposed to become involved, but neither the political nor the local government structure is conducive to the promotion of large-scale, downtown, Baltimore-harbor-type projects led by a dirigiste politician, or from consortia of global entrepreneurs."

Neither is there much chance of a widespread process of gentrification "improving" the urban centre, even though certain governments would like to encourage it. Most élite groups are now resigned to suburban living and in any case the level of crime, pollution, and traffic congestion in the central city discourages a recolonization.

Again, of course, there will be differences. The centres of Rio de Janeiro and São Paulo declined much less than those of most major Spanish American cities because there was much less flight to the suburbs (Violich and Daughters, 1987: 326). As Taschner and Bruna (1994: 96) point out: "In São Paulo the tendency was to shift from the central area quarters to the internal areas of the city ... With few exceptions, these quarters gradually became more dense, and today constitute an extensive verticalized area where high luxury apartments and hotels and small flats co-exist with commerce and retail sales activities."

Similarly, Buenos Aires suffered relatively little deterioration in the central areas. "Unlike the process undergone by other metropolises, Buenos Aires has not seen the expulsion of older residents out of privileged areas claimed by more affluent groups ... The areas with views of parks and the river have been saturated. The old residences ... have been replaced by towers in which apartments of 300 to 400m^2 occupy each floor" (Borthagaray and Igarzabal, 1994: 68).

Conclusion

Latin America's major cities survived remarkably well given the pace of population growth between 1950 and 1980. There was little sign of deterioration in housing conditions and even a general improvement in servicing conditions. Of course, huge problems remained and were accentuated by the economic recession of the 1980s. Today, far too many people are living in poor-quality shelter and far too many peripheral settlements lack adequate infrastructure and services.

Better-quality administration and planning is needed to confront many of these issues and it is time that many local government agencies improved the level of their performance (Bolaffi, 1992). More investment is needed to maintain improvements in service levels. More sensible transport policies are required if the private car is not to suffocate the metropolitan area. More sensible land policies are also needed, policies that will both discourage the excessive holding of building land and reduce tendencies towards urban sprawl.

I do not intend to elaborate on these policies because most are addressed in other chapters of this book. I am also reluctant to produce a long list of recommendations that may never be acted upon. For, despite their manifest ability to cope, few Latin American cities can be said to be well-planned. Indeed, as Violich and Daughters (1987: 378) put it: "in the unregulated form that it has taken, urbanization has become a major new source of national consternation." I am not sure that the quality of planning will improve in the future; indeed, good planning may be impossible given the unequal social and economic structures of Latin America. Perhaps the current belief in the effectiveness of market forces will prove correct and we can all celebrate the demise of incompetent government bureaucracies. Somehow, alas, I doubt it.

Notes

1. Self-help housing is not easy to define. Most planners, however, would probably agree that the distinctive characteristic of self-help housing is that it always begins as a flimsy form of shelter lacking all kinds of service and is developed on land which either lacks planning permission or has been invaded. The adjective "self-help" stems from the fact that the occupier has built some or all of the accommodation, even if some form of professional help has almost always been involved. The typical architect is the local jobbing builder or bricklayer; the building manual is the advice received from family and friends.
2. Of course, two of the eight cities under discussion here, Bogotá and Santiago, largely escaped recession during the 1980s.
3. The *ejido* is a form of commuity landholding established in Mexico as a result of the Revolution. In law, the land cannot be sold, although in practice much of the land occupied by housing in many Mexican cities belongs to *ejidos*.
4. Trivelli (1987: 105) claims that "vacant lots represent one-third of the building space of Brazilian cities."
5. Based on a sample of 446 plots in the three years, drawn primarily from the western, higher-income areas of the city. Not surprisingly, land prices within a given settlement increased more rapidly; lower prices were found in more peripheral locations.
6. In any case, it is uncertain whether prices continue to rise in low-income settlements once they have begun to develop. Indeed, data from Bogotá and Mexico City suggest that plot prices in low-income settlements often fall over time (Gilbert and Ward, 1985). They do not rise partly because the best plots are sold first and partly because it is so difficult to sell such plots.
7. Of course, Brazilian experience during much of that period as hardly typical. The economy was growing rapidly but the poor suffered the consequences of a deliberate attack by the government on their living standards. Under these circumstances, the purchase of land was almost bound to become more difficult over time.
8. For low-income groups the average fell from 132 square metres to 68 over the same period.
9. The latter observation is more true of the eastern US cities. The problem with Ingram and Carroll's argument is that they use figures which record population over a rather wide central area. They also include some figures of dubious value.
10. Table 4.13 presents data on gross population densities over time. While such figures are never totally reliable, they do make sense. The figures have the advantage that they record the urbanized area rather than the administrative area of the city. As such, they record real changes in density over time. The figures contradict the findings of both Portes (1990: 17), who claims that "with the exception of Buenos Aires, densities have continued to increase in urban centers, regardless of their legal boundaries," and Ingram and Carroll (1981), who show that densities increased between 1950 and 1970 in Mexico City, São Paulo, Rio de Janeiro, Bogotá, Recife, Belo Horizonte, Guadalajara, Monterrey, and Cali. Lee (1985) shows the same tendency occurring in Brazil's eight largest cities. Ingram and Carroll's figures also show dramatic increases in density in some cities. The problem with all these sets of calculations is that they have used a constant administrative area of the city over time. Since much of this area was empty at the beginning of the period, any expansion of the city outwards into this empty area is almost bound to increase the population density. All the authors admit the problems with calculating figures in this way but none have modified their figures to take account of them.

References

Allen, E. (1989) "The flood which became a disaster: Housing and the poor in Rio de Janeiro." Centre for Housing Research Discussion Paper no. 25, University of Glasgow.

Amato, P. (1969) "Environmental quality and locational behaviour in a Latin American city." *Urban Affairs Quarterly* 5: 83–101.

Azuela, A. (1989) *La ciudad, la propiedad privada y el derecho*. El Colegio de México.

Bähr, J., and G. Mertins (1985) "Desarrollo poblacional en el Gran Santiago entre 1970 y 1982." *Revista de Geografía Norte Grande* 12: 11–26.

Batley, R. (1982) "Urban renewal and expulsion in São Paulo." In Gilbert et al. (eds.), 231–62.

——— (1983) *Power through bureaucracy: Urban political analysis in Brazil*. Gower.

Bolaffi, G. (1992) "Urban planning in Brazil: Past experience, current trends." *Habitat International* 16: 99–111.

Borthagaray, J.M., and M.A. Igarzabal de N. (1994) *Buenos Aires*. In UNCRD, 63–72.

Castells, M. (1983) *The city and the grassroots*. Edward Arnold.

CED [Centro de Estudios del Desarrollo] (1990) *Santiago: dos ciudades. Análisis de la estructura socio-económica-espacial del Gran Santiago*. CED.

Connolly, P. (1985) "Mexico: state investment in the built environment and the debt problem." Proceedings of the Sixth Bartlett International Summer School, Venice, *The production of the built environment*, 4.1–4.12.

Cordera Campos, R., and E. González Tiburcio (1991) "Crisis and transition in the Mexican economy." In M. González and A. Escobar (eds.), *Social responses to Mexico's economic crisis of the 1980s*. La Jolla: Centre for US-Mexican Studies, University of California, San Diego, 19–56.

Cornelius, W. (1975) *Politics and the migrant poor in Mexico*. University of Stanford Press.

Coulomb, R., and C. Sánchez (1991) *¿Todos proprietarios? Vivienda de alquiler y sectores populares en la Ciudad de México*. Mexico City: CENVI.

Dietz, H.A. (1978) "Metropolitan Lima: Urban problem-solving under military rule." In W.A. Cornelius and R.V. Kemper (eds.), *Latin American urban research*, Sage, vol. 6, 205–226.

Dixon, W.J. (1987) "Progress in the provision of basic human needs: Latin America, 1960–1980." *Journal of Developing Areas* 21: 129–40.

Dowall, D.E., and P.A. Treffeisen (1990) *Urban development and land and housing market dynamics in Bogotá, Colombia*. Institute of Urban and Regional Development Monograph 38, University of California at Berkeley.

Durand-Lasserve, A. (1990) "Articulation between formal and informal land markets in cities in developing countries: Issues and trends." in P. Baross and J. van der Linden (eds.), *The transformation of land supply systems in third world cities*, Avebury, 37–56.

Dwyer, D.J. (1975) *People and housing in Third World cities*. Longman.

Echenique, M. (1982) "Transportation investment and urban land values: Emerging empirical evidence." In M. Cullen and S. Woollery (eds.), *World Congress on Land Policy*, 1980, Lexington Books, 255–73.

Eckstein, S. (1977) *The poverty of revolution: The state and the urban poor in Mexico*. Princeton University Press.

ECLAC (1973) "Some consequences of urbanization for the total social structure."

In G. Germani (ed.), *Modernization, urbanization and the urban crisis*, Little, Brown, 151–67.

FEDELONJAS, [Federación Colombiana de Lonjas de Propiedad Raíz] (1988) *El valor del suelo urbano en Bogotá, 1959–1988*. Bogotá.

Garza, G. et al. (eds.) (1987) *Atlas de la ciudad de México*. Departamento del Distrito Federal and El Colegio de México.

Gavidia, J. (1994) "Housing and land in Latin American large cities." In UNCRD, 19–28.

Germani, G. (1973) "Urbanization, social change, and the great transformation." In G. Germani (ed.), *Modernization, urbanization and the urban crisis*, Little, Brown, 3–58.

Gilbert, A.G. (1978) "Bogotá: Politics, planning and the crisis of lost opportunities." In W.A. Cornelius and R.V. Kemper (eds.), *Latin American urban research 6*, Sage, 87–126.

—— (1989) "Housing during recession: Illustrations from Latin America." *Housing Studies* 4: 155–66.

—— (1990) "The provision of public services and the debt crisis in Latin America: The case of Bogotá." *Economic Geography* 66: 349–61.

—— (1992) "Third World cities: Housing, infrastructure and services." *Urban Studies* 29: 435–60.

—— (1993) *In search of a home*. University College London Press.

—— (1994) *The Latin American city*. Latin America Bureau and Monthly Revision Press.

Gilbert, A.G., and J. Gugler (1992) *Cities, poverty and development: Urbanization in the Third World*. Oxford University Press (second edition).

Gilbert, A.G., J.E. Hardoy, and R. Ramirez (eds.) (1982) *Urbanization in contemporary Latin America*. Wiley.

Gilbert, A.G., and A. Varley (1991) *Landlord and tenant: Housing the poor in urban Mexico*. Routledge.

Gilbert, A.G., and P.M. Ward (1985) *Housing, the state and the poor: Policy and practice in three Latin American cities*. Cambridge University Press.

Glewwe, P., and G. Hall (1992) "Poverty and inequality during unorthodox adjustment: The case of Peru, 1985–90." Living Standards Measurement Study Working Paper no. 86, World Bank.

Gutiérrez, A.T. (1990) *Sobrevivencia y sectores populares en Venezuela*. CENDES (Centro de Estudios de Desarrollo).

Hataya, N., et al. (1993) "Urban problems under the process of fiscal decentralization in Colombia: Public services of the barrios populares in Bogotá." Joint Research Programme Series no. 102, Institute of Developing Economies, Tokyo.

IBASE [Instituto Brasileiro de Analises Sociais e Econômicas] (1982) "Algunos dados sobre solo urbano no Brasil." Mimeo.

IBGE [Instituto Brasileiro de Geografia e Estatistica] (1991) *Anuário Estatistico do Brasil, 1991*. Rio de Janeiro.

Iglesias, E.V. (1992) *Reflections on economic development: Toward a new Latin American consensus*. Inter-American Development Bank.

INE [Instituto Nacional de Estadística] (1986a) *Perú: Compendio estadístico, 1985*. Lima.

—— (1986b) *Gran Santiago: Población y superficie, Censos 1940–1982*. Santiago.

Ingram, G.K., and A. Carroll (1981) "Spatial structure of Latin American cities." *Journal of Urban Economics* 9: 257–73.

Inter-American Development Bank (n.d.) *Water and sanitation*. Washington DC.

Jacobi, P. (1990) "Habitat and health in the municipality of São Paulo." *Environment and Urbanization* 2: 33–45.

Jaramillo, S. (1990) "La estructura urbana y la vivienda en Bogotá." In J.F. López et al., *Vivir en Bogotá*, Ediciones Foro Nacional, 51–88.

——— (1992) *La vivienda en Bogotá*. Documento CEDE 087, Universidad de los Andes.

Jones, G.A. (1991) "The impact of government intervention upon land prices in Latin American cities: The case of Puebla, Mexico." Doctoral dissertation, University of Cambridge.

Jones, G., E. Jiménez, and P. Ward (1993) "The land market in Mexico under Salinas: A real estate boom revisited?" *Environment and Planning A* 25: 627–52.

Kowarick, L. (ed.) (1988) *As lutas sociais e a cidade: São Paulo: Passado e presente*. Paz e Terra.

Kowarick, L., and M. Campanário (1988) "São Paulo: Metrópole do subdesenvolvimento industrializado." in Kowarick, L. (ed.), 29–48.

Kowarick, L., and P. Jacobi (1986) "Crecimiento económico, urbanización y medio ambiente: La calidad de la vida en São Paulo, Brasil." In V. Ibarra et al. (eds.). *La ciudad y el medio ambiente en América Latina*, El Colegio de México, 197–229.

Kross, E. (1992) *Die Barriadas von Lima: Stadtentwicklungsprozesse in einer lateinamerikanischen Metropole*. Schöningh.

Kusnetzoff, F. (1990) "The state and housing in Chile – regime types and policy choices." In G. Shidlo (ed.), *Housing policy in developing countries*, Routledge, 48–66.

Lama, C., and M. Sarabia (1994) "Lima." In UNCRD, 79–84.

Lee, T. (1994) "Water management in the metropolitan areas of Latin America." In UNCRD, 29–40.

Lee, Y.J. (1985) "The spatial structure of the metropolitian regions of Brazil." *World Bank Staff Working Papers*, no. 722. Washington DC.

Mangin, W. (1967) "Latin American squatter settlements: A problem and a solution." *Latin American Research Review* 2: 65–98.

Mills, E.S., and J.P. Tan (1980) "A comparison of urban population density functions in developed and developing countries." *Urban Studies* 17: 313–21.

Mohan, R., and N. Hartline (1984) "The poor of Bogotá: Who they are, what they do, and where they live." World Bank Staff Working Papers no. 635.

Mohan, R., and R. Villamizar (1982) "The evolution of land values in the context of rapid urban growth: A case study of Bogotá and Cali, Colombia." In M. Cullen and S. Woollery (eds.), *World Congress on Land Policy, 1980*, Lexington Books, 217–53.

Molina, H. (1990) "Bogotá: Competition and substitution between urban land markets." In P. Baross and J. van der Linden (eds.), *The transformation of land supply systems in third world cities*, Avebury, 295–308.

Molina, I., et al. (1993) *El futuro de la capital: Estudio perspectivo de vivienda*. Misión Bogotá Siglo XXI, Santafé de Bogotá.

Morris, A. (1978) "Urban growth patterns in Latin America with illustrations from Caracas." *Urban Studies* 15: 299–312.

Necochea, A. (1987) "El allegamiento de los sin tierra, estrategia de supervivencia en vivienda." *Revista Latinoamericana de Estudios Urbanos-Regionales (EURE)* 13–14: 85–100.

Ogrodnik, E. (1984) "Encuesta a los allegados en el Gran Santiago." *Revista de Economía* 22.

Pajoni, R. (1982) "Argentine. La ségregation compulsive. Logiques et pratiques des acteurs de la gestion foncière et de la production immobilière dans les villes des pays en développement." Mimeo, Paris, 18–20 November.

Payne, G. (1989) *Informal housing and land subdivisions in Third World cities: A review of the literature.* CENDEP, Oxford.

Perlman, J. (1976) *The myth of marginality.* University of California Press.

Perló-Cohen, M. (1981) *Estado, vivienda y estructura urbana en el Cardenismo: El caso de la Ciudad de México.* Instituto de Investigaciones Sociales, Universidad Nacional Autónoma de México.

Persaud, T. (1992) *Housing delivery systems and the urban poor: A comparison among six Latin American countries.* World Bank, Latin America and the Caribbean Technical Department Regional Studies Program Report no. 23.

Pineda, J.F., and L.C. Jiménez (1990) "Consideraciones sobre el crecimiento físico de Bogotá D.E." Mimeo, Comisión Bogotá Siglo XXI.

Portes, A. (1972) "Rationality in the slum: An essay in interpretive sociology." *Comparative Studies in Society and History* 14: 268–86.

—— (1979) "Housing policy, urban poverty, and the state: The favelas of Rio de Janeiro, 1972–76." *Latin American Research Review* 14: 3–24.

—— (1990) "Latin American urbanization during the years of the crisis." *Latin American Research Review* 25: 7–44.

Portes, A., and M. Johns (1986) "Class structure and spatial polarization: An assessment of urban trends in the Third World." *Tijdschrift voor Economische en Sociale Geografie* 77: 378–88.

Rakodi, C. (1992) "Housing markets in Third World cities: Research and policy into the 1990s." *World Development* 20: 39–55.

Ray, T. (1969) *The politics of the barrios of Caracas.* University of California Press.

Riofrío, G. (1978) *Se busca terreno para próxima barriada: Espacios disponibles en Lima 1940, 1978, 1990.* DESCO, Lima.

—— (1991) "Lima en los 90. Un acercamiento a la nueva dinámica urbana." *Nueva Sociedad* 114: 143–49.

Rodríguez, A. (1989) "Santiago, viejos y nuevos temas." in F. Carrión (ed.), *La investigación urbana en América Latina: Caminos recorridos y por recorrer. Estudios nationales,* CIUDAD (Quito), 203–36.

Rodríguez, A., and A.M. Icaza (1993) "Procesos de expulsión de habitantes de bajos ingresos del centro de Santiago, 1981–1990." SUR Documentos de Trabajo 136.

Sachs, C. (1990) *São Paulo: Politiques publiques et habitat populaire.* Editions de la Maison des Sciences de l'Homme.

Scarpaci, J.L., R. Pio-Infante, and A. Gaete (1988) "Planning residential segregation: The case of Santiago, Chile." *Urban Geography* 9: 19–36.

Schteingart, M. (1989) *Los productores del espacio habitable: Estado, empresa y sociedad en la Ciudad de México,* El Colegio de México.

Shidlo, G. (1990) "Housing policy in Brazil." In G. Shidlo (ed.), *Housing policy in developing countries,* Routledge, 33–47.

Taschner, S., and G. Bruna (1994) "São Paulo," In UNCRD, 93–104.

Trivelli, P. (1987) "Intra-urban socio-economic settlement patterns, public intervention, and the determination of the spatial structure of the urban land market in Greater Santiago, Chile." Unpublished doctoral dissertation, Cornell University.

Turner, J.F.C. (1967) "Barriers and channels for housing development in modernizing countries." *Journal of the American Institute of Planners* 33: 167–81.

United Nations (1987) *United Nations Statistical Yearbook, 1987.* New York.

────── (1989) *1989 report on the world social situation.* New York.

UNCHS [United Nations Centre for Human Settlements (Habitat)] (1987) *Global report on human settlements 1986.* Oxford University Press.

UNCHS (1989) *Strategies for low-income shelter and services development: The rental-housing option.* Nairobi.

UNCRD [United Nations Centre for Regional Development] (1994) *Enhancing the management of metropolitan living environments in Latin America.* UNCRD Research Report Series no. 1.

UNDIESA [United Nations Department of International Economic and Social Affairs] (1991) *World urbanization prospects 1990.* New York.

Valença, M.M. (1992) "The inevitable crisis of the Brazilian housing finance system." *Urban Studies* 29: 39–56.

Valladares, L. (1978) "Working the system: Squatter response to resettlement in Rio de Janeiro." *International Journal of Urban and Regional Research* 2: 12–25.

Valladares, L. (ed.) (1984) *Repensando a habitação no Brasil.* Zahar.

Villamizar, R. (1982) "Land prices in Bogotá between 1955 and 1978: A descriptive analysis." in J.V. Henderson (ed.), *Research in urban economics* 2, Jai Press.

Villanueva, F., and J. Baldó (1994) "Sobre la cuestión de la urbanización de los barrios." *SIC*, Septiembre–Octubre: 340–6.

Violich, F., and R. Daughters (1987) *Urban planning for Latin America: The challenge of metropolitan growth.* Oelgeschlager, Gunn and Hain.

Ward, P.M. (1990) *Mexico City.* Belhaven.

────── (1993) "The Latin American inner city: Differences of degree or of kind?" *Environment and Planning A* 25: 1131–1160.

Ward, P.M., and S. Melligan (1985) "Urban renovation and the impact upon low income families in Mexico City." *Urban Studies* 22: 199–207.

Webb, R., and G. Fernández (1991) *Perú en números 1991.* Lima: Cuánto.

World Bank (1992) *The housing indicators program.* Volume II: *Indicator tables.* Washington D.C.

────── (1993) *Housing: Enabling markets to work. A World Bank Policy Paper.*

Yujnovsky, O. (1984) *Claves políticas del problema habitacional Argentino,* Grupo Editor Latinoamericano.

5

A hundred million journeys a day: The management of transport in Latin America's mega-cities

Oscar Figueroa

Every day, some ninety-five million motorized journeys are made in Latin America's five largest cities. Most of these journeys are by public transport, which accounts for around three-quarters of the total. As table 5.1 shows, however, there are major variations between the five cities in their dependence on public transport. Lima and Mexico City depend very heavily on public systems, Buenos Aires and São Paulo much less so. These differences can hardly be attributed to differences in the size of each city; they are much more a reflection of differences in the rate of private car ownership, in the organization of the transport system in each city, and in the structure and timing of urban growth. For this reason it is very important to understand the different institutional structures and transport systems in each city as well as the nature of their distinctive forms of historical development.

Urban growth and the evolution of transport systems

At the beginning of the century, when mass transport systems began to develop, few cities contained anywhere near one million inhabitants. In 1900, only Buenos Aires (with 806,000 people) and Rio de Janeiro (with 692,000 people) had more than half a million inhabitants; Mexico City, Santiago, Havana, Montevideo, São Paulo, Sal-

Table 5.1 **Journeys by motorized vehicle and public transport in Latin America's mega-cities, 1980s**

City	Journeys per day (millions)	Journeys by public transport (millions)	Share of public transport (%)
Lima	6.5	5.3	82
Rio	11.5	9.0	78
Buenos Aires	16.4	10.9	66
São Paulo	20.5	11.3	55
Mexico City	39.7	33.0	83
Total	**94.6**	**62.1**	**74**

Sources: Origin–destination surveys, São Paulo (1987) and Buenos Aires (1992). Annual transport and road report, Mexico City, 1991. Various reports, Lima and Rio de Janeiro.

vador, Valparaíso, Lima, Recife, Rosario, Guadalajara, and Bogotá all had between 100,000 and 500,000 inhabitants (Hardoy and Langdon, 1978). Nevertheless, the process of urban improvement through the installation of urban infrastructure and services was already under way, the authorities having realized that economic growth could not occur without it. Improving the transport system formed an important component of this process of urban development; better transport was needed to move the rapidly increasing numbers of people about the city. Fortunately, investment in transport was seldom opposed by business groups; when combined with the opportunities it offered for land speculation, spending on transportation could be highly profitable.

Initially, transport development took a similar form across the five cities. By 1906, for example, all four of the current mega-cities had inaugurated tram systems. The major difference between them lay in the development of railways. Suburban railway systems were developed in São Paulo, Buenos Aires, and Rio de Janeiro because these cities began to grow rapidly at a time when the railway was regarded as an essential component of any urban transportation system. The growth of Lima and Mexico City started later, when a new form of transport, the bus, had begun to sweep all before it. For a number of years, therefore, trams and railways constituted the basis of the public transport system. There were few cars and only Buenos Aires had an underground system.

By 1930, Buenos Aires had 2.2 million inhabitants, Rio de Janeiro 1.5 million, and Mexico City and São Paulo both around 1.1 million. Only Lima, with 273,000 inhabitants, was still a small city (Hardoy and Langdon, 1978). Everywhere, rapid urban growth was putting pressure on the existing transport system; faster industrial development was demanding more efficient methods of moving both people and goods around the city (Navarro, 1986). As a result, governments began to intervene more actively in the transport sector. Sometimes, the form of intervention was rather unhelpful. For example, when they realized that the cost of transport could be a major burden for workers, several governments put pressure on the private tram companies to freeze fares. Populist leaders in Argentina, Brazil, and Peru froze the cost of transport during the 1930s and 1940s, for periods as long as twenty years (Figueroa et al., 1993). With fares frozen, the tram companies began to experience severe financial difficulties. At a time of rapid urban growth, they needed to extend their networks, but they could not afford to invest if they could not raise their fares. The consequence was that few companies attempted to enlarge their networks.

Fortunately, an alternative to the tram was becoming available as small companies began to establish bus routes. This was a process that occurred spontaneously, largely uncoordinated by the urban authorities. The principal advantage of the bus was its flexibility; companies could change their routes quickly and regularly extend their services to the edge of the city.

Increasing competition from the buses worsened the situation of the tram companies. Services declined, bankruptcy threatened, and gradually many of the companies were taken over by the state: in Mexico City in 1946, in São Paulo in 1947, in Buenos Aires in 1948, in Lima in 1955, and in Rio de Janeiro in 1965 (Figueroa, 1991). Nationalization of the tram companies was unavoidable if a transport crisis was to be avoided. Even if buses were carrying the majority of passengers, few cities in the 1940s and 1950s could afford to lose their trams. Such a situation was not to last very long, and, from the 1940s, the bus became the dominant mode of public transport.

The nature of bus operations varied considerably between cities. Whereas Lima and Mexico City permitted private companies to run the buses, municipal companies were set up in Rio de Janeiro and São Paulo. In Buenos Aires, a federal company was established to operate buses within the Federal Capital. However, state efforts to establish a monopoly over transportation in Buenos Aires and São Paulo quickly crumbled in the face of private pressure. The municipal transport authority in São Paulo handed over an important part of its remit to private operators, while the federal company in Buenos

Aires was privatized, leaving only the underground in the hands of the state.

From then on, the bus systems in all of the cities were run mainly by private companies, although the form of those companies differed widely. In the two Brazilian cities, large companies ran the system; in Lima and Mexico City, control remained mainly in the hands of small operators; in Buenos Aires, cooperatives developed with the legal status of companies. One result is that the nature of the bus fleet differs today in the five cities. Whereas minibuses are used extensively in Lima and Mexico City, they are not used at all in the other cities. Medium-sized buses predominate in Buenos Aires, while standard-size single-decker buses are the most common form in São Paulo and Rio de Janeiro. The differences reflect the different histories of transport development in each city.

Gradually, the cities grew so large that their dependence on the bus began to cause difficulties. With increasing levels of private car ownership, the problem of traffic congestion worsened. One response was to develop underground railway systems, and today all five cities contain some kind of metro system. Buenos Aires first established an underground system in 1913 and has extended it over the years (figure 5.1). The metro systems in Mexico City, Rio de Janeiro, and São Paulo are much more recent, having been inaugurated between the end of the 1960s and the middle of the 1970s. Lima is still in the throes of constructing its system, a project which has suffered badly from institutional and funding difficulties.

Of course, underground services are extremely expensive to build and few planners consider them to be an appropriate response to the needs of Latin American cities. Such a view is apparently supported by the relatively small proportion of total journeys carried by the underground in each city (table 5.2). Only in Mexico City does the metro account for more than 10 per cent of all passenger trips, in São Paulo it carries less than 7 per cent of all passengers, and in Buenos Aires and Rio de Janeiro less than 5 per cent. However, since most of the underground networks are very limited in extent, they can hardly be expected to carry the majority of passengers. The logic of the underground is to service routes which carry the largest flows of traffic. Their strategic value lies in their contribution to movement along the key routes where they operate, particularly during rush hours. According to this criterion, it can be said that the performance of the underground systems in Mexico City and São Paulo is satis-

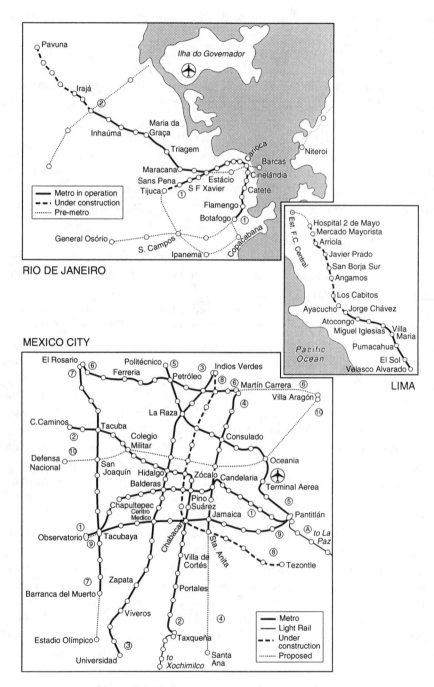

Figure 5.1 **Major underground railway systems**

114

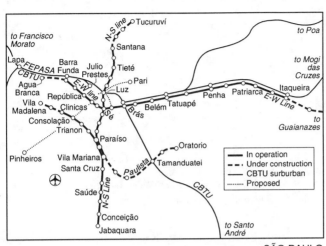

SÃO PAULO

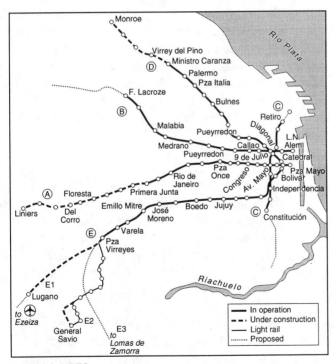

BUENOS AIRES

Figure 5.1 **(cont.)**

Table 5.2 **Journeys by different forms of public transport, 1980s (millions of daily journeys)**

Mode[a]	Buenos Aires	São Paulo	Lima	Rio de Janeiro	Mexico City	Total
Metro	0.7	1.4	–	0.4	4.5	7.0
Train	1.2	1.0	–	1.2	–	3.4
Bus	–	8.4	1.0	7.2	6.7	23.3
Microbus	9.0	–	–	–	–	9.0
Minibus	–	–	4.1	–	21.5	25.6
Trolley	–	0.3	–	–	0.4	0.7

a. The tram systems in Buenos Aires, Rio de Janeiro, and Mexico City are each responsible for less than 100,000 daily journeys. The ferries of Rio de Janeiro carry 175 thousand passengers every day. None is included in the table.

factory, while that of the metros in Rio de Janeiro and Buenos Aires is not. In Rio, a major problem has been the failure to complete the system; in Buenos Aires, an inability to invest in the system has meant that it has been in continuous decline since the 1960s.

Given the cost of metro construction, there has recently been something of a resurgence in the popularity of surface rail systems and even of modern forms of the tram. Buenos Aires has recently modernized its old tram lines and Mexico City has constructed a light rail link as an extension to one of its underground lines. Rio de Janeiro operates an old tram line, which is used mainly as a tourist attraction, as well as a light rail link.

Today, therefore, transport systems in the five cities show considerable differences. While all have some form of metro system, well-developed bus and microbus networks, and, of course, far too many private cars, only Buenos Aires, Rio de Janeiro, and São Paulo have suburban rail systems, only Mexico City and São Paulo have trolley buses, and just Rio has a ferry service. Perhaps the most dominant feature in all of the cities is the widespread use of the bus. Table 5.2 shows that almost 90 per cent of all journeys by public transport are on some kind of bus, and, in Lima, virtually every passenger travels by bus or minibus.[1]

A further similarity between the cities is their increasing dependence on the private car. Unfortunately, as levels of private car ownership have increased so traffic congestion has worsened. Despite major road improvements, there has been little sign of the traffic speeding up. New roads have simply generated more traffic. This worldwide tendency has been worsened by the form that road investment has taken; most new roads have consolidated the existing radial design, fossilizing existing land uses and contributing to worse congestion.

Institutional problems

A number of problems weaken coordination and management of the transport sector in Latin America's largest five cities. The principal problems are as follows.

Fragmentation of urban administration

Fragmentation of responsibility for urban transport is the rule in most of the cities. In part, the problem stems from the fact that the urban area has grown beyond the original limits of the city (see chapters 3 and 4). Because they now form metropolitan conurbations, their government is divided between a number of different municipal areas. This problem spills over into the transport sector. As a result, none of the five cities has a metropolitan authority with full responsibility for transportation.

In São Paulo and Rio de Janeiro, although control of transport is predominantly in the hands of the municipal authorities, the regions have as many regulatory bodies as the municipalities. In Buenos Aires and Mexico City, part of the city is controlled by the federal government and part by the state or provincial government (see chapters 6 and 8). At times, such complicated administrative structures lead almost to anarchy. For example, in Buenos Aires, bus routes regulated by the province or local state are often banned from entering the Federal Capital; passengers must dismount from one bus and get onto another. In Mexico City, the metro operates wholly in the Federal District and no lines penetrate into the State of Mexico. Only now are there plans to remedy that situation.

Only in the Lima-Callao region does one municipal authority have control over transport across the entire metropolitan area. This responsibility, however, dates only from the mid-1980s and has been undermined by the municipality's lack of power over critical issues as well as a general lack of clarity in the legislation. The result has been that the national government has sometimes chosen to override the authority of the municipal administration, for example when it decided to build the Lima underground and when it deregulated urban transport at the beginning of the 1990s.

All five cities also suffer from the complications that arise from different agencies having responsibility over different elements of the transport system. These agencies often take independent decisions. For example, the agency which regulates public transport has no control over the building and maintenance of the roads; hence, bus routes may run along unpaved or poorly maintained roads. At a more general level, there is little or no coordination between the transport authorities and the agencies that control urban land use. Decisions to build a new industrial zone or to permit construction of a new shopping centre may be made without careful consideration of the traffic implications.

Limited regulatory powers

The powers of the government to regulate the transport sector vary considerably between the five cities. For a start ownership structures differ: in Lima, all modes of transport are now in private hands, whereas in Mexico City there is a major state presence (see below). In addition, controls over the private transport companies differ. In Lima, almost all controls were dismantled in 1991 and firms are now free to establish their own routes and fares. In Mexico City, strict centralized controls were maintained in the Federal District until the late 1980s. Since then, greater freedom has been given to the private firms running the minibuses (*peseros*). The public Route 100 network has been reduced and there has been a drastic cut in subsidies to the metro. In São Paulo, bus companies were regulated, until recently, through an innovative practice called "municipalization." The municipality of São Paulo contracted private firms to operate services throughout the metropolitan area. It laid down performance criteria (normally minimum distances to be operated each day) and the companies paid the fares to the municipality. In Buenos Aires, where bus operations have been heavily regulated for years, considerable flexibility has governed official dealings with private enterprise.

Deteriorating public transport systems

Suburban rail links, which have a long history in Brazil and Argentina, have suffered severely from a lack of investment during the last twenty years. Heavily controlled fares have undermined the agencies' ability to generate enough resources to maintain the existing system, let alone improve it. The quality of the service has also been damaged by frequent changes in the management system.

Improvements to the bus services have also been hampered by very low fares. With operators unable to increase revenues, there has been little incentive to expand the fleet. Faced by rising costs, operators have responded by reducing the quality of the service (Figueroa, 1991). Bus fleets have deteriorated, especially in the case of Route 100 in Mexico City and ENATRU in Lima, where the bus fleet has aged considerably. Declines in the quality of the bus fleet and increasing journey times have also been apparent in São Paulo (Trani, 1985), Buenos Aires (Brennan et al., 1993) and Rio de Janeiro (Câmara, 1993).

With uniform fares in operation, few operators have tried to introduce special services which might have tempted higher income groups out of their cars. Under these circumstances, public transport has not fulfilled its social function and has become another source of congestion and disorganization. Most operators have increasingly used smaller buses, a practice which has increased the number of buses in operation and worsened traffic congestion. Too many bus companies run old buses, which contain large numbers of standing passengers, along routes crowded with other traffic.

Recent developments in the transport systems of the five cities

The double privatization of public transport in Buenos Aires

When privatization removed the state's monopoly over transport in 1955, the buses and minibuses were sold to the workers. The cooperative organizations which emerged were very successful in the fierce competition that broke out after privatization. The bus was a flexible mode of transportation and the cooperatives proved very popular with the public. With most urban growth occurring on the edge of the city, the rail systems needed to expand outwards. Faced by mounting financial difficulties, however, neither the trains nor the underground could respond. As a result, the rail network now carries about half the number of passengers it did in 1960. The flexibility of the bus also gave it a major advantage over the tram and the operating companies soon went out of business.

If the bus flourished relative to the train and the tram, the private car did even better; Buenos Aires now has one car for every 16.4

inhabitants (Brennan et al., 1993). While the number of bus journeys has risen by only 5 per cent since 1960, the number of car journeys has increased by 430 per cent. Cars are now responsible for 30 per cent of all motorized journeys within the metropolitan area. The outcome of this development has been totally predictable. First, road congestion has reached chronic levels in the central area and along the main access routes from the north and west. Second, fuel consumption has risen dramatically as a result of the shift from larger to smaller road vehicles and the increase in traffic congestion. Cars now account for 7.4 per cent of all the energy consumed in the country compared to 2.4 per cent by buses and 0.4 per cent by trains. In terms of the relative numbers of passengers carried, the car is a very wasteful form of transport.

The Menem government (1990–date) has tried to address these problems in two main ways. First, because of its lack of confidence in public enterprise, it has been trying to privatize the urban rail systems. It hopes that private companies will improve the efficiency of the train service and will encourage more drivers to leave their cars at home. Second, the bus system has been upgraded and companies have been encouraged to provide a wider range of services. Routes have been modified to avoid the worst traffic bottlenecks and special express services have been introduced which provide a quick, all-seater service. It is hoped that by improving public transport, congestion between the centre and the suburbs will be reduced.

Informality and deregulation in Lima

Lima is different from the four larger cities in so far as it is poorer and its period of peak demographic growth occurred much more recently. In 1965, the city had little more than two million inhabitants and many fewer transport problems than it faces today. The main difficulties were that few buses were being maintained adequately and the bus fleet was failing to expand as quickly as the rapidly increasing population. With the closure of the tram service, the gap between demand and supply was being met mainly through the growth of collective taxi services.

The financial health of the bus companies continued to deteriorate, and during the second half of the 1960s many of the biggest companies went out of business. They were replaced by a series of cooperatives and "social companies" run by the former workers of the bankrupt companies. These new organizations ran whatever old stock was still available (Sánchez-León et al., 1978). Although the state tried to help by establishing the ENATRU-Perú bus company – effectively a rescue of the defunct municipal company APTL – and by merging 16 bus cooperatives into a much larger cooperative company, Transportes Lima Metropolitana, the strategy was only partially successful. The gap between demand and supply was filled by small companies which operated services to the peripheral low-income settlements, using mainly minibuses and collective taxis. By 1989, only 13 companies were running large buses compared to the 94 firms operating small buses, the 39 associations operating minibuses, and the seven committees of collective taxi owners (Transurb-Class, 1989). The increasing number of small vehicles made road congestion very much worse.

Not only did the fleets contain a large number of small vehicles, but many were also very old. In 1988, the average bus was 13 years old, the average minibus 17 years, and the average collective taxi a venerable 25 years. The fleet had aged as firms failed to renew their stock of vehicles (De Wit, 1981).

In the face of continuing deterioration in the public transport system, the central government decided to transfer regulatory responsibility to the municipality of Lima (Vera, 1987), although the government retained ownership of ENATRU. However, the municipality, lacking both experience and resources, failed to create an adequate regulatory system. Responsibility was poorly defined, so the central government retained considerable influence and the operators managed to increase their powers of self-regulation. The inability of the municipal council to run transport efficiently can be seen in the annulling of operational permits without any replacement service, and the introduction of a bidding process for new routes which was never used (Transurb-Class, 1989). Gradually, the central government began to intervene more and more. Such interference was most clearly demonstrated in 1986, when, with a minimum of either consultation or prior study, it decided to build a 35-kilometre-long underground railway.[2] Whether or not this project will survive or die is still in question, even though a considerable amount of money has been invested in building the system.

In 1991, when the central government decided to deregulate public transport in Lima completely (fares, barriers to entry, and routes), the regulatory powers of the municipality came to an end. ENATRU was also dismantled and its fleet sold to its former workers. Deregulation was accompanied by a liberalization in the rules governing

121

the import of both new and used vehicles. The result has been a sharp increase in the number of buses, especially of smaller vehicles, which has added to traffic congestion and led to some deterioration in the quality of the service. Increasing disorder and rising fares have prompted attempts to re-establish some of the authorities' previous powers.

Technological and regulatory development in Mexico City

Mexico City's greatest problem is that over the last 40 years the number of journeys has increased much faster than the population. The authorities have tried to cope with this expansion in highly innovative, if not always consistent, ways. These have included changes to the institutional structure and the introduction of new forms of technology such as the metro. The vast number of experiments is testimony to the severity of the transport challenge facing a city of 16 million inhabitants.

By the early 1960s, traffic congestion in the central area was already extremely serious. In order to deal with this situation, the government agreed to build a massive underground system (Davis, 1994). Work on three lines began and the first line was opened in 1969 (Navarro, 1986). The new lines were an immediate success, carrying nearly one million passengers a day in the first year of operation. Despite the metro's success, however, road congestion continued to be a major problem; the underground merely freed road space for new vehicles to fill. Between 1960 and 1970, the level of private car ownership in the city doubled, rising from 5.1 cars per hundred inhabitants to 10.3 (Figueroa, 1990).

During the 1970s, a different approach was tried. The Echeverría government slowed underground construction and concentrated on the development of the road and bus systems (Davis, 1994). It subsidized the purchase of new buses by private operators and reorganized the bus system. It also began a major road-building plan which would produce 16 new *ejes viales* by 1978.[3] Buses and trolleys were given reserved lanes along these new routes and this programme clearly helped the bus companies. The policy also succeeded in speeding up traffic in the city, but, with its clear encouragement for private car ownership, it soon led to a further rise in the number of road vehicles (Domínguez-Pommerencke, 1987). As a consequence, the number of daily journeys during the 1970s increased at an annual rate of 5.6 per cent (Ibarra, 1981).

By the late 1970s, the construction of new underground lines was again *de rigueur*. Unfortunately, the new lines carried many fewer passengers than the old. In 1976, the 38-kilometre network carried 1.7 million passengers every day: an average of 45,000 passengers per kilometre. By 1992, although 4.5 million passengers were using the expanded system of 158 kilometres, usage had fallen to only 28,000 passengers per kilometre of track. The first three lines, all of which went through the city centre, were carrying 3.1 million passengers; the six new lines, most of which bypassed the centre, only 1.4 million. Currently, the four lines which run into the centre of Mexico City carry 78 per cent of all the network's passengers (Alamys, 1993).

By 1980, it was clear that a new approach was needed. While construction of new underground lines continued, the bus system was reformed. First, the bus companies operating in the Federal District were nationalized and the newly created Route 100 given a virtual monopoly in that area. Second, the General Transport Coordinating Organization was created to coordinate public transport in the metropolitan area. Third, bus and metro fares, which had been heavily subsidized until the middle 1980s, were raised; in future they should reflect the true cost of providing the service (Figueroa, 1990).

The problem with this approach was that it was difficult to maintain investment levels from public funds, particularly during a time of economic recession. The policy of increasing public control over buses in the Federal District also conflicted with the power that private bus and minibus companies wielded in the State of Mexico. Increasingly, the approach was modified and more private companies were allowed to operate within the Federal District; between 1988 and 1991, Route 100's share of passengers fell by half while that of the *peseros* increased two and a half times (México, DDF, 1991). Continued investment in the metro has allowed it more or less to maintain its passenger share (Navarro, 1991).

Changing circumstances demand new forms of intervention. It is clear that the metropolitan area currently relies too much on the *peseros*, which now carry 73 per cent of all passengers. As usual, new ways must be found to improve the quality and efficiency of the city's transport system.

State, metropolis, and municipality: Transport in São Paulo

Metropolitan São Paulo, with its 16 million people living in 38 different municipalities, faces a major transport challenge. Every day, some 30 million journeys are made, a high proportion by car. Not only does the city have one of the highest rates of private car ownership in Latin America but its public transport system is in a state of perpetual decline. Between 1977 and 1987, private cars carried virtually all of the huge increase in passenger trips (Poole et al., 1990). The decline in the availability and affordability of public transport is further reflected in the rapid increase in the number of journeys made on foot. In 1977, the latter accounted for one-quarter of all journeys in the metropolitan area; ten years later they made up one-third. Those with money have become more dependent on the car; the poor have been forced to rely on their feet.

São Paulo has long debated the virtues of private car ownership versus those of public transport. This debate reached its climax when the tram system was closed down. The authorities decided that the city should become much more dependent on the private car and, during the 1950s and 1960s, enormous sums were invested in the road system. Nevertheless, the commitment to a strong state presence in the management of public transport remained intact. The municipal firm (CMTC) converted the old tram routes into bus lines and the federally-owned RFFSA and the State-owned FEPASA ran the railways. When the underground was built in 1975, the State of São Paulo was given majority control in partnership with municipal and federal government agencies.

One of the major difficulties facing the authorities in the city is their lack of control over key variables in the transport equation. As in other large Brazilian cities, regulating the transport situation was rendered all but impossible. The first problem is the fragmentation of powers between different agencies; the second the lack of consensus between those agencies.

Responsibility for regulating transport in the region is divided between the main actor, the municipality of São Paulo, the other municipalities in the metropolitan area, and the largely independent public companies which run the railway, underground, and trolley systems. In addition to the problems of coordinating policy between the different public agencies, the power of private operators has been gradually increasing. This is reflected in the loosening level of state control over the bus system. The close monitoring exercised over the bus companies in the 1960s, including rationalization of the firms and a division of the city into sectors, later led to the CMTC's contracting private firms to operate under its name and eventually, in

1993, to privatization of the CMTC. Today, most passengers are carried by independent companies; there is little in the way of state control.

Faced by major difficulties in confronting and resolving their problems in a concerted way, the authorities in São Paulo have been forced to give more and more responsibility to independent actors. The lack of coordination, combined with the nature of urban growth in the city, has led to a major decline in the quality of transport in the city. This deterioration has been particularly marked for those using the buses, average journey times having increased from 52 to 57 minutes between 1977 and 1987. Since the poor form the bulk of the passengers, they have suffered most. Today, 26 per cent of the lowest income group take an hour and a half to get to work; by comparison, only 12 per cent of the richest group take that long. One consequence is that mobility rates are very low among the poor: while the very poor average only 0.44 journeys per day, high-income people make 1.86 journeys every day (Poole et al., 1990).

Changes in transport policy in Rio de Janeiro

Rio de Janeiro's ten million inhabitants face major transport problems. With an institutional framework as disorganized as that of São Paulo, transportation in Rio is further complicated by the unique physical layout of the city (see chapter 9). With the sea and the mountains limiting transport options, a radial road network system has developed, funnelling traffic into the highly congested centre. Not only is the central area the principal generator of journeys, it is also the major transit point: 84 per cent of all journeys begin or end in the municipality of Rio de Janeiro. What makes the situation worse is that most of these journeys are made by road. Consequently, traffic congestion is a serious problem. Journeys, particularly for the poor moving into the centre from the distant periphery, are long, slow, and relatively expensive (Câmara, 1993).

The transport authorities in Rio have generally shown little determination in their attempts to ameliorate these conditions. Design of the road network has been influenced more by political pressures than by the needs of travellers. Whereas the network in the low-income north of the city remains poorly developed, high-cost solutions, such as the Rebouças tunnel, have improved communication to the affluent south (Montenegro, 1987). The authorities have also

125

failed to maintain control over the numerous private bus companies. Despite severe traffic congestion, there has been little investment in alternative modes of transport. The suburban train system has deteriorated badly, the ferry service between the city centre and Niterói is stretched to breaking point, and the underground system has a very limited capacity.

Poor coordination, both between the government and the private companies and within the public sector, is a major problem. Although private buses carry the vast majority of Rio's passengers, they have a rudimentary level of organization and have never been adequately regulated by the authorities. There is also a small public bus company, which accounts for 3–5 per cent of bus journeys. The federal train company (previously RFFSA and now CBTU) operates what must be the most badly run suburban system in Brazil. Even when the authorities start from scratch, they seldom manage to do the job effectively; the new underground is a poorly designed and inefficient system.

Adequate transport solutions have hardly been facilitated by the changing political organization of the city, which became a city-state (Guanabara) when the federal government was moved to Brasília in 1956 and lost its independence when it was merged with the neighbouring State of Rio de Janeiro in 1975. Today, the state authorities exercise most responsibility over the city's transport system (Britto Pereira, 1987). The city has also suffered from extreme swings in policy as municipal, state, and federal administrations have changed. The list of major swings in urban transport policy is long. Several private bus companies were taken over by the authorities in 1987, but, with a change in the state government in 1991, were returned to the private sector. In terms of roads, the decision to allow private companies to construct a toll road (Vermelha Road) to link the north and the centre of the city was soon reversed. The road was built with public funds and with no charge for users (Nassi, 1987a). Plans for the development of the underground have changed constantly over the last ten years, as new lines have been opened and even closed (Nassi, 1987b). Indeed, Rio must be the only city in the world to have opened a new underground line and then to have closed it almost immediately!

It is the combination of difficult terrain, the physical layout of the city, and a long record of maladministration that has produced Rio's current traffic chaos. By contrast with almost any other city in Brazil, Rio has an extraordinarily inefficient system.

Do mega-cities have special transport problems?

It is clear from the above account that each of the "mega-cities" has distinct transport problems. Transport conditions are far worse in Lima and Rio de Janeiro than in Buenos Aires or Mexico City. And, in so far as the transport characteristics of Lima are much more similar to those of Bogotá than they are to those of Buenos Aires, it is possible to argue that city size is less important than other factors in determining the nature of transport problems. Whatever their size, Latin American cities share certain organizational and management problems.

A particular problem is that all large Latin American cities rely excessively on their roads. Private car ownership is rising in practically every Latin American city and everywhere the bus dominates the public transport system. While justified in terms of the lower short-term costs, the longer-term social cost of road transport is high. Increasing diseconomies have rarely been passed on in the form of higher charges; most of the consequences of worsening traffic conditions have been assumed by the society at large.

In this sense, the problems of the mega-cities are no different from those of most other large Latin American cities. Traffic congestion begins whenever the bus system becomes saturated. This is determined less by the size of the city than by its shape and land-use structure, which, in turn, dictate the frequency and direction of most journeys. As a result, all Latin American cities suffer from severe traffic congestion, air pollution, too many accidents, and lengthening journey times.

In so far as new kinds of solutions are adopted to remedy traffic problems, mega-cities show few differences from other large cities. Although all five mega-cities have metros in operation or in construction, so do many smaller cities (including Caracas, Medellín, Pôrto Alegre, and Santiago). Attempts to reduce congestion by increasing road capacity lead to similar kinds of problems whatever the size of the city. The building of motorways tends to fragment urban space. While Mexico City and São Paulo suffer particularly badly from this process, so does Caracas.

Nevertheless, transport systems in very large cities in Latin America do appear to suffer more seriously from three particular problems. First, the absolute numbers of passengers needing to be transported along key access routes is much higher than in smaller cities. Second, the largest cities tend to suffer from worse levels of traffic congestion. Finally, average journey times tend to be much longer than in smaller cities. Each of these problems tends to become more acute as cities grow in size.

(a) Congestion along key access routes:

All Latin American cities have grown through territorial expansion and through densification along their principal transport corridors. The existing roads have had to carry ever-increasing numbers of vehicles, a problem accentuated by the huge growth in private car ownership. Although some forms of economic activity have decentralized and new sub-centres have begun to compete with the historic centre, the latter remains the major destination point of a high proportion of journeys. Significant numbers of journeys between sub-centres also pass through the city centre. In response, transport improvements have naturally concentrated on improving communications to the central city. Although similar problems occur in smaller cities, the volume of passengers moving towards the city centre in metropolitan areas is much greater. A good illustration of this can be seen in the case of the underground networks in Mexico City and São Paulo. During rush hour, several central lines carry around 60,000 passengers an hour, the highest figure for any underground system in the world. Despite a recent tendency for economic deconcentration to occur, radial axes from the centre have continued to develop.

(b) Overall congestion levels:

Road capacity has increased to accommodate the growing flows of traffic. Unfortunately, the seemingly inevitable response has been for the number of road journeys to increase. In Caracas, São Paulo, Buenos Aires, and Rio de Janeiro, massive motorway and road programmes soon resulted in new routes becoming saturated. Although the *ejes viales* road construction programme in Mexico City did reduce congestion for a time, this was very much an exception.

(c) Journey times:

As congestion has worsened, journey times have lengthened. Surveys in Rio de Janeiro, São Paulo, and Buenos Aires all show increasing journey times to key destinations (Câmara, 1993; Poole et al., 1990; Brennan et al., 1993). Of course, there is no precise relationship between size of city and journey times. In many cities in developed countries, average journey times have remained constant despite urban expansion through expensive technological improvements. In

Latin America, however, few innovations have been made in the transport sector. With the exception of new metro systems, motorways, and occasional experiments in bus transportation, as in Curitiba, life carries on with little change. As a result, increasing size leads almost inevitably to slower journeys.

Of course, size is only one feature affecting transport conditions. The morphology of the city plays an important part in determining the seriousness of these problems. Equally, the quality and layout of the road system, the level of car ownership, the quality of public transport, and the level of income are all important contributory variables. Nevertheless, size generally worsens the transport situation because it is superimposed upon fossilized road and rail networks.

Conclusion

The traffic problems of smaller cities such as Bogotá, Caracas, Santiago de Chile, Guadalajara, and Pôrto Alegre do not appear to be very different from those of the five mega-cities. Severe congestion sets in well before a city's population has reached eight million people. It begins when the saturation threshold for bus systems is reached and is worsened by the urban land-use structure of particular cities. Certain organizational and management problems are common to most cities in the region, whatever their size. The most obvious similarity is that all are too dependent on road transport. The burden of rising levels of car ownership is growing throughout the region, even if the rate of growth varies from city to city.

The tendency to rely on private cars, buses, and taxis is explained by the lower costs of road solutions in the short term. The longer-term social costs and negative externalities have been ignored and are rarely passed on to users in terms of higher private costs. Apart from lost time and, recently, a tendency for public transport to raise its fares, the majority of these externalities are passed on as social costs. As a result, there has been little sign of improvement in the transport sector in Latin America's major cities; most of the evidence points to worsening congestion, longer journeys, and slower traffic speeds.

It is difficult to say who suffers most from this deterioration. Bus passengers are certainly paying more in terms of longer journeys, and in recent years fare levels have also risen as transport subsidies have been cut. These changes have clearly hit the poor, as the bus is their principal method of transport. But car-owners have also suffered from growing congestion in terms of longer journey times. Their main protection is that at least they can sit in comfort as the traffic crawls along.

The critical question for the future is whether the situation will continue to deteriorate. If levels of car ownership continue to rise and the authorities refuse to place limits on where people can drive, congestion is bound to worsen. There is a clear need for more investment in public transport systems and for their better management; but whether government budgets will be able to bear such costs and whether the private sector can be tempted to invest in public transport are open questions. Deregulation and privatization may help improve public transport facilities, but current evidence is ambivalent with respect to the likely outcome. Certainly, if deregulation and privatization mean that the real costs of public transport improvements are passed on to passengers, then they may hurt the poor. In so far as such a strategy will increase the cost to poor people of getting to work or to local supermarkets, it will clearly reduce their living standards.

Presumably the answers to these questions will vary from city to city and, consequently, so too will the severity of transport problems. For whatever else this chapter has managed to show, it should be clear that despite certain similarities between the mega-cities, there are just as many differences. Traffic congestion may be bad in every large city in the region, but it is still easier to travel around Buenos Aires and São Paulo than Lima.

Notes

1. At the time of the survey the metro in Lima was not in operation.
2. There had long been a wish to construct a mass transport system in the city and a detailed plan for the construction of an underground system was first drawn up in 1973. This was designed to relieve pressure on the most congested routes at a time when the city's population had reached 3.5 million.
3. Freeways in the English, not the American, sense are probably the best term to describe the concept. They were not motorways but very wide surface-level roads along which cars and buses could run quickly in a single direction. A large number of homes were destroyed in the construction of these *ejes*.

References

Barat, J. (1975) *Estructura metropolitana e sistema de transportes: Estudo do caso do Rio de Janeiro*. Rio de Janeiro: IPEA/INPES.
——— (1991) *Transporte e energia no Brasil*. Rio de Janeiro: Bertrand Brasil.

Brennan, P., and O. Vicente (1988) "Genèse, organisation et fonctionnement des transports privés à Buenos Aires." *Proceedings of CODATU IV*. Jakarta.

Brennan, P., et al. (1993) "Urban transport deregulation and the evolution of mobility in Buenos Aires." *Proceedings of CODATU VI*. Tunis.

Britto Pereira, V. (1987) *Avaliação da política de transportes públicos no Rio de Janeiro*. Brasília: Empresa Brasileira de Transportes Urbanos.

Brizzi, J. (1991) "Ahorros energéticos en el transporte urbano de la Argentina." *Actas del V Congreso Latinoamericano de Transporte Público y V Encuentro Latinoamericano de Transporte Urbano*, Santiago, II, 1–13.

Casal, H. (1971) *Historia del colectivo*. Buenos Aires: Centro Editor de América Latina.

Câmara, P. (1993) "Rio de Janeiro public transport provision: Characteristics and spatial inequalities." *Actas de la CODATU VI*. Tunis.

Davis, D.E. (1994) *Urban leviathan: Mexico City in the twentieth century*. Temple University Press.

De Wit, H. (1981) *El transporte público en Lima metropolitana*. Lima: Centro de Investigaciones Urbanas del Perú.

Domínguez-Pommerencke, L. (1987) "Vialidad." In G. Garza (ed.), *Atlas de la ciudad de México*, DDF and El Colegio de México, 191–3.

Duarte, E., and E. Hiroi (1990) "A mobilidade na região metropolitana de São Paulo." In *Actas de la CODATU V*, São Paulo.

Figueroa, O. (1981) "L'organisation des transports collectifs urbains en Amérique Latine." *Review RTS* 15: 29–36.

―――― (1990) "La evolución de las políticas de transporte colectivo en la ciudad de México entre 1965 y 1988." *Revista Estudios Demográficos y Urbanos* 5(2): 221–35.

―――― (1991) "Les politiques de transport en commun dans les villes d'Amérique Latine." Doctoral dissertation, Institut d'Urbanisme de Paris, Créteil.

Figueroa, O., and E. Henry (1987) "Les enjeux des transports dans les villes latino-américaines." *Synthèse INRETS no. 6*. Arcueil.

―――― (1991) "Analysis of the underground systems in Latin America." In M. Heraty (ed.), *Urban transport in developing countries*, London, PTRC, 230–40.

Figueroa, O., et al. (1993) *Transports, tramways, technologies: Splendeur et décadence des tramways en Amérique Latine*. Paris: Collection INRETS-CODATU Transport Transfert Développement.

Hardoy, J.E., and M.E. Langdon (1978) "Análisis estadístico preliminar de la urbanización de América Latina entre 1850 y 1930." *Revista Paraguaya de Sociología* 15: 115–74.

Henry, E., and O. Figueroa (eds.) (1986) *Transporte y servicios urbanos en América Latina*, vol. I. Paris: INRETS-CIUDAD.

―――― (1987) *Transporte y servicios urbanos en América Latina*, vol. II. Paris: INRETS-CIUDAD.

Ibarra, V. (1981) *El transporte de pasajeros en el área metropolitana de la ciudad de México*. El Colegio de México.

Kogan, J. (1993) "Reestructuración de los servicios ferroviarios metropolitanos en Buenos Aires." *Actas del VI Congreso Latinoamericano de Transporte Público y VI Encuentro Latinoamericano de Transporte Urbano*, San José, 357–64.

Krantzer, G., and A. Muratorio (1993) "Los servicios rápidos con tráfico restringido

131

en la región metropolitana de Buenos Aires." *Actas del VI Congreso Latino-americano de Transporte Público y VI Encuentro Latinoamericano de Transporte Urbano*, San José, 303–14.

México, DDF [Departamento del Distrito Federal] (1991) *Anuario de transporte y vialidad*. México DDF.

Montenegro, A. (1987) "Problemas de operación y de política del metro de Rio de Janeiro." In Henry and Figueroa (eds.), 605–20.

Nassi, C. (1987a) "The impacts of Rio de Janeiro Metro in urban transport system." In *Transport, communication and urban form*, Clayton, Australia, 317–30.

—— (1987b) "Impasses do serviço público: O caso do setor transporte no Estado do Rio de Janeiro." In R. Piquet (ed.), *Crise urbana e a privatização dos serviços públicos*, Rio de Janeiro, UFRJ, 198–207.

Navarro, B. (1986) "La evolución del metro de México DF." In Henry and Figueroa (eds.), 257–71.

—— (1991) "Metropolización y transporte masivo: La experiencia mexicana." In Delgado and Villareal (eds.), *Cambios territoriales en México: Exploraciones recientes*, UAM-Xochimilco.

Pacheco, R. (1986) "Coexistence des secteurs privé et public de transports colectifs à São Paulo." *Actas de la CODATU III*. Cairo.

Pinheiro Machado, D. (1988) "Sistema metro y efectos sobre la estructura urbana. El caso de Rio de Janeiro." *Revista EURE* 42: 43–62.

Poole, A.D., R. Pacheco, and M. Campelo (1990) "Urban and collective transport policy in developing countries: A case study of Brazil." Report to International Development Research Centre, São Paulo.

Sánchez-León, A., et al. (1978) *¿Paradero final? El transporte público en Lima metropolitana*. DESCO.

Trani, E. (1985) "L'aggravation des conditions de déplacements domicile-travail dans la région métropolitaine de São Paulo." Doctoral dissertation, Institut d'Urbanisme de Paris, Créteil.

Transurb-Class (1989) *Plan de transporte de Lima metropolitana y el Callao*. Lima.

Vera, D. (1987) "La oferta de transporte en Lima y la política municipal." In Henry and Figueroa (eds.), 449–621.

Ward, P.M. (1991) *México: Una megaciudad*. Mexico City: Alianza.

6

Buenos Aires: A case of deepening social polarization

Luis Ainstein

The city of Buenos Aires was founded by the Spanish on low-lying land on the right bank of the River Plate. This was a magnificent choice. At the mouth of the country's major river and on the edge of one of the most fertile regions in the world, the city was bound to expand as Argentina became incorporated into the world economy. By the beginning of the twentieth century, Buenos Aires had become one of the world's greatest cities. During the next half-century its population was to increase massively. Again its location brought a major benefit; the flat terrain allowed the city to expand with virtually no physical constraint. Over the years, the site has posed only one real problem, poor drainage. The Reconquista and Matanza-Riachuelo river systems have never managed to cope with a climate prone to sudden bursts of rain; certain parts of the city have always had to face the danger of floods.

Population growth and structure

Buenos Aires played an insignificant role in the Spanish Empire. It had little of the economic and political importance of Lima and Mexico City and did not develop significantly until the end of the colonial period. It was only when independence permitted Argentina

Table 6.1 **Population of Buenos Aires and Argentina**

Year	Buenos Aires	Average growth rate	Argentina	Average growth rate
1869	181,000		1,830,000	
1895	671,000	5.2	4,045,000	3.1
1914	1,973,000	5.8	7,904,000	3.8
1947	4,643,000	2.6	15,894,000	2.1
1960	6,750,000	2.9	20,014,000	1.8
1970	8,353,000	2.3	23,364,000	1.6
1980	9,766,000	1.6	27,949,000	1.8
1991	10,887,000	0.8	32,423,000	1.3

to trade directly with Europe that the country's rich resources guaranteed Buenos Aires an international role. With its port located at the heart of the rich *pampas*, the city began to flourish as a major transshipment centre. When Juan Manuel de Rosas, the governor of Buenos Aires, established political control over the country during the 1830s, the city's economic future was virtually guaranteed (Scobie, 1963: 77). It began to expand rapidly and during the latter half of the nineteenth century its growth was spectacular. By 1914, it had become one of the world's great cities.

Table 6.1 shows how quickly the populations of both Greater Buenos Aires and Argentina grew between 1869 and 1914. Both received large flows of immigrants from Europe and, in 1914, 30 per cent of the country's population had been born abroad. After 1914, when the number of immigrants into Argentina began to fall, Buenos Aires grew more slowly. Slower growth was accentuated by the fact that national fertility rates fell very early. Thereafter, the urban population was never to grow as rapidly as that in most other Latin American countries.

Buenos Aires and the *pampas* have long dominated Argentina. The *pampas* provided most of the country's export revenues and after 1920 industrial development further increased the region's economic importance. Throughout the twentieth century, seven out of ten Argentines have lived in the *pampas* region and around one-third in the national capital. For more than a century, Buenos Aires has been an extreme example of a "primate" city. In 1971, no fewer than 36 per cent of all Argentines lived in the capital.

It was only when Argentina's economy started to languish in the

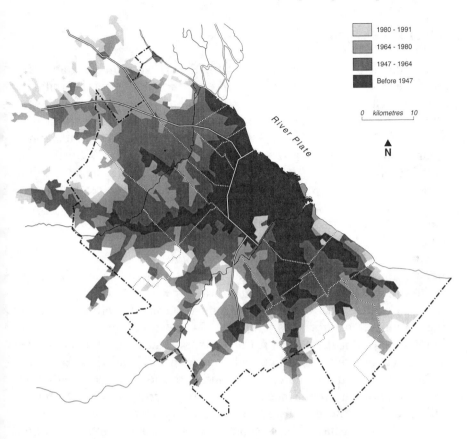

	1980 - 1991
	1964 - 1980
	1947 - 1964
	Before 1947

0   *kilometres*   10

N

Figure 6.1 **Urban expansion of Greater Buenos Aires, 1536–1991**

1960s and import-substituting industrialization ran out of steam that the national dominance of Buenos Aires began to weaken. During the 1970s and 1980s, the city's share of the national population gradually fell. The decline in national prominence, however, should not be exaggerated. In 1991, Greater Buenos Aires still had ten times more people than Córdoba, the country's second largest city.

Today, the metropolitan area covers a vast area of some 3,900 square kilometres. It overspilled the 200-square-kilometre area of the Federal Capital as early as 1869 (figure 6.1) and most of the city's subsequent expansion has taken place in the Province of Buenos Aires. Since 1947, the population of the the Federal Capital has barely changed and, in 1991, it contained only 37 per cent of the city's total population.

The urban economy

It is difficult to find economic data for the whole metropolitan area, because most statistics are computed either for the Federal Capital or for the vast area covered by the Province of Buenos Aires. Nevertheless, the city's key role in the national economy is clearly indicated by the fact that the Federal Capital alone generates almost one-quarter of Argentina's gross national product. The city's dominance is most obvious in tertiary activities: in 1989, the Federal Capital generated one-third of the nation's value added from tertiary activities. Buenos Aires contains most of the federal government's offices and the headquarters of many major businesses, particularly those concerned with trade and finance.

Since 1980, however, the economic health of Buenos Aires has been poor. Economic activity in the Federal Capital declined between 1980 and 1985, although it managed to grow slowly during the rest of the decade. The city's fortunes mirror the difficulties faced by the Argentine economy as a whole. They also reflect the impact of industrial deconcentration on the metropolitan area; the secondary sector declined by almost 9 per cent between 1980 and 1989. Between 1974 and 1985, more than 200,000 industrial jobs disappeared from the metropolitan area. Since 1985, economic growth has been maintained only by the expansion of the tertiary sector. Finance, insurance, and real-estate services have constituted the most dynamic activities in the city.

During the 1980s and early 1990s, Greater Buenos Aires suffered from a serious employment problem. Unemployment rose from 2.3 per cent in April 1980 to 7 per cent in October 1989. By May 1993, unemployment had achieved a twenty-year peak of 10.6 per cent. Underemployment also increased, from 4.7 per cent in 1980 to 8.2 per cent in 1993. Women and young people, particularly those with low levels of formal education, have been the worst affected.

Rising unemployment and underemployment reflect longer-term trends in the national economy. Trade liberalization has meant that more manufactured imports have entered the country and, since 1985, employment in the secondary sector has been in decline. Fortunately, the expanding tertiary sector has absorbed more workers. Between 1974 and 1985 some 120,000 new jobs were created. By 1992, tertiary activities provided 70 per cent of all jobs in the metropolitan area (INDEC, 1992).

Continuing economic problems, secular shifts in lifestyles, and

Table 6.2 **Population growth of Buenos Aires by municipal area, 1970–1991**

Municipality	Area (km²)	1970 population	% change 1970/80	1980 population	% change 1980/91	1991 population
Federal Capital	200	2,972,453	−1.67	2,922,829	1.3	2,960,976
First Ring District						
Avellaneda	55	337,538	−1.00	334,145	1.33	338,581
Lanús	45	449,824	3.81	466,980	−0.33	465,454
Lomas de Zamora	89	410,806	24.18	510,130	12.19	572,318
La Matanza	323	659,193	44.04	949,566	17.97	1,120,225
3 de Febrero	46	313,460	10.20	345,424	1.10	349,221
Gral. San Martín	56	360,572	6.95	385,625	4.64	403,515
Vicente López	39	285,178	2.07	291,072	−0.71	289,005
(Subtotal)	653	2,816,572	16.56	3,282,942	7.77	3,538,319
Second Ring District						
Quilmes	125	355,265	25.70	446,587	14.08	509,449
Almte. Brown	122	245,017	35.47	331,919	33.54	443,251
Esteban Echeverría	377	111,150	69.97	188,923	44.92	273,779
Morón	131	485,983	23.13	598,420	7.18	641,416
Gral. Sarmiento	196	315,487	59.43	502,926	29.30	650,285
San Isidro	48	250,088	15.66	289,170	3.24	298,540
(Subtotal)	999	1,762,880	33.75	2,357,945	19.46	2,816,720
Third Ring District						
Berazategui	188	127,740	58.02	201,862	21.27	244,796
Florencia Varela	206	98,446	76.19	173,452	47.28	255,462
Merlo	170	188,868	54.92	292,587	31.86	385,821
Moreno	180	114,041	70.50	194,440	47.75	287,295
San Fernando	924	119,565	11.76	133,624	6.96	142,925
Tigre	360	152,355	35.46	206,349	23.60	255,041
(Subtotal)	2,028	800,995	50.10	1,202,314	30.69	1,571,340
Total for 1st, 2nd and 3rd Ring Districts	3,860	5,380,477	27.19	6,843,201	15.83	7,926,379
Total Buenos Aires	3,879	8,352,900	16.92	9,766,030	11.48	10,887,355

Source: Author, based on data from the National Population and Housing Censuses of 1970, 1980, and 1991.

Table 6.3 **Occupation and employment in Greater Buenos Aires**

	1980	1989/90	1992
Secondary sector	n.a.	30.6	29.3
Tertiary sector	56.6	68.5	70.0
Rate of participation in labour force:			
Men	54.7	54.6	41.7
Women	25.6	28.2	29.3

Sources: INDEC, 1992; Lindenboim, 1985.

Table 6.4 **Labour contracts in Greater Buenos Aires, 1990 (percentages)**

Labour contracts[a]	Federal Capital	Rest of Buenos Aires
Without written contract	76.3	81.0
Below monthly minimum wage	22.9	31.7
Temporary contracts	14.2	16.6
Without social security coverage	33.7	37.8
No union affiliation	55.9	53.0

Source: INDEC, 1990.

a. Because these are non-exclusive categories they add up to more than 100 per cent.

major reforms introduced by the administration of Carlos Menem have brought important changes in the structure of the labour force. Female participation has increased significantly, from 25.6 per cent of the workforce in 1980 to 29.3 per cent in 1992, and is principally explained by the need to sustain family incomes at a time of rising unemployment and falling wages. Casualization of the labour force has also been increasing and working conditions have deteriorated substantially. Official rules and regulations are increasingly being ignored and, as table 6.4 shows, illegality has become the norm. Many new jobs have been created in activities with very low levels of productivity.

Income distribution

Argentina began to suffer from economic decline and falling per capita incomes in the early 1970s. Economic problems generated political unrest, which gave rise to an extended period of military rule (1975–83). The authoritarian phase introduced a development model which accentuated income inequality.

Table 6.5 **Distribution of income in metropolitan area, 1984 and 1989 (percentages)**

Decile	1984	1989	Variation 1984/1989
Poorest 10%	2.6	1.8	−31.0
2	3.9	2.9	−25.3
3	4.7	3.2	−32.5
4	6.0	4.1	−31.2
5	7.4	5.2	−29.7
6	8.6	6.4	−25.9
7	10.6	8.1	−23.7
8	12.7	10.6	−16.2
9	16.5	16.1	−2.7
Richest 10%	27.0	41.6	54.2
Total	**100.0**	**100.0**	

Source: INDEC, 1992.

Unfortunately, the return of democracy in 1983 made the distribution of income in Buenos Aires even more unequal. Table 6.5 shows that the difference between the income share of the richest and poorest deciles rose from 10 times in 1984 to a startling 23 times in 1989. Growing inequality was associated with increasing poverty during a period when the gross domestic product grew by only 1.4 per cent and when the country was suffering from hyperinflation. Whereas the incomes of the richest 10 per cent increased by almost 60 per cent, those of the poorest seven deciles fell by approximately 30 per cent. Whether considered in absolute or relative terms, the rich have become much richer, the majority much poorer.

Living standards

A major comparative study of poverty in Latin America has used two different criteria of impoverishment. An Index of Unsatisfied Basic Needs attempts to identify the "structural poor" and is based on indicators such as the physical quality of housing, the level of overcrowding within the home, sanitary conditions, schooling of the children, and the earnings potential of the household. The second measure is designed to identify those who have become "impoverished." It is based on a poverty line below which a family cannot afford to purchase a basket of essential goods and services. Those who cannot even buy the food in the household basket are classified as living in extreme need.

Studies comparing living conditions in Buenos Aires and the rest

Table 6.6 **Poverty in the metropolitan area of Buenos Aires (percentage of house-holds)**

Type of poverty	1980	1988	1990	1980/1990
Structural poor	16.4	16.2	16.1	−1.8
Impoverished	4.2	16.8	18.4	338.1
Total poverty	**20.6**	**33.0**	**34.5**	**67.4**

Source: Minujin, 1992.

of Argentina show that structural poverty is much less marked in the metropolitan area than in the country as a whole (CEPA, 1992; CEPA, 1993). However, averages can be deceiving and parts of peripheral Buenos Aires are just as deprived as other regions of the country.

Table 6.6 shows that, during the 1980s, although the share of the population living in "structural poverty" remained virtually stationary, the proportion living below the poverty line increased dramatically. Indeed, by 1990, the latter group made up 35 per cent of the Buenos Aires population. Many of the poor included families previously classified as middle-income.

The effect of poverty is apparent in terms of differences in health care between income groups. The proportion of pregnant women receiving medical attention during the first three months of pregnancy is 83 per cent for the non-poor but only 62 per cent for the "structural poor" and 67 per cent for "impoverished" groups. The poor also have more children, the structurally poor averaging 6.6, the impoverished 4.4, and the non-poor 2.9 (INDEC, 1990). Family size is clearly linked to rates of contraceptive use: whereas only 23 per cent of the "structural poor" use some form of contraception, the rate rises to 33 per cent among the "impoverished" groups, and to 45 per cent among the non-poor.

Hyperinflation during the late 1980s had a major impact on the number of people living in poverty or in extreme need. The latter category made up a startling 12.7 per cent of the total population in October 1989, although this had fallen to 2.4 per cent by May 1992.

Levels of poverty vary greatly between different areas of the metropolitan area. At its peak in 1989, indigence in 10 districts of outer Buenos Aires reached 22 per cent compared to 13 per cent in the city as a whole (CEPA, 1992).[1] Table 6.7 shows how housing and sanitary conditions vary between inner and outer areas of the city; access to the main drainage system varies considerably. It also compares

Table 6.7 **Buenos Aires: Quality of life by area, 1980 and 1991**

Variable	Federal Capital		Rest of Buenos Aires		Vicente López		General Sarmiento		Florencio Varela	
	1980	1991	1980	1991	1980	1991	1980	1991	1980	1991
H/H without schooling	1.6	−1.0	3.7	2.6	2.1	1.2	4.5	3.2	5.0	3.8
H/H with incomplete primary education	11.1	7.4	29.0	21.5	13.8	9.3	36.3	26.5	40.3	29.3
6–12 year olds not attending school	3.7	1.2	6.7	1.5	3.3	0.9	8.3	1.6	8.8	1.6
Population in poor housing	4.1	5.1	28.0	28.1	4.7	5.5	45.5	43.6	58.9	53.2
Homes with overcrowded conditions	1.5	2.0	8.5	6.5	1.9	1.5	13.4	9.7	18.4	13.0
Houses without sanitation	0.9	2.2	14.3	7.3	2.6	1.8	23.5	11.0	34.7	16.9

Source: CEPA, 1993.

living standards in three areas of the city with very different average incomes (Vicente López in the north of the First district, General Sarmiento in the west of the Second district, and Florencio Varela in the south of the Third district; see figure 6.2). There are major differences in terms of the education of heads of household, with some 29 per cent of heads having an incomplete primary education in Florencio Varela compared to 7 per cent in the Federal Capital.

Urban administration

The institutional framework

Argentina is a federal republic. The government is democratically elected and has three tiers of administration: national, provincial, and municipal. The federal government is by far the dominant force in the country, controlling the public finance system and exercising the key executive functions. Provincial government is responsible for anything that is not reserved for the federal administration. It also controls the activities of the municipalities.

Administrative responsibility for Greater Buenos Aires is divided between a large number of different bodies. The key distinction is between the Federal District and the municipalities which belong to the Province of Buenos Aires. In the Federal Capital, the federal government controls every important administrative matter and the president appoints the district's highest officer, the Intendent of the Municipality of the City of Buenos Aires. Although the municipal council is elected, its decisions are largely controlled by the national parliament.

Beyond the Federal Capital, administrative responsibility rests with the Province of Buenos Aires and the 19 municipalities which make up the remainder of the metropolitan area. The provincial government negotiates its duties with the federal authorities. Administration is complicated by the fact that the headquarters of the provincial government is based in the city of La Plata, 35 miles south-east of Buenos Aires.

Each of the nineteen municipal districts is governed by an intendent and a council. Since both are popularly elected, political conflicts with the provincial authorities not infrequently occur, especially when the political complexions of the two sets of administrations differ.

Attempting to prevent anarchy is the function of two bodies with responsibility for administrative coordination: the Metropolitan Area

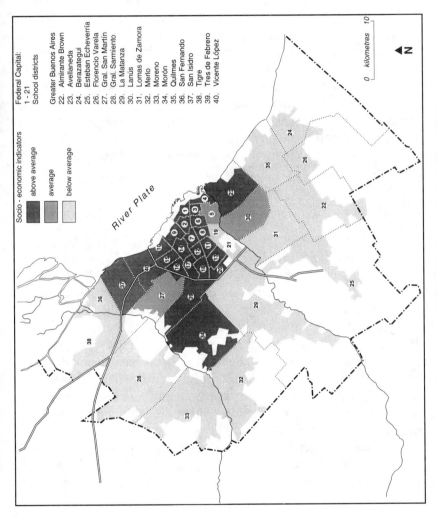

Figure 6.2 **Residential segregation in Buenos Aires, 1991**

of Buenos Aires (AMBA) and the National Commission for the Metropolitan Area of Buenos Aires (CONAMBA). AMBA is responsible for coordinating links between the federal government, the municipality of the City of Buenos Aires and the province of Buenos Aires. CONAMBA is exclusively concerned with overseeing national concerns within Greater Buenos Aires. Unfortunately, neither body has much power and, since 1984, neither has managed to integrate government policy in the metropolitan area.

Independent public agencies carry out certain specialized functions in the city. One agency is responsible for solid waste disposal and land recovery, another for managing the city's waterways. A number of public bodies are also responsible for regulating and supervising the newly privatized service companies. Since these regulatory agencies have responsibility only for parts of the city, there is no way of preventing highly varied standards of service delivery and the consequent exacerbation of social inequalities.

Public finance

Each level of government has an independent income. Federal revenues come mainly from income and company taxes, municipal revenues principally from a progressive property tax. Provincial governments obtain their revenues from a variety of sources. Common funds at the municipal and provincial levels are intended to even out financial inequalities between various areas in the country. Given that Buenos Aires is the richest province in the country, it loses out from this system. Similarly, the Federal Capital has received practically nothing from national funds intended for new road construction.

Each level of government is responsible for providing a range of public services within its jurisdiction. Given the wide variation in service provision in the different parts of the city, however, the population tends to use services in the best-serviced area, the Federal Capital. Given the lack of a satisfactory charging mechanism between authorities, this means that the centre is effectively subsidizing the periphery.

Changing administrative systems

The Menem administration has attempted a fundamental restructuring of government in Argentina. The key changes include a move towards functional decentralization, privatization of public services, and deregulation of the private sector. These reforms have had important repercussions within the Buenos Aires urban area, few of which are likely to have helped the poor.

"Decentralization" involves the delegation of national and provincial government functions to the municipal level. Decentralization is also occurring at the municipal level, where subdivisions are being created in each of the metropolitan municipalities. Official rhetoric has justified these changes in terms of the need to reduce bureaucracy and to increase the level of public participation. Unfortunately, the changes have been made with insufficient funding. A further problem is that there has been little attempt to improve coordination between the different levels of government in the metropolitan area. For the poorest areas, however, the major problem is that the reforms have cut the transfer of funds from more prosperous parts of the city. This means that existing inequalities in public service provision are likely to increase further.

Privatization has had a number of rather harmful effects. First, the transfer of service and infrastructure provision to private companies has led to steep price increases, a tendency accentuated by the removal of government subsidies. This has cut use by very poor groups, particularly now that illegal users are regularly disconnected. Second, privatization has reduced the supply of housing, education, and recreational facilities, at a time when demand has risen owing to the needs of an increasingly impoverished middle class.

Finally, deregulation of the private sector has led to important changes in operating hours and, most importantly, in the relative prices of goods and services. Rents, fares, the cost of leisure facilities, and charges for health care have all risen in real terms. Deregulation has had a harmful impact on the poorest people in the city.

Service provision

Energy

The metropolitan area receives its electricity from the national distribution network. Two thermal power stations operate within the Federal Capital and a nuclear station just outside it. Among the main utilities, electricity offers the widest spatial and social coverage. Practically every home in the city is linked to the electricity network, helped in some poor neighbourhoods by illegal connections (although, as a result of recent privatization, this situation is now being regularized).

Buenos Aires has a very well-developed gas system. In 1990, some 20,000 industrial companies and some 2.6 million homes, three-quarters of the city's total, were connected to the network.

Water and sanitation

Between 1980 and 1991, the proportion of homes connected to the mains water system increased despite a severe reduction in the level of investment (Novaro and Perelman, 1994). The proportion of households in Greater Buenos Aires with a link to the mains water supply increased from 44 per cent to 50 per cent. The authorities achieved this feat by giving high priority to the connection of new households in the periphery. The problem was that they were unable to maintain the quality of the water supply. Regular maintenance procedures were cut, the rate of water loss rose, and there were frequent interruptions to the household water supply (Novaro and Perelman, 1994).

The organization of water and sanitation services has been modified in recent years. Until 1992, both water and sanitation were provided by the state-run Obras Sanitarias de la Nación (OSN).[2] In most of the metropolitan area, water is now provided by a private company, Aguas Argentinas, which supplies the Federal Capital and thirteen municipalities in the Province of Buenos Aires. In four outer municipalities water is supplied by the Province of Buenos Aires' water company, and in two others, Quilmes and Berazategui, by the respective municipalities.

Administration of the drainage system has also been restructured. Until 1992, it was operated by the OSN but it is now the responsibility of each municipality. The drainage system is seriously deficient and, with rainfall heavily concentrated between October and March, Buenos Aires regularly suffers from floods.[3] Occasionally, there have been major disasters, the most serious occurring at the end of May 1985, when 300 millimetres of rain fell in 30 hours. Fifteen people were killed and 120,000 people had to be evacuated. The danger of floods has been worsened by the way in which the city has expanded. Too many poor neighbourhoods are located on low-lying land in areas where few attempts have been made to improve the drainage system.

The sewerage system is also deficient and untreated sewage is regularly discharged into the ground. With one-half of all homes in the metropolitan area lacking connection to the mains water system, many low-income neighbourhoods face serious health problems. This is a particular problem in the Province of Buenos Aires, where only 25 per cent of homes are connected to the mains.[4] In the worst-served municipality, Merlo, only 4 per cent of homes have either mains water or sewerage provision.

Rubbish collection in most of the metropolitan area is the responsibility of a mixed enterprise which is also in charge of its treatment and final disposal. In practice, large areas of the city are excluded from this service, and in the peripheral neighbourhoods rubbish is simply dumped onto open sites. This creates major environmental and health problems.

This combination of sanitary problems has led to serious outbreaks of cholera, hepatitis, and meningitis in recent years. There was a particularly serious outbreak of hepatitis in 1988 and 1989.[5] Poor diet and limited access to health facilities for the groups most at risk have increased the dangers of epidemics breaking out in Buenos Aires.

Transportation

Close to 12 million trips are made every day in Buenos Aires, an average of about 1.1 trips per person. This figure represents a significant decrease since 1970, when the average was 1.9 trips per person.

Table 6.8 shows that use of the private car has increased markedly since 1970 and now accounts for one-quarter of all journeys. Government policy implicitly supports use of the private car, with few restrictions on movement and an abundance of parking spaces. Since there were approximately 2.4 million cars in the metropolitan area in 1992, one for every 4.5 people, the city suffers from chronic road congestion.

Table 6.8 **Major modes of transport in Buenos Aires, 1970 and 1992 (percentage of journeys)**

Mode	1970	1992
Car	15.4	24.3
Taxi	6.7	1.4
Bus	54.3	49.8
Rail	7.0	6.4
Underground	5.4	3.6
Other	11.2	14.5

Sources: Arcusin et al., 1992; MOSP, 1972.

Unfortunately, the road system is not well adapted to the growing use of private cars. Buenos Aires has too few motorways and roads capable of handling the large volume of traffic. The best-developed part of the road system leads to the historic centre and roads deteriorate in quality closer to the edge of the city. Outside the Federal Capital, only the main roads are paved.

The way in which the road network developed aggravates traffic congestion. The city grew on the basis of a grid system, with 100-metre-square blocks divided into lots with a frontage of ten metres. Most streets are narrow, less than 18 metres wide, although avenues more than double the width of the ordinary streets run along every fourth block. Although this road system was more or less adequate for the time when it was designed, and is still suitable for areas with a low residential density, it is not appropriate for a city where land-use densities and rates of car ownership have been growing so rapidly.

Traffic congestion has been aggravated by a relative decline in the use of public transport and by the shape of the road and railway systems. Most journeys starting in the First Ring, and a considerable proportion of those beginning in the Second and Third Ring districts, involve travelling to, or through, the Federal Capital. Overall, one-fifth of journeys in the metropolitan area begin or end in the Federal Capital (Arcusin et al., 1992).

There are six railway lines, five of which terminate at three central stations. The lines fan out from the city centre and disrupt road traffic because there are few bridges or tunnels. Buenos Aires has also had an underground railway since 1913. Today, the network is consists of five lines with a total length of 28 miles. The lines form a radial pattern and complement the surface rail system in so far as they link up with the main rail termini.

Coordination of transport services in the city is poor and is currently subject to major policy changes. Both the underground and the train companies are being privatized, although they continue to receive subsidies. Bus services are already managed privately and no longer receive a subsidy. The benefits of bus privatization are widely questioned both in terms of the excessively high profits earned by the companies and by the limited service that local monopolies provide to poorer settlements (Zajac, n.d.). With the exception of the underground, the city lacks a coordinated fare structure, and, with subsidies in decline, the cost of public transport is rising in real terms. This is clearly a serious problem for low-income groups living in the periphery of the city. Higher fares and a deteriorating system help to explain why use of the public transport system fell relatively between 1970 and 1992 (table 6.8). It also suggests why journeys on foot and by bicycle increased in importance.

Population density and land-use structure

Land use in Buenos Aires takes the form of a series of concentric rings spreading outwards from the historic centre. Most government offices, many commercial and financial services, and the headquarters of the larger manufacturing companies are concentrated in the centre. The dominance of this area in terms of producer services seems to have increased over time; new service companies are moving into the area as manufacturing activity moves out.

Of course, commercial activity has also developed in the suburbs. A major commercial sub-centre has been developed in the Belgrano area, eight miles north-west of the central area (figure 6.3), and many smaller centres, and increasingly shopping malls, have appeared in more distant suburbs. These commercial centres have catered mainly for families with their own car; few have been well located for families dependent upon public transport.

Land use in Buenos Aires has developed a strong radial pattern beyond the historic centre. This results from the flatness of the terrain and the way that the original road network was laid out. This pattern was reinforced over time, first by the layout of the rail network and later by that of the tram and underground systems. Not surprisingly, a classic population density gradient has developed. Population densities in the city decrease sharply from the centre to the periphery. In 1991, 15,000 people per square kilometre lived in the Federal Capital, 5,419 in the First Ring, 2,820 in the Second Ring, and 774 in the Third Ring. (The average density of the metropolitan area was 2,800 persons per square kilometre.)

Social segregation in the city is acute and leaves an indelible mark on the pattern of land use. High-quality shopping and personal services are concentrated in the northern and western neighbourhoods of the Federal Capital, where most of the affluent live (figure 6.2). In the rest of the area, there has been an unprecedented decline in the physical fabric, including the growth of large areas of slums. Low-income settlements have developed in all parts of the periphery, but particularly in the south and west.

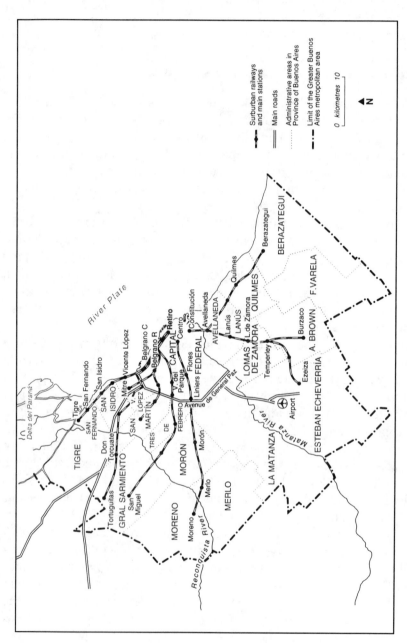

Figure 6.3 **Buenos Aires: Administrative divisions and railway lines**

The environment

Despite the strong winds, which quickly disperse most contaminants, levels of air pollution in the central area regularly exceed World Health Organization norms. Since the burning of solid waste and liquid fuels was prohibited in 1977, road vehicles have been the principal source of air pollution in the city.

It is water pollution, however, which represents the most serious environmental problem. The Reconquista and Matanza-Riachuelo rivers are so polluted that they have become virtually open sewers, and the central drainage system discharges around one million cubic metres of untreated sewage directly into the River Plate. Close to the city, the river's oxygenation level has fallen to 40 per cent. Illegal dumping of industrial toxins into the water system has been a recurrent problem and there have been numerous episodes of mass poisoning.

A final source of pollution comes from domestic and industrial rubbish, which is dumped on over a hundred open sites in populated areas. More than two million tons of waste have been left on 600 hectares of dumps in the metropolitan periphery.

Although environmental regulations are far from adequate, the critical problem is the failure to implement those that do exist. A combination of political pressure from powerful economic interests and the inefficiency of the state agencies which are meant to regulate them has meant that controls have been far too lax.

Conclusions

During the 1980s, Argentina suffered from a combination of debt, economic recession, and growing poverty. Like most major cities in the region, Buenos Aires suffered badly from the "debt crisis" and its aftermath. Fortunately, the national economic growth record has improved during the 1990s, even if the future is anything but certain. As a consequence, it is difficult to predict how the national capital will fare. Clearly, its prospects are integrally linked to Argentina's ability both to generate new export products and to increase sales of its traditional products.

Poverty and inequality in Buenos Aires have increased markedly in recent years. Housing conditions have deteriorated and the failure to improve the quality of the water and sewerage systems has rebounded on the poor living in the urban periphery. Incomes have fallen, levels of unemployment have risen, more people are employed in casual forms of work, and labour conditions in the "formal" sector have been badly affected by deregulation. In the process, the distribution of income has deteriorated: the very rich have prospered, and everyone else has got much poorer.

Given current circumstances, it would be unwise to expect much improvement in the next few years. Adjustment policies are likely to reduce incomes further and to increase levels of unemployment. Subsidies are being phased out and the privatization of transport and public utilities may well hurt the poor. It is less than certain that the quality of urban management will improve. Decentralization of administration is leading to a fragmentation of responsibility. While rich neigbourhoods can cope with the new responsibilities they are being given, poorer districts are being forced to take on new tasks with few additional resources. For the rich, a high-quality lifestyle is assured; for the poor, living conditions may well get even worse.

Notes

1. These districts were Almirante Brown, Berazategui, Esteban Echeverría, General Sarmiento, Florencio Varela, La Matanza, Merlo, Moreno, San Fernando, and Tigre.
2. In 1981 OSN had delegated its functions to each province (Novaro and Perelman, 1994: 4).
3. Between 1981 and 1990, 72 per cent of rainfall fell in this period. The driest months are June to September.
4. In the Federal Capital virtually every home is connected.
5. Its incidence increased by 140 per cent in the Federal Capital and by 386 per cent in Buenos Aires Province; the rest of the country was less badly affected (INDEC, 1992).

References

Ainstein, L. (1991) "El proceso de formación y administración territorial de Buenos Aires." *Ciudad y Territorio* 86/7: 499–511.
Ainstein, L., J.L. Karol, and J. Lindenboim (1992) "Evaluation methods and structuring policies of urban networks and components." In Facultad de Arquitectura ..., 391–441.
Arcusin, J., P. Brennan, A. Ternavasio, and O. Vicente (1992) "Desregulación del transporte y evolución de la movilidad en Buenos Aires." Mimeo, Buenos Aires.
Archenti, N., and A. del Franco (1990) "Los sectores sociales medio-bajos y bajos del Gran Buenos Aires. Crisis y actitudes políticas." Buenos Aires: FUCADE (mimeo).
Bourdé, G. (1987) *La classe ouvrière argentine (1929–1969).* L'Harmattan.
Brunstein, F., and S. Finquelievich (1992) "Transferring responsibilities to users: Water and sanitation cooperatives in Greater Buenos Aires." In Facultad de Arquitectura, ..., 363–78.

CEPA [Comité Ejecutivo para el Estudio de la Pobreza en la Argentina] (1992) *Evolución reciente de la pobreza en el aglomerado del Gran Buenos Aires 1988–1992.* Buenos Aires: MEOSP.

—— (1993) *Necesidades básicas insatisfechas. Evolución intercensal 1980–1991.* Buenos Aires: MEOSP.

Clichevsky N., M.F. Prévôt Schapira, and G. Schneier (1990) *Loteos populares, sector inmobiliario y gestión local en Buenos Aires. El caso del Municipio de Moreno.* Buenos Aires: CREDAL–CEUR.

Cuenya, B. (1988) *Inquilinatos en la ciudad de Buenos Aires.* Buenos Aires: Cuadernos del CEUR no. 24.

Cuenya, B., E. Pastrana, and O. Yujnovsky (1984) *De la villa miseria al barrio autoconstruido.* Buenos Aires: CEUR.

Facultad de Arquitectura, Diseño y Urbanismo, Universidad de Buenos Aires (1992) Proceedings of the International Seminar "Metropolitan areas: Network dynamics and sustainable development." Buenos Aires.

Herzer, H. (1992) "La ciudad de Buenos Aires: Inundaciones y Concejo Deliberante." In Facultad de Arquitectura . . . , 279–94.

Hintze, S. (1992) "Consecuencias de la crisis en los sectores populares de Buenos Aires." In Facultad de Arquitectura . . . , 295–322.

IIED/AL [International Institute of Environment and Development – América Latina] (1991) "Problemas ambientales en las ciudades argentinas." *Medio Ambiente y Urbanización* 37: 3–123.

INDEC [Instituto Nacional de Estadística y Censos] (1984) *La pobreza en la Argentina.* Buenos Aires: INDEC Estudios.

—— (1989) *La pobreza en el conurbano bonaerense.* Buenos Aires: INDEC Estudios.

—— (1990) *Módulo de precariedad laboral de la Encuesta Permanente de Hogares.* Buenos Aires.

—— (1991) *Conurbano bonaerense: Aproximación a la determinación de hogares y población en riesgo sanitario a través de la Encuesta Permanente de Hogares.* Buenos Aires.

—— (1992) *Situación y evolución social.* Buenos Aires.

Lindenboim, J. (1985) "La tertiarización del empleo en Argentina. Una perspectiva regional." Buenos Aires: United Nations Development Programme. (mimeo).

—— (1992) "Reestructuración industrial y empleo. Mitos y realidades." *Desarrollo Económico: Revista de Ciencias Sociales* 32: 227–50.

Minujin, A. (ed.) (1992) *Cuesta abajo. Los nuevos pobres: Efectos de la crisis en la sociedad argentina.* Buenos Aires: UNICEF-Losada.

MOSP [Ministerio de Obras y Servicios Públicos] (1972) *Estudio preliminar del transporte de la región metropolitana de Buenos Aires.* Buenos Aires.

Novaro, M., and P. Perelman (1994) "La provisión de agua en el Gran Buenos Aires." *Medio Ambiente y Urbanización* 49: 3–16.

Pírez, P. (1992) "La ciudad metropolitana de Buenos Aires y las relaciones políticas." In Facultad de Arquitectura . . . , 323–40.

Rouquié, A. (1987) *Amérique Latine: Introduction à l'Extrême Occident.* Editions du Seuil.

Schvarzer, J. (1983) "Implantación industrial." in J.L. and L.A. Romero (eds.), *Buenos Aires, historia de cuatro siglos*, vol. II. Buenos Aires: Editorial Abril.

L. Ainstein

———— (1991) "Del transporte ferroviario al ómnibus: Cambios en las prácticas urbanas en Buenos Aires." In Coloquio Internacional, *Grandes metrópolis de Africa y América Latina*, Toulouse.

Scobie, J. (1964) *Argentina: A city and a nation.* New York: Oxford University Press.

Torres, H.A. (1993) *El mapa social de Buenos Aires (1940–1990).* Buenos Aires: Facultad de Arquitectura, Diseño y Urbanismo, Universidad de Buenos Aires, Serie Difusión.

Vapñarsky, C.A., and N. Gorojovsky (1990) *El crecimiento urbano en la Argentina.* Buenos Aires: GEL–IIED/AL.

Yujnovksy, O. (1983) "Del conventillo a la villa miseria." in J.L. and L.A. Romero (eds.), *Buenos Aires, historia de cuatro siglos*, vol. II. Buenos Aires: Editorial Abril.

Zajac, H. (n.d.) "Monopolios en el transporte público: La otra cara de la 'desregularización'." Universidad de Buenos Aires.

7

Lima: Mega-city and mega-problem

Gustavo Riofrío

The origins of Lima's problems

Lima's problems began when it was founded on the Pacific coast by the Spanish in 1535. It was not a good place to locate Peru's new capital city. It was chosen in part because the Spanish did not want a highland capital like Quito or Bogotá. They ignored Cusco, the Inca capital, and Jauja, the first capital of Peru, both of which were located in the *sierra*. They wanted a maritime capital that would link South America with Europe; Lima was established to act as the point of contact between Spain and the Inca civilization.

Lima's founders were no doubt misled by the weather when they established the city. January is one of the few months of the year when dank mist does not cover the city like a grey blanket. Lima's climate is boring. From February until October, there is neither wind nor sun, the weather is neither hot nor cold, simply dull and humid. *Limeños* have to travel into the mountains to see the sun or to look at the stars. Except for the occasional sea breeze, there is little or no wind in Lima. Beneath the layer of mist, smoke and dust accumulate, a perfect recipe for atmospheric pollution and for the development of respiratory diseases. The colour of the city reflects the leaden sky, the buildings impressing the visitor only with their greyness. While the summer is pleasant, it rarely lasts more than four months.

It is the cold Humboldt current, running northwards along the Peruvian coast, that creates the winter mist and prevents the formation of rain clouds. Peru's rain comes from the Atlantic Ocean, soaking Amazonia but never crossing the Andes.[1] A desert extends almost the whole length of the Pacific coast, some 2,000 kilometres from north to south.

Lima is located at the mouth of one of the fifty or so alluvial valleys that periodically irrigate the Peruvian coastline. Location in another valley would have served the future city better. Either the Santa valley (450 kilometres to the north) or the Cañete (150 kilometres to the south) would have provided the new capital with both more space and more water. The problem with the Rimac valley is that the river's regime is highly seasonal, varying from an average of 30 cubic metres per second during the winter months to as much as 400 cubic metres in the summer. In the winter there is not enough water; in the summer there is always the danger of floods, made worse by the narrowness of the valley.

Demographic growth

Until the beginning of this century, most of Peru's political power was concentrated in Lima. It was an administrative city that gradually extended its grip on the wealth of the nation. Most of the country's imports were channelled through the port of Callao; most of Peru's export revenues found their way back to the city. After the Second World War, Lima became even more dominant, finally managing to destroy its rivals by establishing a virtual monopoly over the newly emerging industries and commercial services. By 1986, Lima generated 69 per cent of industrial value added and collected 87 per cent of the nation's taxes. It also contained 76 per cent of the nation's telephones, 51 per cent of its public employees, and 73 per cent of its doctors. In the same year, Lima attracted 83 per cent of all Peru's bank loans and 98 per cent of private investment outside the mining sector. By 1993, Lima had no rivals; it was nearly 10 times larger than Arequipa, Peru's second city, and more than one-quarter of all Peruvians lived there.

Lima's growth, like that of most cities in Latin America, had accelerated after 1940. In the next half-century, its population grew tenfold. By 1993, seven out of ten Peruvians were living in urban

Table 7.1 **Lima: Population growth, 1940–1993**

	Lima		Peru	
	Population (000s)	Annual growth rate	Population (000s)	Annual growth rate
1940	649		6,208	
1961	1,846	5.1	9,907	2.2
1972	3,303	5.5	13,538	2.9
1981	4,608	3.1	17,005	2.5
1993	6,423	2.7	22,639	2.2

Source: INEI, 1994.

areas, two out of five of these in Lima. The last census showed that Lima-Callao contained 6.3 million people.

Fortunately, the city's growth rate began to slow in the 1970s (table 7.1), the result of a drop both in the rate of natural increase and in the pace of cityward migration. The slower pace of growth means that the population pyramid is no longer dominated by children. The 1993 census showed that the most populous sections of the age pyramid were the 15–19 and the 20–24-year age groups. Neither is Lima any longer a city of migrants: most of the population has been born in the city.

Employment and poverty

The changing age structure of the city has brought new problems in its wake. Today, Lima lacks sufficient jobs and needs more facilities for higher education; there are plenty of primary schools now that the wave of youngsters has passed, especially in the low-income districts of the city (Driant, 1991). The youth that seeks work in Lima today is literate and is no longer satisfied with the unskilled construction work that once employed so many of its migrant forebears. The proportion of the economically active population born in the city rose from 40 per cent in 1981 to 50 per cent in 1993. Most of the young people now seeking to enter the labour force share the unsatisfied desires of their parents. The difference is that they are not strangers to the city, they were born there.

Unlike many other Latin American cities, Lima has experienced little or no economic growth since the petrol crisis of 1973. Since 1980, the economic situation has deteriorated severely. Peru has suf-

157

Table 7.2 **Un- and underemployment in Lima (percentage of economically active population)**

	1979	1990	1993
Unemployment	6.5	8.3	9.6
Underemployment	33.0	73.1	77.6
Satisfactorily employed	60.6	18.6	12.8

Source: Ministerio de Trabajo, Household surveys.

fered badly from inflation, which rose to a peak of 7,660 per cent in 1990, and its per capita income has declined consistently, by almost 30 per cent between 1981 and 1993 (CEPAL, 1993).

Changes in economic policy have brought few benefits. Fluctuations in economic policy during the import-substituting industrialization phase of the 1980s gave way in the 1990s to a neoliberal model of economic adjustment and trade liberalization. Although the latter has reduced the monthly inflation rate to single figures and has recently brought an increase in per capita income, there has been little effort to compensate poorer groups in society. These have seen no improvement in their incomes or in their prospects for employment.[2] The minimum wage in Lima in 1992 was only one-sixth of its value in 1980 and average salaries in 1994 one-half of their earlier value; some kind of social compensation package is badly needed.

Economic decline has reduced the number of decent jobs available. Cuts in the national government's budget reduced the number of government employees, a high proportion of whom worked in Lima, by 300,000 between 1990 and 1993. There has also been a major decline in manufacturing employment. Table 7.2 shows that only 13 per cent of the economically active population in Lima currently earn an adequate income and that the level of unemployment has risen to almost 10 per cent. Some of the unemployed are highly qualified; others, with less education and skills, remain unemployed because the informal sector can no longer absorb them.

Much informal-sector work is contributing little to national development, providing only a way in which families can survive their poverty. According to the census, there were half a million street traders working in Lima in 1993. Public space is being invaded by the informal sector. The streets of the city are full of traders, many of whom have established stalls that permanently occupy space in the central areas of the city. All sorts of activities are now conducted in the city streets: food is sold and eaten, vehicles are repaired and resprayed, there is a lot of crime. The authorities have no answer to this phenomenon. They hope that if existing rules and regulations are relaxed the informal sector will prosper and contribute to economic regeneration. They trust that some businesses will discover new market niches, improve their productivity, and develop into formal enterprises. Despite these hopes, there are clearly too many people working in informal-sector activities. Incomes have fallen dramatically in this sector since 1980, a trend matched by wages in the formal sector.

Recent reports show clearly how falling incomes have affected poverty in the city. Between 1985/86 and 1990, it is estimated that the proportion of households living below the poverty line rose from 17 per cent to 44 per cent. After a single year of structural adjustment, the proportion had risen to 49 per cent in October/November 1991. By 1992, the proportion was 55 per cent, with 90 per cent of the labour force earning less than US$400 per month. When poverty is measured in terms of those unable to buy the minimum basket of goods, the proportion of Lima families living in poverty rises to a staggering 60 per cent (DESCO, 1993).[3]

Of the 49 per cent of *limeños* living below the poverty line in 1991, 20 per cent could be classified as living in structural poverty and the other 29 per cent as newly poor. The first group suffers not only from a low income but also from poor housing and low levels of education; the second group has an income below the poverty line.

Households are coping with increasing levels of poverty by putting more people into the labour force. While this allows them to survive, their employment in low-income activities only serves to lower wages further, so that "poverty tends to reproduce itself" (Gamero et al., 1994).

Although not everyone in Lima is poor, some three-quarters of the population of Lima are now considered to be working-class or "lower." The only slight consolation is that this proportion is far smaller than the 89 per cent recorded for the country as a whole.

Housing

The most distinctive feature of Lima's growth over the years has been the proliferation of low-income settlements. These are known locally as *barriadas* or, since the military regime of Juan Velasco Alvarado (1968–75), more euphemistically as *pueblos jóvenes*, or "young towns". Given the lack of cheap public housing, Peruvian govern-

159

Table 7.3 **Population by social class in metropolitan Lima, 1993**

Social class	Population (000s)	%
Upper	184	2.8
Middle	1,310	20.1
Below poverty level[a]	2,483	38.1
Below extreme need level[a]	2,540	39.0
Total	**6,518**	**100.0**

Source: Compañía Peruana de Investigación de Mercados (CPI), Market report.

a. The poverty line is measured as twice the cost of purchasing a minimum basket of food goods; the extreme need line as the cost of purchasing a minimum basket of goods.

ments have built even less than those in most other Latin American countries, so the poor have been forced to build their own accommodation. Both natives and migrants have occupied undeveloped land on the edge of the city: between 1955 and 1961 the share of Lima's population living in *barriadas* jumped from 10 per cent to 17 per cent (see also chapter 4). Housing policy became two-faced: the poor were permitted to invade land and build their own shelters, while the state and the private sector sought to provide housing for the middle class (Riofrío, 1978). As far as the state was concerned, housing for the poor became simply a matter of providing a plot of land. After 1961, the occupation of peripheral desert land came to be accepted officially.

Sites and service schemes were pioneered in Peru during the 1960s. Land was reserved for the poor, and when invasions of different areas took place the authorities responded by regularizing these settlements. If the community took on the burden of upgrading the settlement, the authorities would quickly recognize its leaders. The settlers would be guaranteed security of tenure. Most "young towns" were laid out in a highly ordered manner. The lots were all the same size, there was a recognizable street plan, and certain areas were left for the subsequent provision of public facilities and open spaces. Compared to the situation in other Latin American cities, families living in the "young towns" had plenty of space.

At one level the process worked well. Individual families gradually improved their homes, following similar designs to the houses of the middle class. Depending on their financial resources, they built quickly or slowly. They were free to build the kind of home they wanted and the final housing solution was often superior to what they would have received in a public housing project. Better the home in a *barriada* at a time when most architects tended to design only "small, cheap, modular, and uncomfortable" units for the poor.

The problem with the *barriadas* was that the uncoordinated self-help process was a highly inefficient way to develop a city: it was expensive, it was slow, and it forced many families to live for long periods in inadequate accommodation. The standard of construction was often very low and many families were forced to live in crowded conditions. The authorities did far too little to help the poor build their homes. They did not make cheap credit available. They did not organize any kind of technical assistance. They did not even ensure that the buildings being constructed were safe to live in. After 1961, the *barriadas* were freed from any requirement to obtain a building licence. The authorities accepted that they would receive no payments from the *barriadas*; in return they would not interfere. The only planning was that done by the community itself.

The process of self-help construction produced a city of relatively low density. Compared to other Latin American cities, few families rented accommodation. Central Lima had few slum areas because most people preferred to live in their own self-help home and could obtain their own plot and begin construction. The fact that the state owned large areas of flat desert land allowed this process to continue unhindered for many years. Low-density shelter also accommodated most higher-income groups. Urban sprawl was the result.

The problem with this process was that it could not continue for ever (Riofrío, 1991). By the 1990s, the city faced major problems with this housing model. Unoccupied land was scarce and therefore expensive. Any land close to the main service lines had several potential developers competing to settle it. The stock of state land was exhausted and the "young towns" began to occupy less suitable sites. New settlements began to occupy land on steep slopes, in valleys subject to flooding, in areas reserved for public projects. It was expensive to service these areas and the new settlements were as badly organized and serviced as the *barriadas* of the 1940s and 1950s.

As the amount of accessible, serviceable land became scarcer, population densities began to rise in the established areas. Lots increasingly accommodated more than one household. While the more foresighted or affluent built additional rooms at the side or above their own homes to accommodate newcomers, others were forced to share their own quarters. The young and poor could no longer obtain free plots in the periphery. They were forced to share or rent in the existing settlements, which caused increasing problems in terms of service provision and overcrowding. More and more households did not easily fit into settlements conceived as low-density residential areas and which had long been neglected by planners and politicians.

If there are increasing problems in the established "young towns," the situation is even worse in the new settlements. In part, this is because of the difficulty and cost of obtaining services in distant and unsuitable locations. In part, it is because the nature of the settlers has changed. Many are refugees from the guerrilla war which was raging in the countryside until 1993. They arrived with few resources, unprepared for urban life, expelled by the actions of either guerrillas or the military. The rest are native to the city. Educated they may be, but they do not know how to build homes; in any case, given the perilous work situation, they have few resources with which to consolidate and improve a shelter.

New and old settlements alike face a further problem, the inability of the authorities to provide adequate services and infrastructure. Lima coped in the 1960s and 1970s by extending services without improving basic facilities. The authorities lengthened the power lines without increasing overall capacity. They put more water into the existing pipes without upgrading or even maintaining the system. The city is now reaping the consequences of this improvisation.

Infrastructure and services

The lack of infrastructure and services in now a major problem in Lima, one aggravated both by rapid population growth and by economic decline. In contrast to the improvement that occurred in the 1970s, the quality of servicing deteriorated badly during the 1980s. Water, sewerage, and electricity provision was hampered by the decline in public investment as well as by concerted guerrilla attacks on the national electricity grid. Admittedly, the quality of some kinds of service, notably roads and rubbish collection, did improve during the 1980s. These services were in municipal hands and the improvement can be attributed to the fact that since 1980 the municipal councils in Lima have been elected.

The combination of terrorist attacks and drought brought particular problems for the electricity sector. Between 1989 and 1992, the city suffered from severe rationing; at particularly difficult times the electricity supply was reduced by 35 per cent. Guerrilla attacks and a lack of water aggravated a crisis that had long been in the making; at its heart lay the lack of adequate planning and foresight.

Table 7.4 **Water, sewerage, and electricity provision in Lima, 1993 (percentage of households)**

Piped water provision in the home	63.6
Link to the main sewer	60.2
Electricity in the home	82.1
Total homes	1,399,530

Source: INEI, 1994.

Capacity had been reduced because too little investment had taken place. The authorities had responded only to crises: for example, they built a new coal-driven power station between 1992 and 1994 as an emergency response to the shortage of 300 megawatts of power.

The water sector was no better planned. Water had been scarce since the middle 1960s, when poorer settlements first began to be rationed. Too little water was supplied from outside the city and, as a result, the level of the water table gradually dropped and sea water penetrated the aquifer. The shortage of water meant that, during the 1980s, fewer homes in the "young towns" were being connected to the network. Table 7.4 shows that by the 1990s services were lacking in many parts of the city. Even homes linked to the mains were suffering water shortages; 4.5 million *limeños* suffered from rationing during the drought of 1992.

It remains to be seen whether current plans to privatize some of the major utilities will yield better results. Certainly, any reactivation of the economy will help the situation, and public investment has already increased the supply of water to the city. So far, however, there is little sign of any improvement in the quality of maintenance or of any extension of the supply network.

Transport

Current road conditions and the state of public transport are perfect examples of the urban disorder that rules in Lima today. During the 1980s, there had been signs of hope. More investment was put into transport than into any other sector. With the newly elected municipal authorities attempting to improve traffic conditions, the road system improved in leaps and bounds. A World Bank loan helped the Municipality of Lima to build new roads and to pave or repave 100 kilometres of existing road. Paved roads reached most settlements, including the larger "young towns." The principal problem was how to handle the massive amount of traffic in the city without saturating the main roads. Lacking adequate funds, the Municipality of Lima was unable to build enough road interchanges or to improve the system of traffic lights. International loans could not be used because these were cut in 1986, when the national president insisted on the construction of an electric train system in the city and, as a result of this project, the Municipality of Lima could not comply with the terms of its contract with the World Bank. The construction of three new road interchanges in the last six years has helped, but any real improvement has been hampered by the fact that road spending has been cut by the national government's attempts to cut municipal funding.[4]

The system of public transport has been in progressive decline since the 1970s. Long-term municipal plans to reorganize mass transport in the city were rudely interrupted by the imposition of the electric train project in 1986. The national president established a new authority to "plan" and operate the new railway, and building work commenced in the absurdly short period of nine months. Ten kilometres of line were built in the south of the city between 1986 and 1990, but the line has still not been completed and is currently out of service.

Public transport in Peru is mainly in the hands of large numbers of small enterprises. They operate fleets of small vehicles which are rarely well maintained. In Lima, the bus routes are poorly planned and have grown haphazardly in response to changing demands for transport. During the 1990s, economic restructuring has brought several important changes. First, with the lowering of import tariffs, large numbers of new vehicles have been imported. The number of public transport vehicles in Lima increased from 7,000 to 27,000 between 1990 and 1993. While this has helped modernize some of the fleet, new legislation has also allowed the import of used vehicles, and even used tyres, into the country.[5] The result is that there are far too many small vehicles on the roads. Second, large numbers of unemployed workers have set up in business, driving the newly imported taxis and "combis." Unfortunately, few of these drivers have been properly trained and the municipal authorities estimate that only half hold a driving licence. The huge expansion in unauthorized taxi services has increased the rate of accidents and has also led to frequent attacks on passengers by drivers. The "combis" are even worse than the taxis and the police estimate that 40 per cent of road deaths in Lima involve such a vehicle.

Public transport in the city is in chaos because the authorities no longer exert any real level of control. The standard of driving has deteriorated as the numbers of vehicles have increased. People park their vehicles where they want and no-one prevents illegal parking. In terms of transport, Lima appears to have become ungovernable (see also chapter 5).

Crime, violence, and terrorism

Lima faces many of the same problems as most other Latin American cities with respect to crime. Ordinary crime and police corruption have increased in line with rising levels of poverty. Crime rates are higher in Lima than in the rest of Peru, and during the 1980s crimes of violence rose considerably. Well-armed and organized gangs emerged during the late 1980s. As in other Latin American cities, the authorities have been unable to cope with the rising wave of violent crime. However, the situation in Lima is worse than in most other parts of the region because of the influence of drugs and terrorist violence.

Special mention needs to be made of the problem of drugs. For some years, coca paste has been exported from the Peruvian Amazon directly to neighbouring countries. Recently, however, new networks have developed which have involved Lima in the production of refined cocaine. Peru is now an important exporter in its own right and the local mafias, subsidiaries of the Colombian cartels, have acquired a great deal of power. So far, the authorities have scarcely confronted the new drug mafias. Only two arrests of important dealers have been made in Lima, the first in 1985 and the second in 1994.

Crime rates in Lima have been affected by the recent rise in the level of drug addiction. For decades, Peru exported drugs, but it only began to consume drugs in the late 1970s. Local drug producers started to sell cocaine paste, the equivalent of crack, on the streets. Its cheapness and highly addictive characteristics soon turned many young people into addicts. A form of drug-related violence, previously unknown in the city, became common. Ordinary killings in Lima increased from 5.2 deaths per day in 1992 to 9.9 per day the following year (Otárola, 1994). By 1994, few families in the city had not been touched in some way by crime, terrorism, or drug addiction. Whatever their income, everyone had been affected.

A wave of terrorist violence during the 1980s also brought a major

165

shift in criminal behaviour throughout Peru. Lima suffered when the rural-based Shining Path guerrillas realized that the most fertile ground to sow their political seeds lay in the city. Lima became an important recruitment centre and also the principal target by which national and international attention could be attracted. From 1980, the guerrillas attacked the national electricity network, particularly that supplying Lima. The authorities responded by defending only one of the three transmission lines to the city, increasing Lima's vulnerability. Shining Path also launched a wave of assassinations of *barriada* leaders and of leading national personalities. From around 1985, the focus of assassinations was in Lima. Car bombs and dynamite explosions reached dramatic proportions in 1992, generating a widespread feeling of fear in the city. Security services proliferated to protect both offices and high-income residential property. In addition to Shining Path, another guerrilla group, the Tupac Amaru Revolutionary Movement (MRTA), launched a wave of kidnappings and attacks on rich and powerful people. The authorities contributed to the atmosphere of insecurity by their indiscriminate and exaggerated form of response.

It is only since the leader of the Shining Path guerrillas was arrested that the level of terrorist violence has fallen. Since Abimael Guzmán's capture in 1993, guerrilla activity has declined remarkably. From a high in 1992 of 8.5 deaths per day, the number of deaths in Lima from political violence was almost halved in 1993 and fell again in 1994. This has brought huge relief in Lima, although whether the peace will last is uncertain; for, although the security forces were immensely successful in capturing the leaders of Shining Path, government attempts at confronting poverty and at improving political participation among lower-income groups have been far less convincing.

By the early 1990s, no-one in the city felt safe. Many ordinary people started to carry guns and the police estimate that today there are around a quarter of a million armed civilians. As a result of widespread fear, there has been a huge increase in the demand for security services. By 1993, some 500 firms were operating in the country, employing some 125,000 people; the security industry was the one business that was doing well. During the 1990s, armed escort vehicles began to proliferate in Lima and cars ceased stopping at red traffic lights. Professional companies fitted more and more electric fences round high- and middle-income settlements.

Table 7.5 **Major causes of violent death in Lima, 1993 (persons killed)**

Traffic accidents	1,353
Terrorist attacks	680
Community leaders assassinated by Shining Path	24
Political violence	284
Common crime (estimated)	1,800
Politically motivated disappearances	6
Total	**4,147**

Sources: Policía Nacional, División de investigación de accidentes de tránsito, reported in *El Comercio*, 7 March 1994: A6; *Perú Paz* 18, January 1994: 16 and 18; Policía Nacional, *Caretas*, 21 April 1994: 34; DESCO, *Quehacer* 76 (1992): 42.

Urban management

The overriding impression given by the city's management is one of being unable to coordinate the actions of the different administrative agencies. Lima and Callao lie in different municipalities and, in spite of their common problems, their councils have never even managed to organize a meeting to coordinate future plans for the conurbation's development. The two municipalities are divided into 49 districts, each with its own mayor and council, which are elected every four years.[6] Each district is administratively autonomous in most respects, although the budget has to be approved by the respective municipality. Since 1994, however, a new law has increased the amount of money each district receives from central government. While increased funding is welcomed by the districts, it has been achieved at the expense of coordinated planning. The funds have been taken from the budget of the Metropolitan Investment Fund (INVERMET), which used to coordinate programmes across the districts. So far, there has been little sign of cooperation between the districts, and this will always be difficult to achieve given their differences in age, socio-economic needs, and financial and managerial capacity.

Public services in Lima are organized in ways which often impede the making of sensible decisions and which reduce the chances of coordination. For example, rubbish collection is in the hands of the districts but final disposal is the responsibility of the two municipalities. The result is that the districts often dump rubbish in unauthorized areas. A different kind of problem afflicts the electricity and water services. Each is run by central government agencies whose boards contain no municipal representatives. The municipalities have

167

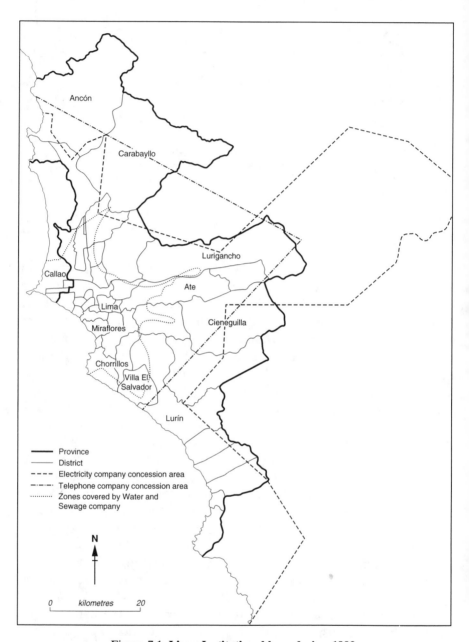

Figure 7.1 **Lima: Institutional boundaries, 1993**

never managed to coordinate the actions of these different agencies. Figure 7.1 shows the responsibilities of the different agencies that administer telephones, water, and electricity.

The formulation of housing policy in the city is equally flawed. State housing agencies have always acted autonomously and have never sought permission for their projects from the municipal authorities. The likelihood of coordination has hardly been helped by the reallocation of central government functions that occurred in 1992. The Ministry of Housing now forms part of the Ministry of Transport and Communications, while the state housing agencies are responsible to the Ministry of the Presidency.

The two municipal authorities are responsible for most forms of planning in the conurbation. However, they have little control over the public service agencies and given their failure to liaise there is little real planning going on in the city. This tendency was encouraged in the 1990s by the neoliberal attitudes which rule national government thinking. The National Planning Institute was abolished in 1991 and the only real planning entity now operating in the country is the Ministry of Economy and Finance!

Towards a more participative, denser, and more polycentric metropolis

For Lima to be administered competently it is necessary to create stronger planning processes and to develop ways of coordinating the activities of the different groups who are responsible for changing the city. It is vital to include the mass of the population in the decision-making process; after all, the poor have already taken on the task of building much of the city themselves. There is no lack of suggestions and ideas bubbling up from the bottom; the difficulty is to get the authorities to take such views seriously. Officials do not like ideas that conflict with their own plans and ways of thinking, especially given the social divide that exists in Peru between the top officials and the poor. In turn, the poor are extremely suspicious of the ways in which important decisions are made in Lima. Although it will not be easy to overcome this mutual hostility and lack of respect, it is essential to do so.

Such a change in official attitudes is necessary for both growth and equity reasons. First, it is by no means obvious that the Peruvian economy can grow without the dynamism of the informal sector; certainly few parts of the formal sector in Peru will be able to compete in the world market (de Soto, 1987). Second, if the government does not help the informal sector, there is little hope that the benefits of growth will trickle down to the poor.

The informal sector needs official help in the form of more credit and the provision of business advice centres and industrial facilities. What it does not need are the kinds of policy that emerged in the past when the poor were not consulted: for example, the development of industrial parks with facilities for companies with more than 50 employees.

The shape of Lima also has to change. Current tendencies towards urban sprawl and a unicentric city need to be reversed, and most professional planners are agreed that Lima has to develop a more polycentric form. Fewer people should have to travel to the central area and alternatives need to be found to reduce the number of trips passing through the city centre. The creation of a polycentric city is important for economic reasons, particularly to reduce traffic congestion and to save people's time, but it is also of social significance. Ordinary people cannot possibly identify with a city as large as Lima; they need a local identity, to belong to lively neighbourhoods of which they can be proud. Fortunately, there are already signs that certain commercial and service centres are developing in the suburbs (figure 7.2). It is important to encourage this trend.

At present, however, official efforts to encourage the decentralization process have been confined to discussing the legal implications of administrative change. To move forward it is necessary to obtain political agreement on what form the new administrative structure of the city should take and to determine which of the incipient secondary centres should have priority in terms of private and public investment.

If the shape of the city needs to be modified, so too does the unfortunate tendency towards low-density development. The outward spread of the city has occurred in an uncontrolled and highly irresponsible way. This process needs to be slowed so that scarce resources can be used more efficiently. There are already some signs of a shift in this direction, but it is occurring in too spontaneous a fashion. Public intervention is required to prevent future crises in service provision. Much greater coordination is necessary between the authorities and private investors at every social level. In future, infrastructure investment should be used to encourage densification.

There is great scope for such intervention in the "young towns," where as many as 300,000 buildings could be extended to produce additional homes. Densification could also be encouraged by improving living conditions in the deteriorating areas of the city. The civil defence authority has drawn attention to the fact that 110,000

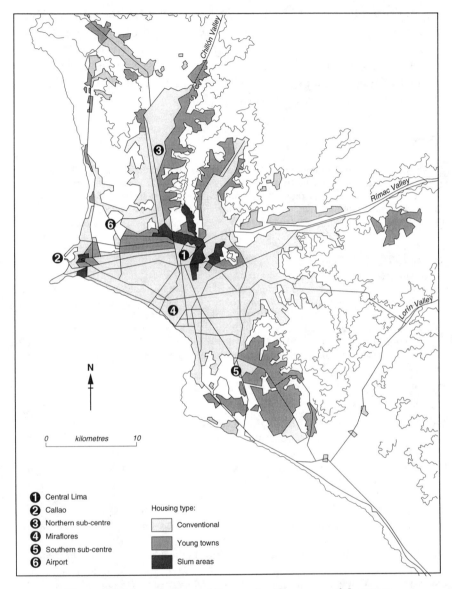

Figure 7.2 **Lima: Settlement type and main commercial centres**

dwellings in central Lima, Rimac, La Victoria, and the centre of El Callao are in danger of collapse. In such areas, conventional forms of urban renewal will not necessarily help if they encourage gentrification and expel the existing population. If existing population densities are to be maintained, major public programmes are required to help

171

the small-scale enterprises already functioning in these areas. Small projects, especially those that never get beyond the pilot stage, are of little help. What is required is larger-scale investment and better planning aimed at restructuring the city. More infrastructure investment in low-income areas would both improve living conditions and help slow the outward growth of the city.

Notes

1. Only occasionally does this situation change, as it did for example in 1971, when the warm waters of the El Niño current reached the Peruvian coast. Floods replaced the drought because Lima, with its flat roofs and lack of drainage system, is not equipped for rain.
2. The minimum monthly wage in June 1994 was the equivalent of US$72.
3. The monthly cost of the basket of essential goods (calculated as twice the cost of a basket of basic foods) was US$323 at a time when the highest decile of income earners averaged US$321 per month.
4. The largest interchange cost US$22 million; it was the largest civil engineering project in the city in 1991.
5. This has led to abuses such as the importing of right-hand-drive buses from Japan which are then modified by local firms. The number of accidents caused by badly modified steering has risen dramatically.
6. The mayors were voted in for a period of three years in the last election, in January 1993, but the new constitution, approved at the end of 1993, states that the municipal period lasts four years. It seems, therefore, that the present mayors will be in power for four years.

References

Allou, S. (1989) *Lima en cifras*. CIDAP/IFSA.

CEPAL (1993) "Balance preliminar de la economía de América Latina y el Caribe." *Notas sobre la economía y el desarrollo* 552/3.

DESCO [Centro de Estudios y Promoción del Desarrollo] (1993) "Canasta de la pobreza." *Coyuntura Laboral* 77: 14–15.

de Soto, H. (1987) *The other path*. I.B. Taurus.

Driant, J.C. (1991) *Las barriadas de Lima*. DESCO/IFEA.

Gamero, J., R. Guzmán, and L. Valverde (1994) *La pobreza en el área de Lima Metropolitana*. DESCO.

INEI [Instituto Nacional de Estadística e Informática] (1994) *Censos nacionales de 1993*. Lima.

Ministerio de Trabajo (1986) *Encuesta nacional de niveles de vida* 1. Lima.

——— (1990) *Encuesta nacional de niveles de vida* 2. Lima.

——— (1992) *Encuesta nacional de niveles de vida* 3. Lima.

Otárola, A. (1994) "El otro desborde popular." *Perú Paz* 3: 18.

Riofrío, G. (1978) *Se busca terreno para próxima barriada: Espacios disponibles en Lima 1940, 1978, 1990*. DESCO.

——— (1991) *Producir la ciudad (popular) de los noventa: Entre el mercado y el estado*. DESCO.

8

Mexico City: No longer a leviathan?

Allison Rowland and Peter Gordon

Introduction

When the United Nations issued a report on Mexico City in 1991, it concluded that "in recent years ... projections of Mexico City's population have converged, with most now assuming a population of 25 to 27 million by the end of the century" (UNDIESA, 1991: 7). Only two years later, however, new data combined with assessments of the effects of new national policies cast doubt on whether the city will ever reach this size, let alone do so in less than a decade. An important factor in this reassessment has been the subsequent release of the 1990 population census, which added to a growing conviction that the 1980 data upon which many of the more spectacular projections rested was significantly incorrect. The 1990 data show a much more modest rise than previously expected in the city's population since 1970.

Forecasting error is not the only cause for reconsidering estimates of the future size of Mexico City. The scope and rapidly spreading consequences of economic reforms brought about by President Carlos Salinas de Gortari since 1988 have added credence to projections of a smaller Mexico City.

Internationalization of the Mexican economy since 1986 has had a marked effect on the country's urban structure. Examination of the 1990 population census confirms that on balance people and jobs are no longer moving to Mexico City or to the central region of the country. Recent economic census data tell a similar story, suggesting that these trends will continue because new investment in manufacturing has tended to occur outside the Mexico City region.

If population movements continue to follow the current pattern of deconcentrated economic expansion, the doomsday scenarios for an overcrowded, unmanageable Mexico City should be rethought. More importantly, the policies and proposals designed to cope with traffic congestion, air pollution, water, housing, and solid waste disposal have to be reassessed. The cost of dealing with these problems may be less than previously predicted.

The Mexican urban structure: The roots of centralism

Mexico is similar to most other Latin American countries in so far as a high degree of urban primacy has become the norm. The roots of this pattern are found in the historical concentration of political power, economic activity, and population (Davis, 1994; Garza and Schteingart, 1978; Gwynne, 1985; Scott, 1982). Subsequent industrialization accentuated this pattern; investment was concentrated in the largest cities: Mexico City, Guadalajara, and Monterrey. The availability of jobs attracted large numbers of migrants to those cities (figure 8.1).

By 1950, Mexico City was home to 12.3 per cent of the national population, while the two next largest urban areas, Guadalajara and Monterrey, together accounted for only 3.2 per cent of the national total (table 8.1). By 1970, the shares of all three cities had grown, to 17.9 per cent for Mexico City, 3.0 per cent for Guadalajara, and 2.4 per cent for Monterrey; by 1990, the shares were 18.5 per cent, 3.5 per cent, and 3.2 per cent respectively. By 1950, Mexico City accounted for 25 per cent of all persons employed in manufacturing industry, a level of dominance that peaked at 42.1 per cent in 1970 (table 8.2).

Spatial concentration in Mexico was accentuated by import-substituting industrialization (Gwynne, 1985: 84–5; Portes, 1990). Other government policies aggravated these centralizing tendencies. During the 1960s and 1970s, most public investment in water, education, power, and transport was directed at urban areas, with Mexico City receiving the highest share. In addition, direct and indirect subsidies for water, corn, electric power, diesel fuel, and public transport

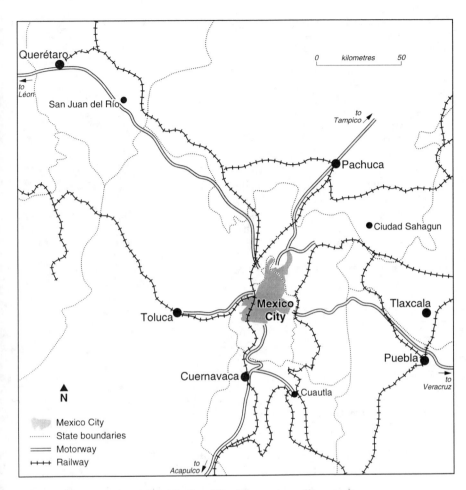

Figure 8.1 **Mexico City: The metropolitan region**

offered special advantages to Mexico City (Garza and Schteingart, 1978; Scott, 1982).

Deliberate government efforts to reverse this concentration of industrial activity were ineffective and sometimes counterproductive. The most serious problem was that few decentralization policies took the differing potentials of the regions into account. Thus, a limited amount of public investment was spread over a wide and undifferentiated periphery – not surprisingly, to limited effect (Scott, 1982). More targeted policies during the 1970s, for example industrial complexes and parks, had little effect on industrial location (Aguilar-Barajas, 1990).

175

Table 8.1 **Population of Mexico's ten largest urban areas, 1950, 1970, and 1990**

Rank	Urban Area	State	Population (000s)		
			1950	1970	1990
1	Mexico City	Federal District/México	3,167	8,624	14,685
2	Guadalajara	Jalisco	440	1,456	2,870
3	Monterrey	Nuevo León	375	1,177	2,574
4	Puebla	Puebla/Tlaxcala	235	533	1,420
5	León	Guanajuato	157	420	868
6	Toluca	México	115	239	820
7	Cd. Juárez	Chihuahua	131	424	798
8	Torreón	Coahuila/Durango	260	438	792
9	Tijuana	Baja California	65	341	747
10	Mérida-Progreso	Yucatán	159	242	665
	National population		**25,791**	**50,417**	**81,250**

Source: Respective national censuses.

Table 8.2 **Manufacturing employment, 1950, 1970, and 1988 (numbers of employees)**

	1950	1970	1988
Mexico City	156,697	672,446	745,387
National total	626,285	1,596,816	2,587,013
Mexico City as % of nation	25.0	42.1	28.8

Sources: Derived from Garza, 1987, and Gordon et al., 1993.

While the *maquiladora* programme has successfully increased economic activity on the border with the United States and has attracted substantial migration to the border cities, the *maquilas* have generally failed to generate significant industrial linkages or to stimulate growth in other parts of Mexico (Scott, 1982; Wilson, 1992).

The debt crisis and its aftermath

The import-substituting industrialization model came to an abrupt end with the Mexican debt crisis of 1982. Subsequent macroeconomic policies, implemented at the behest of the International Monetary Fund and foreign banks as a condition for loan rescheduling, attempted to restrain public spending, liberalize the economy, and attract foreign investment. The initial result of these policies was severe recession. However, since 1986 real GDP growth has revived, reaching 1.4 per cent in 1987, 3.1 per cent in 1989, and 2.6 per cent in 1991.[1]

Table 8.3 **Growth in manufacturing, commercial, and service sectors, 1985–88**

	1985	1988	Average annual growth (%)
Border states	859,434	1,105,217	8.4
Mexico City	1,764,101	1,715,050	−0.9
National	5,716,065	6,235,537	2.9
National minus border states	4,856,631	5,130,320	1.8

Sources: Derived from Rowland, 1992, and INEGI, 1989.

Domestic and foreign investment flows responded to the liberalization measures – in some cases in anticipation of the implementation of the North American Free Trade Agreement (NAFTA). Direct foreign investment of only US\$491 million in 1985 had increased to \$4,762 million by 1991; as a proportion of GNP this represents a rise from 0.3 per cent to 1.7 per cent.

The new export-oriented economic model, combined with the effects of structural adjustment, has had striking effects on the distribution of manufacturing, commercial, and service employment nationwide. The most significant changes are the decline in Mexico City and the growth of the northern border region. Between 1985 and 1988, employment in the border states grew at almost three times the national average, while the net number of jobs in Mexico City fell (table 8.3). Export-oriented production favoured cities with ports, those along the northern border, and those in areas with natural resources (Gordon et al., 1993; Pradilla, 1990; Rowland, 1992). Most such cities are outside the previously favoured region of central Mexico.

Entry into NAFTA is likely to continue this trend and bring benefits for particular industrial sectors. In the context of an overall rise in employment, the "winners" are generally predicted to be apparel, footwear, pottery, leather, furniture, services, construction materials, beverages, plastics, and rubber. The "losers" are expected to be chemicals, machinery, paper, non-ferrous metals, and tobacco (Gordon et al., 1993).

Mexico City may well continue to lose out relative to other areas if these forecasts are correct. Gordon et al. (1993) suggest that supplier links with growing areas and sectors of the economy are weak for those establishments located in the capital. Therefore the impact of the country's economic liberalization will depend primarily on the extent to which the city remains a national centre for finance and capital.

177

The other, less quantifiable, national trend affecting economic growth in Mexico City lies in the country's political structure. Traditionally highly centralized and tightly controlled by the dominant political party, the Institutional Revolutionary Party (PRI), the political system has in recent years become more open to opposition parties and more responsive to local conditions. If this trend continues, the need for large companies to put their headquarters in Mexico City may diminish. The vast labour force employed in the government bureaucracy may also be reduced or even dispersed to other parts of the country.

In the past, agglomeration economies, local market size and wealth, and direct contact with the national government played important roles in the spatial structure of the Mexican urban system. However, in the 1980s, as export markets became more significant, production processes worldwide changed, and transportation and communication facilities in Mexico improved, traditional location factors lessened in importance for many firms. At the same time, congestion costs in Mexico City increased and evidence of polarization reversal began to appear (Gilbert, 1993b: 731; Portes, 1990; Richardson, 1989). One outcome was the gradual emergence of a polycentric spatial structure in central Mexico: an antidote to both the exhaustion of agglomeration economies and crippling congestion.

Mexico City's changing urban structure

Population growth and decentralization

The results of the 1990 census suggest that two significant changes have occurred in Mexico City. First, population growth has slowed (table 8.4). Between 1970 and 1990, average annual population growth for Mexico City was half of what the 1970 to 1980 data suggested. The explanation for this depends on the credibility accorded the 1980 census figures. If they are discarded, we can conclude that population growth fell gradually over the twenty-year period. If not, the 1980 data suggest that rapid metropolitan growth continued through the 1970s and then fell off sharply in the 1980s, presumably in response to the economic crisis beginning in 1982. However, this view implies that average annual growth plummeted from 4.4 per cent in the 1970s to 0.2 per cent in the 1980s. A drop of this extent is unlikely.

Table 8.4 **Population growth in Mexico City, 1970–1990**

	Total population		Average annual growth (%)		Share of population	
	1970	1990	1970–80	1970–90	1970	1990
Mexico City total	9,210,853	14,685,098	4.4	2.3	100.0	100.0
Central City	3,002,984	1,930,267	−1.1	−2.2	32.6	13.1
First Ring	4,874,557	7,126,731	4.5	1.9	52.9	48.5
Second Ring	1,321,813	4,628,213	9.6	6.3	14.4	31.5
Third Ring	11,499	999,887	38.7	22.3	0.1	6.8

Source: Gordon, 1992.

Mexico City Ring definitions:
Central City:
DF: Benito Juárez, Cuauhtémoc, Miguel Hidalgo, Venustiano Carranza.
First Ring:
DF: Azcapotzalco, Coyoacán, Cuajimalpa, Gustavo A. Madero, Iztacalco, Iztapalapa, Alvaro Obregón. *State of Mexico*: Naucalpán, Netzahualcóyotl.
Second Ring:
DF: Magdalena Contreras, Tláhuac, Tlalpán, Xochimilco. *State of Mexico*: Atizapán de Zaragoza, Chimalhuacán, Coacalco, Cuautitlán Izcalli, Ecatepec, Huixquilucán, La Paz, Tlalnepantla de Baz, Tultitlán.
Third Ring:
DF: Milpa Alta. *State of Mexico*: Chalco, Chiautla, Chicoloapán, Chiconcuac, Cuautitlán, Ixtapaluca, Melchor Ocampo, Nicolás Romero, Tecamac, Tultepec.

The second change has been an acceleration in the pace of decentralization of population from the centre of the city towards more recently urbanized areas. Beginning in the 1950s, the Mexico City Metropolitan Zone has grown beyond the original boundaries of what is now referred to as the Central City (the present-day delegations of Benito Juárez, Cuauhtémoc, Miguel Hidalgo, and Venustiano Carranza) to include increasing numbers of delegations in the Federal District and municipalities in the adjoining State of Mexico (Garza and Schteingart, 1978) (figure 8.2). Three additional "rings" of settlement have been incorporated into Mexico City since that time (Negrete-Salas et al., 1993). The movement of population from the Central City toward the outermost rings began in the 1950s and accelerated through the following decades (Garza and Schteingart, 1978: 70). The bulk of the population now lives in the First and Second Rings, while the Second and Third Rings have been growing most rapidly. The Central City is in decline; its population in 1990 was only two-thirds of its 1970 total.

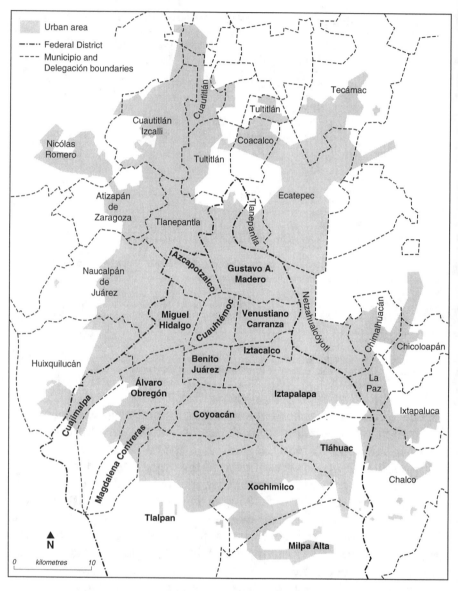

Figure 8.2 **Mexico City: Administrative divisions**

Trends in employment location in Mexico City

Garza and Schteingart (1978: 63) report that Mexico City's share of the country's industrial firms has been in decline since the early 1960s. Table 8.5 shows that industrial employment in Mexico City

Table 8.5 **Industrial employment by ring, 1960–1988**

	1960	1970	1975	1980	1985	1988
Mexico City total	407,005	672,446	733,389	1,059,182	859,432	745,387
Central City	214,769	252,238	221,209	271,666	211,033	176,350
First Ring	133,864	297,555	334,544	481,455	414,917	376,539
Second Ring*a*	52,248	115,837	172,293	290,394	215,769	172,533
Third Ring*a*	6,124	6,816	5,343	15,667	17,713	19,965

Sources: Derived from Garza, 1987, and INEGI, 1989.

a. For consistency with historical records, the municipalities of Huixquilucán and Chimalhuacán have been excluded from the Second Ring data for 1985 and 1988, while Chiautla, Chicoloapan, Chiconcuac, Melchor Ocampo, and Tultepec have been excluded from Third Ring data for 1985 and 1988.

Table 8.6 **Average annual growth rates in industrial employment by ring, 1960–1988 (percentages)**

	1960–70	1970–80	1980–88	1980–85	1985–88
Mexico City total	16.7	15.1	−11.6	−7.0	−4.8
Central City	5.4	2.5	−14.4	−8.4	−6.0
First Ring	26.6	16.0	−8.2	−5.0	−3.2
Second Ring*a*	26.5	30.6	−17.2	−9.9	−7.5
Third Ring*a*	3.6	27.7	10.8	4.1	4.0

Sources: Derived from Garza, 1987, and INEGI, 1989.

a. For consistency with historical records, the municipalities of Huixquilucán and Chimalhuacán have been excluded from the Second Ring data for 1985 and 1988, while Chiautla, Chicoloapán, Chiconcuac, Melchor Ocampo, and Tultepec have been excluded from Third Ring data for 1985 and 1988.

peaked around 1980, and has declined since then. Within the capital there has been a strong trend towards decentralization. Table 8.6 shows that the central city has been growing less rapidly than the outer rings ever since the 1960s, a process that intensified in the 1980s.

Not surprisingly, the most recent data show a pattern of employment decentralization within Mexico City similar to the movement in population. Table 8.7 shows that employment grew only in the Third Ring. There were large job losses in manufacturing in the Second Ring, but the commerce and services sectors recorded high growth rates, albeit less than those of the Third Ring. At higher levels of disaggregation some sectors did grow in the inner rings (for example wholesaling and some service sectors), but the general trend is for faster growth outside the central area.

181

Table 8.7 **Average annual growth of employment by sector, 1985–1988 (percentages)**

	Total	Manufacturing	Commerce	Service
Mexico City total	−0.9	−4.7	1.1	3.8
Central City	−0.9	−6.0	−0.2	2.6
First Ring	−1.0	−3.2	0.4	3.3
Second Ring	−2.3	−7.4	4.6	12.4
Third Ring	9.6	4.9	13.8	15.4

Source: Derived from INEGI, 1989.

Table 8.8 **Metropolitan employment by sector, 1985 and 1988**

	Total		Manufacturing		Commerce		Service	
	1985	1988	1985	1988	1985	1988	1985	1988
Central City	666,506	649,185	211,033	176,350	222,366	220,931	233,107	251,904
Share	37.8	37.9	24.5	23.6	43.4	41.7	59.7	57.6
First Ring	753,776	731,199	414,917	376,539	213,980	216,791	124,879	137,869
Share	42.7	42.6	48.2	50.3	41.8	40.9	32.0	31.5
Second Ring	308,709	287,907	216,611	173,506	63,613	73,122	25,485	41,279
Share	17.5	16.8	25.2	23.2	12.4	13.8	7.3	9.4
Third Ring	35,110	46,759	18,683	21,636	12,403	18,741	4,024	6,382
Share	2.0	2.7	2.2	2.9	2.4	3.5	1.0	1.5
Total	**1,764,101**	**1,715,050**	**861,244**	**746,031**	**512,362**	**529,585**	**390,495**	**437,434**

Source: Derived from INEGI, 1989.

Examination of the changing shares of economic activity presents a less clear picture of decentralization (see table 8.8). Overall, the Third Ring increased its share of employment, but at the expense of the First and Second Rings rather than the Central City. While the Second Ring lost manufacturing employment to the First and Third, it gained in commerce and services. These apparently contradictory trends can be explained by the observation that between 1985 and 1988, the metropolitan area as a whole lost over 113,000 jobs in manufacturing – 5 per cent of its total employment in this sector.

Aguilar (1993) has documented this general pattern of spatial de-concentration in manufacturing between 1975 and 1985. Working with more highly disaggregated employment data, he shows how certain types of manufacturing and service activities are more likely to de-centralize from the city centre than others. Firms serving local mar-kets move out, presumably following the suburbanizing population

while those with links to national and international markets are mo
likely to remain in the centre. He sees a resurgence of "high technology" industries, such as electronics, as well as printing and publishing in the central area, between 1975 and 1985. His disaggregated
service-sector data show decentralization in consumer services, while
business services remained in the central city.

Both the employment data and the population data tell the same
story: Mexico City continues to decentralize rapidly. The doomsday
scenarios regarding pollution, traffic congestion, and other problems
associated with a large and concentrated population are being chal-
lenged by adjustments in patterns of economic activity in the metropolitan region and nationwide. However, a number of serious difficulties remain for the city in the areas of urban administration and
finance, housing, urban services, air pollution, and traffic management.

Administration and finance

Urban administration

City management, service provision, and the coordination of public
agencies are inevitably complex in an urban area the size of Mexico
City. However, these tasks are further complicated by the fact that
Mexico City has spilled across the political boundaries of the Federal
District (DF) into the State of Mexico (figure 8.3). This process began
in the early 1950s, when restrictions on residential and industrial
expansion, rent control, rising land costs, and increasing congestion
in the DF encouraged new households and businesses to locate just
over the border. There, land-use regulations – including restrictions on
sales of previously non-urban land – were less likely to be enforced,
offering business opportunities for land developers and *ejidatarios*,
as well as lower-priced land for impoverished families (Cymet, 1992;
Garza and Schteingart, 1978).[2] At the other end of the income spec-
trum, new developments in the hilly western parts of the city offered
attractive sites for high-income residents fleeing the congestion and
deterioration of the central area.

Newly arrived migrants to the city, as well as relocating residents,
have tended to settle increasingly at the urban periphery, where
housing densities are lower (Gilbert and Ward, 1982; Negrete-Salas
et al., 1993). The metropolitan municipalities located in the State of
Mexico now have nearly as many residents as the Federal District,
and one-third of all formal-sector jobs. Despite this, these municipal-

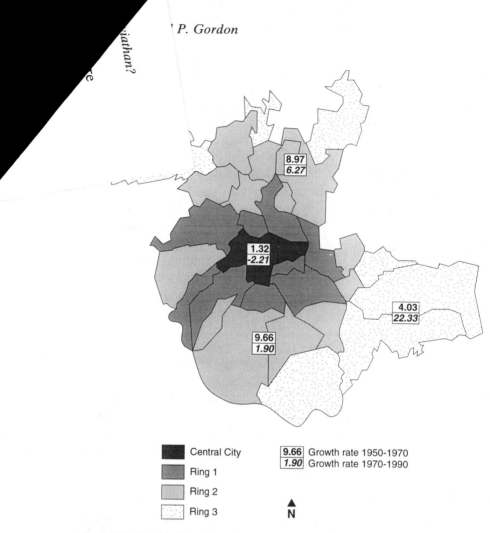

Figure 8.3 **Mexico City: Changing rates of population growth by rings of metropolitan development, 1950–1990 (Source: Negrete-Salas et al., 1993)**

ities have enjoyed minimal official contact with the DF in terms of planning, regulation, and service provision.

A number of difficulties are posed by the dual government jurisdictions. Mass transit rarely crosses boundaries between the DF and the State of Mexico, forcing mid-trip transfers for most passengers. Prices for basic services, including public transportation, water, and electric power, are also several times higher in the State of Mexico than in the DF (Damián, 1991). Worst of all, public-service levels and living standards are much lower in the State of Mexico; unemployment and fertility rates are higher while school attendance and literacy rates are lower (Rowland, 1993).

184

Part of the explanation for this differential lies in the very different governmental systems which operate within the two political jurisdictions. In the DF, government is headed by a mayor (*regente*), who is appointed by the national president and holds a cabinet post. Most city-wide planning tasks are undertaken by the Departamento del Distrito Federal (DDF), whose leaders are appointed by the mayor. For administrative purposes, the DF is divided into sixteen delegations, each of which is headed by a *delegado*, also appointed by the mayor in consultation with the national president. These *delegados* are in charge of most forms of local service provision, including street maintenance, water, and drainage. Community representation is formally provided by block representatives (*jefes de manzana*), who serve on a neighbourhood council (*junta de vecinos*) and are directly elected by residents. The neighbourhood councils select a president to serve on a delegation-wide neighbourhood council, and these sixteen delegation-wide councils each send a representative to the DF's Consultative Council.

There are four major problems with this structure. First, the system produces elected bodies that have no executive powers; they serve only in an advisory role on matters selected by the mayor's team. The main purpose of this system, according to most analysts, is to control rather than to satisfy community demands. The second major criticism is that even these local elections are apparently manipulated by the *delegados* to ensure compliant delegation councils and consultative councils (Aguilar, 1988; Gilbert and Ward, 1985; Jiménez, 1989; Ward, 1990b). Third, the effectiveness of the block committees is undermined by other significant channels of community participation, including PRI organizations like the National Confederation of Popular Organizations (the official PRI channel for urban popular demands), urban *ejido* commissioners, and the National Coordination of the Urban Popular Movement (an umbrella organization of leftist, non-PRI, urban popular movements), all of which may circumvent the formal structure of community participation and deal directly with *delegados* or even the DDF. Finally, many of the most important community demands, for example for land regularization or electricity services, fall beyond the power of the *juntas* and *delegados* (Aguilar, 1988).

Municipalities in the State of Mexico benefit to some extent from metropolitan-wide activities undertaken by the DDF. For all other matters, they depend on the governor of the State of Mexico, the only formal link between them and between this part of the metropolitan area and the DF. The governor is elected by popular vote; municipal representatives are similarly elected to the State legislature. Each municipality elects a municipal president and council, but their roles are curtailed by their very limited funding.

Urban finance

Analysis of urban finance is complicated by the jurisdictional division between the DF and the State of Mexico and by the status of the Federal District as national capital. The jurisdictional division means that resources available for different parts of the city and different projects vary greatly. The DF benefits both from resources available through the DDF and from direct allocations from various federal ministries and programmes. The complexities of these arrangements are beyond the scope of this chapter, but it is clear that the DF does much better than the State of Mexico. For example, Rodríguez (1993: 138) discovered that of the 19 per cent of the 1987 federal budget allocated to regional development nationwide, more than half was spent on the DF. As a result, when compared with other cities in developing countries, the degree of dependence on federal grants in the DF is very high and its dependence on local taxes low (table 8.9). In addition, because the DF is the national capital, any financial mismanagement is more likely to be tolerated. In 1985, when the DDF managed to accumulate loan obligations amounting to nearly half of

Table 8.9 **Financing of local public expenditure in selected LDC cities and Mexico City**

	Locally raised revenue (%)			Revenue from outside sources (%)	
	Local taxes	Self-financing services	Other	Grants and shared taxes	Net borrowing
Median LDC cities, 1979–1986	39	18	8	22	7
Mexico City, 1987					
DF	5	23	14	51	7
Non-DF*a*	30	11	22	37	–

Sources: Bahl and Linn, 1992: 34–5, and derived from INEGI 1990: 92–9 and 149.
a. Conurbated municipalities of the State of Mexico only.

Table 8.10 **Mexico City revenue and expenditure, 1987 (thousands of pesos per capita)**

	Total revenue	Federal revenue sharing	Taxes	Duties	Products	User fees
DF	229	125	12	14	21	56
Non-DF[a]	20	7	6	4	1	2
Total Mexico City	135	72	9	9	12	32

	Total expenditure	Administrative costs	Public works & promotion	Transfers
DF	224	102	106	16
Non-DF[a]	14	11	3	1
Total Mexico City	130	61	60	9

Source: Derived from INEGI, 1990b: 92–9 and 149.
a. Conurbated municipalities of the State of Mexico only.

Notes:
Does not include expenditures for debt service and interest on debt.
Data not available for State of Mexico municipalities of Tultepec and Melchor Ocampo.

its budget, the federal government came to its aid with credits and subsidies (Villalpando, 1989).

In contrast, the amount of money available to the conurbated municipalities of the State of Mexico is much smaller than the DDF budget. The municipalities do benefit from spending by state and federal agencies, particularly for infrastructure and environmental projects, but total state spending in the municipalities is far less than the amount spent by federal agencies in the DF. The DDF is much more effective than its counterparts in the State of Mexico at collecting taxes, duties, and user fees (table 8.10). Part of the explanation lies in the greater number of corporate headquarters located within the DF, as well as the higher number of collection points for duties and user fees. Again, however, the importance of federal transfers to the DF is critical.

Although Mexico is structured on the principles of fiscal federalism, the pattern of transfers from the central government serves to limit the ability of the system both to respond efficiently to local

187

needs and and to link services received to payments in the form of service fees and property taxes. The problem is exacerbated by the federal government's tendency to rely on parastatal agencies for much of its income (despite recent waves of privatization), and the lack of local accountability, stemming from weak levels of local political competition (Crane, 1990: 4). Thus, the system leaves little opportunity for local initiative or discretion.

Two major, but unsuccessful, attempts have been made to reform the system. The 1980–81 tax reform replaced most state and local revenue sources with a national value-added tax, to be allocated to the local authorities on a basis proportional to amounts collected. In 1982–83, another attempt at fiscal reform, Article 115 of the Constitution, ostensibly devolved power from the federal and state authorities to the local level. This gave local governments responsibility for many new local service functions, which they were to finance through their newly established monopoly over property taxes. Neither of these policies functioned as designed, because steps that were subsequently taken to make the reforms more palatable to state governors allowed them to maintain control over local government finance (Crane, 1990; Davis, 1991; Rodríguez, 1993).

A role for metropolitan government?

Many observers have suggested that a single metropolitan institutional structure would provide a simplification and clarity of purpose that is currently lacking in Mexico City's administration. The coordination of planning between the two jurisdictions would encourage greater compatibility in terms of goals, rules and regulations. Several attempts have been made to coordinate better the wide range of activities and regulations of the two jurisdictions, beginning in 1976 with the Commission of the Conurbation of the Centre of the Country, and followed in 1988 by the Council of the Metropolitan Area of the Federal District and the State of Mexico. These efforts were largely ineffective and short-lived, both suffering from a lack of executive power and a lack of will to cooperate among agencies (Cornelius and Craig, 1991; Rowland, 1993; Ward, 1990b; Wilk, 1992). A recent exception to this pattern is the creation of the Metropolitan Commission for the Prevention and Control of Environmental Pollution in the Valley of Mexico. Formed in 1992, the Commission consists of representatives from eight national ministries, three parastatal agencies, and the governments of the DF and the State of Mexico. It appears to have achieved some success in planning, monitoring, and enforcing air-quality programmes (Lacy, 1993; Wilk, 1992). Cooperation on a wider range of issues is more difficult, both administratively and politically. Combining finance and expenditure processes, for example, would require that the rules for such processes be more transparent and well-regulated than they are now. It might also run the political risk of increasing public pressure to do more for the poorer municipalities in the State of Mexico.

The ongoing shift in population and economic activity from the DF to the suburbs within the State of Mexico will have significant effects on both jurisdictions. Revenues, especially from taxes, are likely to decline in the DF as the deconcentration continues. Meanwhile, municipalities beyond the DF continue to grow, primarily owing to migration from older parts of the city, and will soon surpass the DF in population. This will put additional pressure on already strained municipal governments and may increase the demand for changes in the administrative system.

Current issues and policy approaches

Income, employment, and social services in the 1980s

When harmful macroeconomic policies are abandoned, there is often a further deterioration in economic conditions before any sort of turnaround is achieved. This has been the experience in much of Latin America, Eastern Europe, and the countries of the former USSR. In addition, the conditions for optimal policy transitions are not yet well understood (Van Wijnbergen, 1992). Both factors apply to Mexico, where the 1980s are often referred to as "the lost decade." Government-imposed wage restraints and a new system for setting minimum wages resulted in substantial drops in formal-sector real wages between 1982 and 1985–86. Nationwide, real average wages dropped by 30 per cent during this period, minimum wages saw a similar decline, and general manufacturing wages fell by 35 per cent in real terms (González and Escobar, 1991; Lustig, 1990).

However, Lustig (1990) points out that a drastic decline in wages may not translate into an equivalent loss in total household income. Wage income represents a smaller share of poor families' incomes than it does of that of wealthier families. It appears, then, that middle- and upper-middle-income households (who generally rely more on wage income than do poorer families) bore more of the brunt of adjustment arising from this decline in real wages. On the other hand, non-wage incomes actually rose slightly between 1981 and 1984. However, this gain is explained more by a rise in profits (generally accruing to the rich) than to increases in the incomes of self-employed owners (generally the informal sector), so it is unlikely that these small increases could compensate households for larger losses in wage incomes. Finally, as Lustig (1990) notes, even small absolute and relative declines in incomes of the poorest households can exacerbate already severe conditions.

Falling real wages help explain how, while output declined sharply for Mexican firms in the early 1980s, the open unemployment rate did not rise dramatically. Firms were able to reduce their labour costs and the government could cut its own expenditure through a combination of layoffs and wage cuts. In spite of this the actual number of unemployed is reported to have risen from 2.7 million to 4.6 million between 1981 and 1984. In addition, underemployment rose, as workers were forced into lower-paying and less productive jobs, often in the informal sector (Lustig, 1990). Indeed, according to one report, informal employment in Mexico rose faster between 1980 and 1987 than in most other Latin American countries (González and Escobar, 1991).

Not surprisingly, the effects of falling wages and shifting employment patterns on the distribution of income is not straightforward. In fact, it is not clear whether income inequality rose or fell in Mexico in the 1980s.[3] Lustig asserts that the economic crises and subsequent structural-adjustment process decimated the Mexican middle class, while wealth was increasingly concentrated in the hands of the rich between 1981 and 1985 (Lustig, 1990). Lorey and Mostkoff-Linares (1993) examine the economic fortunes of various occupational groups and income strata through the 1980s. They conclude that "... the evidence from the 1990 census is perplexing. Data on both income and occupation imply that the situation in the 1980s was characterized by a clustering of population in the lowest middle-class and highest lower-class subgroups rather than by a dramatically increasing misery at the lowest levels of Mexican society."

Other standard social indicators for the 1980s, also point to an ambiguous picture of the impacts of Mexico's economic crisis. Indeed, Hirschman (1994: 344) reports that "during the 1980s, when indexes of economic performance leveled off or declined in some Latin American countries under the impact of the debt crisis, important social indicators, such as infant mortality, illiteracy, and the extent of birth control continued showing improvement." Adjustments at the household level to falling incomes and to workers involved in lower-productivity activities appear to have had an effect on school enrolments and infant nutrition. Primary and secondary school enrolment dropped relative to the number of eligible children in the early 1980s. Although aggregate health indicators, such as infant mortality rates, did not rise, illness and mortality were more frequently related to poor nutrition. These nutritional deficiencies may also be related to the government's move away from general food subsidies toward more targeted programmes. Though defensible from a fiscal standpoint, rising food prices for those poor households no longer included in these programmes may have led to nutrition problems (Lustig, 1990). On the other hand, shrinking per capita outlays on education, public health, and social security are not necessarily an indication of lower service levels. Lustig (1990: 1337) concludes that these figures actually reflect the declining wages of workers and a lack of new investment in these sectors.

Housing and urban services

Over half of all housing in Mexico City consists of self-help structures in various states of consolidation (Azuela, 1990; UNDIESA, 1991). Self-help housing is concentrated primarily in the State of Mexico, where enforcement of prohibitions on construction on unauthorized sites has traditionally been less stringent. Unlike the situation in other Latin American cities, land invasions have not been common in recent decades. More typical are illegal subdivisions of private and *ejido* land: it is estimated that 9 to 10 million people live on land that has been developed in these "irregular" ways (Connolly, 1988; Coulomb and Duhau, 1989; Schteingart, 1989; Ward, 1990a). The result has often been settlements on land poorly suited for service provision; on the steep, rocky slopes of volcanoes to the south-west of the city and on the desiccated lake beds to the east, prone to flooding during the rainy season and dust storms during the dry months.

Few other options for home ownership exist for the poor, given the limited reach of public-sector housing (see below). The traditional, irregular forms of providing land for housing the poor in Mexico City may be drying up, as bans on squatting in territorial reserves, as well as on illegal subdivisions and *ejido* sales, are being more stringently enforced (Ward, 1990a). This is partly a response to competition in the land market from developers of middle-class housing (Connolly,

1988). As a result, population densities and land prices are increasing in low-income areas. Rental accommodation is the tenure choice of increasing numbers of Mexico residents, even though the proportion of renters is declining (Coulomb and Sánchez, 1991; Gilbert, 1993a: 55).

Questions about the legality of landholdings plague housing development of all types. But while some high-income neighbourhoods have been built on irregularly obtained land, the issue of land tenure is particularly vexing in low-income, self-help settlements. Security of tenure is generally cited by residents of irregular settlements as the single most important issue they face (Aguilar, 1988; Jiménez, 1989; Varley, 1993). Unfortunately, regularization is often complicated by uncertain land records and the overlap of jurisdictions of various government agencies, particularly for former *ejido* lands. In addition, tenure issues offer ample opportunity for the political jockeying and influence-peddling which often accompanies highly sensitive and rather arbitrary procedures in Mexico.

There is some disagreement among researchers over the degree to which regularization continues to be used by local officials primarily as a political tool. Ward maintains that since the late 1970s, land regularization has become more systematic and technical, a process motivated by concern to incorporate residents into the tax base, recover costs of service infrastructure investment, and exert greater authority over planning and building (Ward, 1990a; Ward, 1990b). Varley (1993), in contrast, argues that in spite of increased bureaucratization, the PRI still exercises a great deal of control over the timing and location of regularization. In her view, land-tenure regularization continues to serve as a means for demobilizing non-PRI political movements in low-income neighbourhoods and maintaining political stability in the city.

Political patronage and cooptation is also a motive for constructing public housing. Mexico City is notable for the large number of agencies which have been involved with public housing construction, sometimes working cooperatively, and at other times at odds with one another. The most prominent agency in the construction of housing for low-income residents is the Trust Fund for Popular Housing (FONHAPO), which has also been important in sites and services schemes and in the earthquake rebuilding programme. Two major housing funds for employees are also active in public-sector housing: the National Institute of the Fund for Workers' Housing (INFONA-VIT), whose membership is limited to registered blue-collar workers, and the Housing Fund for State Workers (FOVISSSTE), which serves state employees. Both funds are supported by mandatory payments in the form of fixed percentages of workers' salaries (Ward, 1990b: 417). State credit guarantees toward the purchase of privately built housing are also available to certain low-income workers through Central Bank of Mexico programmes called the Fund for Banking Operations and Discounts to Housing (FOVI) and the Fund for the Guarantee and Support of Housing Credit (FOGA). These public-sector housing agencies have played a significant role in housing provision in Mexico City since 1970. Whereas only 10 per cent of the population lived in housing produced by one of the various forms of government intervention in 1970, by 1985 over 20 per cent benefited from state assistance (Connolly, 1988: 168; Ward, 1990b: 419). A special agency, Popular Housing Renewal, was also set up following the 1985 earthquake; it built 54,000 units in the central area for highly subsidized purchase by newly homeless low-income residents (Gilbert, 1993a; Ward, 1990b).

Only about 15 per cent of the housing in Mexico City consists of private, single-family units built on legally obtained land (Dowall and Wilk, 1989). This type of housing is concentrated in a relatively small number of expensive neighbourhoods, populated by the wealthiest Mexico City residents.

Urban service provision is a major problem in the city. Of course, those who can afford to pay the prevailing user fees for urban services have no difficulty obtaining them; heavy government investment in basic water, drainage, electricity, and other systems, as well as generally competent and non-politicized management of these agencies, has greatly increased capacity (Gilbert and Ward, 1985). However, the situation is very different in low-income and irregular neighbourhoods. There the inhabitants are more likely to find themselves at the mercy of political manoeuvring. Indeed, some authors posit a link between regularization and the ability to demand and receive urban services (Ward, 1990b), although others cite examples of illegal settlements dealing directly with the utilities to obtain water or electricity services (Aguilar, 1988; Varley, 1993). What is clear is that services are obtained gradually by lower-income residents, and servicing depends in part upon their ability to organize and make their demands known.

In Mexico City, 91 per cent of housing units have some type of sewerage connection, 94 per cent have piped water, 64 per cent have in-house water, and 99 per cent have electricity. But household service provision varies widely both between neighbourhoods and between the DF and the conurbated municipalities of the State of Mexico. Sewer connection rates are 95 per cent in the DF and 85 per cent in the State of Mexico, piped water 97 per cent and 91 per cent, and in-house water 72 per cent and 54 per cent (Rowland, 1993).

Water provision and disposal

Water has to be pumped up to Mexico City over the surrounding mountains from areas far from the metropolitan area. The cost of provision has become increasingly high as the main local supplies, the water table beneath the city and the agricultural lands to the south, have become depleted. At the same time, the frequent failure to collect service fees has also discouraged maintenance and extension of service to newly settled low-income areas.[4]

Water disposal is an even more serious problem. Because the Valley of Mexico lacks a natural outlet, both sewage and storm water tend to accumulate. Sewage-treatment plants do not run at full capacity and cannot satisfy the city's needs. The collection system is also in disrepair, suffering from old age as well as from damage sustained in the 1985 earthquake. As a result, particularly in poor areas, sewage is collected in poorly maintained septic tanks or left in the open air. In the wet season, surface runoff must be pumped out of the valley or allowed to run northward with the sewage, where it is often used for irrigation. The highly permeable soil to the south of the city is not able to cleanse the drainage water and the subsoil aquifer is increasingly contaminated.

Air pollution

The most pressing environmental problem faced by Mexico City is its air pollution. In 1991, international norms were exceeded in the city centre on no less than 307 days. In other parts of the city they were exceeded anywhere from 232 days in the north-eastern zone to 325 days in the south-west (Lacy, 1993: 27). The source of the problem is similar to that in other large cities, but an unfortunate combination of natural phenomena accentuates what would otherwise just be a major nuisance. Surrounded by mountains in a basin 2,240 metres above sea level, the metropolitan region suffers from very stable air. In winter, thermal inversions trap cold, stagnant air beneath the level of the mountains. At the same time, the sunshine at this latitude produces photochemical smog 60 per cent more efficiently than the sunshine in Los Angeles (Lacy, 1993: 45). In addition, altitude increases automobile emissions and the high-octane gasoline required for combustion at this level also has a high lead content. To make matters worse, people are more susceptible to the negative effects of pollution at high altitude. As Walsh (1989, quoted in UN, 1991: 22) puts it: "if one was asked to design a city with characteristics conducive to high air pollution, one could not do a much better job than has been done in the Valley of Mexico."

Transport is the primary source of air pollution in Mexico City, with the private automobile contributing almost half of all emissions (table 8.11). Exacerbating the problem is the deteriorated state of so many vehicles. Even rudimentary pollution-control devices are rare. In a voluntary emission-testing programme of 600,000 vehicles conducted from 1986 to 1988, 70 per cent of petrol-driven vehicles and 85 per cent of diesel vehicles failed to meet the standards (Walsh, 1989: 23). Unfortunately, as the number of private cars increases, petrol consumption is growing rapidly: deliveries to retailers in 1991 were 22

Table 8.11 **Sources of emissions, Valley of Mexico, 1989**

Sector and source	% of total emissions	Weighted by toxicity of emission
Transportation	**76.6**	**42.4**
Private automobiles	34.9	
Gasoline trucks	19.9	
Combis and minibuses	10.5	
Taxis	7.9	
Diesel trucks	1.6	
State of Mexico buses	1.1	
Ruta-100 (DF buses)	0.5	
Others (trains, planes, etc.)	0.2	
Industry and Trade	**4.4**	**16.9**
Industry	3.7	
Trade	0.7	
Energy	**4.0**	**10.8**
PEMEX	2.4	
Thermo-electric production	1.6	
Ecological factors	**14.9**	**29.9**
Eroded areas	9.6	
Fires and other processes	5.3	
Total	**100.0**	**100.0**

Source: Derived from Lacy, 1993.

per cent higher than in 1986 (Lacy, 1993: 50). Should car ownership continue to increase, air pollution is likely to become worse.

Industry is not a major source of pollution, although it does contribute most of the sulphur dioxide. In addition, the number of commercial and service establishments using polluting processes, such as restaurants, hotels, dry cleaners, public baths, and bakeries, is growing.

The first serious attempts to reduce air pollution were begun in 1986. In 1991, these efforts were stepped up with the announcement of the Integrated Programme against Atmospheric Pollution (PICCA). This programme was undertaken by the Salinas administration in conjunction with the Comisión Metropolitana and the private sector. The total cost of the programme between 1990 and 1994 has been estimated at over US$4.7 billion (Lacy, 1993: 61).

Perhaps the best-known anti-pollution effort is the *Hoy no circula* programme, which forbids driving one day per week in the Federal District. A variety of other measures directed toward private vehicles include mandatory catalytic converters, a compulsory vehicle-inspection programme, and improvements to traffic controls and roads. New types of fuel including unleaded petrol and low-sulphur diesel fuel, have also been developed by PEMEX to lower harmful emissions.

Measures are also being taken to increase usage of the mass-transit system. These include the gradual extension of the metro system into the State of Mexico, the expansion of the trolley-bus network, the construction of a light train along Avenida Zaragoza, and the introduction of luxury buses. A major programme is also under way to reduce pollution from public transport, including fitting catalytic converters to taxis, *combis*, and microbuses and replacing 3,500 Ruta-100 buses with newer models (Lacy, 1993: 64).

The closure of PEMEX's 18 de Marzo refinery in 1991, at a reported cost of US$500 million, was the most dramatic step yet taken against industrial pollution. However, additional measures include a ban on new contaminating industries, agreements with existing companies aimed at controlling their emissions, continuous monitoring of the worst polluters, and mandatory switching from petrol and diesel fuels to natural gas. The two thermo-electric power plants serving the metropolitan area have been almost entirely converted to natural gas. They have been also instructed to suspend operations during thermal inversions (Lacy, 1993: 65–6).

The likelihood of success of these pollution-abatement programmes remains to be seen. Even if fully enacted – rarely the case in previous

Table 8.12 **Modal split of transportation in Mexico City, 1985**

Mode	% of total daily person-trips[a]
Private autos	24.0
Metro	18.5
DF Buses	27.0
State of Mexico buses	15.0
Combis and shared taxis	10.8
Trolleys and streetcars	3.0

Source: UNDIESA, 1991.
a. Figures are rounded.

efforts – many programmes will take years before they are effective. This is particularly true of those that rely on improvements to the fleet of private road vehicles, since the average age of these is so high. Retrofitting with improved pollution-control equipment is difficult to implement and virtually impossible to enforce. Other programmes, such as *Hoy no circula*, are easily subverted and possibly contribute to increased vehicle sales. What is more, progress in some areas may actually worsen other types of environmental damage. For example, the unleaded fuel introduced by PEMEX may have led to increased ozone levels (Walsh, 1989: 23).

Fortunately, the deconcentration of population and economic activity from the city centre to the suburbs and from Mexico City to other regions of the country suggests that the problem of air pollution may not be wholly intractable. The development of urban sub-centres may help to contain average commuting times and reduce industrial pollution (Gordon and Richardson, 1993).

Transport policy

Transport congestion is a major problem. The government's main response has been to try to reduce reliance on the private automobile and to increase the use of public transport. Unfortunately, the main tool used to achieve this goal, highly subsidized fares, has had little impact on the modal split (table 8.12). Those presently without cars take the metro if it goes near their destination, but otherwise rely on buses or collective taxis (Walsh, 1989: 26). The real problem, however, is rising car ownership. Once people own a car, they use it. With car ownership likely to grow faster than population and incomes, congestion is bound to get worse.

Of course, the current trend towards deconcentration of population and employment can be expected to help traffic management. As Ward (1990b: 97) points out, the emergence of new centres of employment, commerce, and services has allowed people to fulfil most of their daily needs within a limited sector of the city. He claims that average journey times for most residents have not increased much in recent years, an observation which is consistent with data from cities in developed countries.

Conclusions

The recently observed tendency for the rate of population growth in Mexico City to slow, together with the spatial deconcentration of population and employment within the metropolitan area, is good news for national and local policy-makers. Many doomsday scenarios had been based on the expectation of housing, infrastructure, and services falling further behind the rapidly growing population. It now appears that the authorities may finally have a chance to catch up with these problems. There is much scope for improvement in living conditions for low-income residents in particular. Unfortunately, the effectiveness of policy in this area, for example, greater "rationalization" of land-tenure regularization, depends greatly on changes in the political system. Such changes are extremely difficult to predict, especially given the current volatility of Mexican politics. In addition, difficulties in financing and implementing projects will continue to be complicated further by the conflicts and overlaps between the city's two political jurisdictions. However, the PICCA programme, designed by the Comisión Metropolitana, offers evidence that these difficulties can be overcome once the political will has been mustered.

It is interesting that many of the changes in Mexico City and the national urban system have come about after a decade of severely constrained resources. During the 1980s, the country's efforts were more closely focused on international debt problems and macro-economic policy than on metropolitan and regional goals. The economic liberalization undertaken by Mexico, however, has done more in less than a decade to further the goals of regional decentralization than any set of programmes devised for that purpose. In this irony Mexico is not alone; the same trends have been noted in other developing countries as well. As Gilbert (1993b: 733) points out: "The great paradox of polarisation reversal is that regional policy has contributed very little to it. Deconcentration has occurred in practice when regional planning was at its weakest."

While Mexico City will continue to face the tough problems of housing and service provision and environmental degradation, the evidence presented here suggests that in terms of settlement patterns the effects of continued liberalization are mostly benign. Now that NAFTA has been signed it is to be hoped that the effects of continued integration into the world economic system will work in the same direction.

Notes

1. This paper was written before the devaluation of December 1994 and Mexico's subsequent economic recession.
2. *Ejidos* were established after the Mexican Revolution as inalienable areas of community land; *ejidatarios* are members of the community.
3. Gini coefficients for the country have stayed remarkably stable for decades, according to a variety of sources (Ahluwalia et al., 1979; Paukert, 1973). For example, nationwide Gini coefficients between 1950 and 1990 remained near 0.53 with no obvious trend (1990 value calculated by E. Zepeda). Although metropolitan data are seldom available, Gini coefficients derived for Mexico City reflect a distribution that is less unequal than that of the nation as a whole, with a value of 0.49 (E. Zepeda, personal communication, 1994).
4. System losses may reach as high as 30 per cent (UNDIESA, 1991: 21).

References

Aguilar-Barajas, I. (1990) *An evaluation of industrial estates in Mexico, 1970–1986.* Pergamon Press.

Aguilar, A.G. (1988) "Community participation in Mexico City: A case study." *Bulletin of Latin American Research* 7: 33–46.

——— (1993) "La ciudad de México y las nuevas dimensiones de la reestructuración metropolitana." In L.F. Cabrales-Barajas (ed.), *Espacio urbano, cambio social y geografía aplicada*, Universidad de Guadalajara, 25–51.

Ahluwalia, M.S., N.G. Carter, and H.B. Chenery (1979) "Growth and poverty in developing countries." *Journal of Development Economics* 6: 299–341.

Azuela, A. (1990) *Institutional legal arrangements for the administration of land development in urban areas: The case of Mexico.* Mimeo, UNDP/UNCHS Urban Management Program. Cited in Gilbert, 1993a.

Bahl, R., and J. Linn (1992) *Urban public finance in developing countries.* Oxford University Press.

Connolly, P. (1982) "Uncontrolled settlements and self-build: What kind of solution? The Mexico City case." In P.M. Ward (ed.), *Self-help housing: A critique*, Mansell, 141–74.

—— (1988) "Sector popular de vivienda: Una crítica al concepto." *Medio Ambiente y Urbanización* 24: 3–14.

Cornelius, W.A., and A.L. Craig (1991) *The Mexican political system in transition.* Center for US-Mexican Studies, University of California, San Diego.

Coulomb, R., and E. Duhau (eds.) (1989) *Políticas urbanas y urbanización de la política.* Universidad Autónoma Metropolitana.

Coulomb, R., and C. Sánchez (1991) *¿Todos proprietarios? Vivienda de alquiler y sectores populares en la Ciudad de México.* Mexico City: CENVI.

Crane, R. (1990) "Notes on fiscal federalism in Mexico: 1976–1986." Unpublished draft, University of California, Irvine.

Cymet, D. (1992) *From ejido to metropolis, another path.* Lang.

Damián, A. (1991) "Infraestructura, equipamiento y segregación urbana." In J. Delgado and D.R. Villareal (eds.), *Cambios territoriales en México: Exploraciones recientes,* Universidad Autonoma Metropolitana – Xochimilco, 259–77.

Davis, D.E. (1991) "Urban fiscal crisis and political change in Mexico City: From global origins to local effects." *Journal of Urban Affairs* 13: 175–200.

—— (1994) *Urban leviathan: Mexico City in the twentieth century.* Temple University Press.

Dowall, D.E., and D. Wilk (1989) "Population growth, land development, and housing in Mexico City." Working Paper 502, University of California at Berkeley.

Garza, G., and M. Schteingart (1978) "Mexico City: The emerging metropolis." In W.A. Cornelius and R.W. Kemper (eds.), *Latin American Urban Research 6,* 51–86.

Garza, G. (1987) "Distribución de la industria en la ciudad de México (1960–1980)." In G. Garza (ed.) *Atlas de la ciudad de México,* El Colegio de México, 102–8.

Gilbert, A.G. (1993a) *In search of a home: Rental and shared housing in Latin America.* University College London Press and University of Arizona Press.

—— (1993b) "Third world cities: The changing national settlement system." *Urban Studies* 30: 721–40.

Gilbert, A.G., and P.M. Ward (1982) "Residential movement among the poor: choice or constraint?" *Transactions of the Institute of British Geographers* 7: 129–49.

—— (1985) *Housing, the state and the poor: Policy and practice in three Latin American cities.* Cambridge University Press.

González, M., and A. Escobar (eds.) (1991) *Social responses to Mexico's economic crisis of the 1980s.* University of California, San Diego.

Gordon, P. (1992) "The impacts of the internationalization of Mexico's economy on Mexico City." School of Urban and Regional Planning, University of Southern California.

Gordon, P., and H.W. Richardson (1993) *Trends in congestion in metropolitan areas.* Washington DC: National Research Council.

Gordon, P., J. Nugent, H. Park, H.W. Richardson, and A. Rowland (1993) *The implications of NAFTA for the Mexican urban system,* The Planning Institute, University of Southern California.

Gwynne, R.N. (1985) *Industrialization and urbanization in Latin America.* Croom Helm.

Hirschman, A.O. (1994) "The on-and-off connection between political and economic progress." *American Economic Association Papers and Proceedings* 84: 343–8.

International Institute for Applied Systems Analysis (1993) "Economic instruments for pollution control." *Options*, Winter 1993.

INEGI [Instituto Nacional de Estadística, Geografía e Informática] (1989) *Censo económico 1989*. Aguascalientes.

INEGI (1990) *Finanzas públicas estatales y municipales, 1978–1987*. Aguascalientes.

Jiménez, E. (1989) "A new form of government control over *colonias* in Mexico City." In A.G. Gilbert (ed.), *Housing and land in urban Mexico*, University of California, San Diego, 157–72.

Lacy, R. (ed.) (1993) *La calidad del aire en el valle de México*. El Colegio de México.

Lorey, D.E., and A. Mostkoff-Linares (1993) "Mexico's 'lost decade' 1980–90: Evidence on class structure and professional employment from the 1990 census." In J.W. Wilkie, C.A. Contreras, and C.A. Weber (eds.), *Statistical abstract of Latin America* 30: 1341–60.

Lustig, N. (1990) "Economic crisis, adjustment and living standards in Mexico, 1982–85." *World Development* 18: 1325–42.

Negrete-Salas, M.E., B. Graizbord, and C. Ruiz (1993) *Población, espacio y medio ambiente en la Zona Metropolitana de la Ciudad de México*. El Colegio de México.

Paukert, F. (1973) "Income distribution at different levels of development: A survey of evidence." *International Labour Review* 112: 97–125.

Portes, A. (1990) "Latin American urbanisation during the years of the crisis." *Latin America Research Review* 25: 7–44.

Pradilla, E. (1990) "Las políticas neoliberales y la cuestión territorial." *Revista Interamericana de Planificación* 22: 77–107.

Richardson, H.W. (1989) "The big, bad city: Mega-city myth?" *Third World Planning Review* 11: 355–72.

Rodríguez, V.E. (1993) "The politics of decentralization in Mexico: From *municipios libres* to *Solidaridad*." *Bulletin of Latin American Research* 12: 133–45.

Rowland, A. (1992) "Wage rates and real estate maxims: What really matters for Mexico?" School of Urban and Regional Planning, University of Southern California.

Rowland, A. (1993) "Managing a metropolis: Options for improving urban service delivery in Mexico City." School of Urban and Regional Planning, University of Southern California.

Scott, I. (1982) *Urban and spatial development in Mexico*. Johns Hopkins University Press.

Schteingart, M. (ed.) (1989) *Los productores del espacio habitable: Estado, empresa y sociedad en la ciudad de México*. El Colegio de México.

UNDIESA [United Nations Department of International Economic and Social Affairs] (1991) *Population growth and policies in mega-cities: Mexico City*. Population Policy Paper No. 32.

Van Wijnbergen, S. (1992) "Should prices be decontrolled gradually or in a big bang?" In A. Cukierman, A. Hercowitz, and L. Leiderman (eds.), *Political economy, growth and business cycles*. MIT Press.

Varley, A. (1993) "Clientelism or technocracy? The polities of urban land regularization." In N. Harvey (ed.), *Mexico: Dilemmas of transition*, Institute of Latin American Studies, London, and British Academic Press, 249–76.

Villalpando, R. (1989) "Costos, financiamiento y subsidios de la Zona Metropolitana de la Ciudad de México." In C. Bustamante and F. Burgueño (eds.), *Eco-*

nomía y planificación urbana en México. Universidad Nacional Autónoma de México.

Walsh, M.P. (1989) "Motor vehicle emissions in Mexico: A strategy for progress." Paper prepared for the World Bank.

Ward, P. (1990a) "The politics of housing production in Mexico." In W. van Vliet (ed.), *The international handbook of housing policies and practices.* Greenwood Press.

———— (1990b) *Mexico City: The production and reproduction of an urban environment.* Boston: G.K. Hall and Co.

Wilk, D. (1992) "Formas y mecanismos de coordinación metropolitana de la Ciudad de México." Unpublished draft, Mexico City.

Wilson, P. (1992) *Exports and local development: Mexico's new maquiladoras.* University of Texas Press.

9

Rio de Janeiro: Urban expansion and structural change

Hamilton Tolosa

Introduction

Until the mid-1970s, the Brazilian economy grew consistently at an annual rate of slightly over 6 per cent. At the beginning of the 1980s, economic conditions changed radically. Falling rates of investment led to a widespread recession, and a distorted price structure completely upset business expectations and disorganized national production. A series of unsuccessful stabilization experiments distorted prices further and increased social inequalities.

National economic problems had a significant impact on the urban system. During the boom, the major cities were expanding but industrial deconcentration in the hinterland of these cities led to the rapid growth of a number of secondary cities in the south and south-east of the country. During the 1980s, urban poverty increased markedly, both in the largest cities and in small cities based in backward agricultural regions or dependent upon consumer-goods industries. With the recession, many small industrial companies simply vanished.

This chapter considers how the Rio de Janeiro metropolitan area (RJMA) fared during the recession of the 1980s. How did its national urban role change and how was the quality of life in the city affected?

These questions are considered through an examination of the dynamics of population change, employment, poverty and income distribution, housing, supply of services, transport provision, pollution and environmental policies, and crime. The final section considers the city's future prospects.

Population growth

Rio de Janeiro was formally constituted into a metropolitan area (RJMA) in 1973. The RJMA contained fourteen counties: Rio de Janeiro, Duque de Caxias, Itaborai, Itaguaí, Magé, Mangaratiba, Maricá, Nilópolis, Niterói, Nova Iguaçu, Paracambi, Petrópolis, São Gonçalo and São João de Meriti.[1] With around 10 million inhabitants, the metropolitan area is Brazil's second largest city and its second most important port. It is located some 400 kilometres north of its greatest national rival, São Paulo. Together, these two cities contain over 25 million people and almost half of Brazil's manufacturing activity. They dominate the south-east, the most prosperous region in Brazil, and in recent years have maintained their combined share of the national population.

In contrast to São Paulo, however, Rio's economic situation has been in decline for some years. Its economic future was damaged when the federal capital was moved to Brasília in 1960, along with a huge amount of public investment. Rio has also suffered badly from the Brazilian economic recession and has been losing out in the struggle with São Paulo for commercial and industrial dominance. In 1985, São Paulo accounted for 26 per cent of the country's manufacturing production compared to Rio's share of 7 per cent. Many of Rio's leading banks, industries, and research and development companies either relocated or moved their headquarters to São Paulo. Earnings from tourism also declined as the media drew international attention to Rio's escalating crime rate. As a result, an increasing gap opened up between the two largest metropolitan areas. Since 1970, the population of São Paulo has grown nearly twice as fast as that of Rio. In 1988, average household earnings per capita were 22 per cent higher in São Paulo than in Rio; in 1970 the difference had been only 10 per cent; in 1976, 18 per cent. This was not just a relative decline. As a result of the national recession, Rio's population became much poorer. Between 1976 and 1988 real earnings in Rio de Janeiro fell by 29 per cent.

Over the last thirty years, Brazil's urban population has grown at

Table 9.1 **Metropolitan growth in Brazil, 1970–1991**

Metropolitan Area	Population (000s)			Annual growth (%)	
	1970	1980	1991[a]	1970/80	1980/91
Rio de Janeiro	6,891	8,872	9,600	2.4	0.8
Capital city	4,252	5,091	5,336	1.8	0.4
Periphery	2,639	3,681	4,264	3.4	1.3
São Paulo	8,139	12,588	15,199	4.4	1.7
Capital City	5,924	8,493	9,480	3.6	1.0
Periphery	2,215	4,095	5,719	6.3	3.1
Southern cities[b]	4,053	6,334	8,451	3.8	2.7
Capital Cities	2,729	3,929	4,600	3.7	1.4
Peripheries	1,324	2,405	3,851	6.2	4.4
Northern cities[c]	4,629	6,692	8,959	3.8	2.7
Capital Cities	3,558	4,942	6,350	3.3	2.3
Peripheries	1,071	1,750	2,609	5.0	3.7
Brazil	**93,165**	**119,002**	**146,154**	**2.5**	**1.9**

Source: Demographic Census, 1970, 1980, and 1991.
a. Preliminary results.
b. Includes the following metropolitan areas: Belo Horizonte, Curitiba, and Pôrto Alegre.
c. Includes the following metropolitan areas: Belém, Fortaleza, Recife, and Salvador.

Note:
Statistical information throughout this paper was obtained from two major sources: the population censuses for 1970, 1980, and 1991 (preliminary results) and the National Household Survey, which is conducted annually. The National Household Survey covers the nine metropolitan areas and the federal capital, Brasilia. Unfortunately, the sampling design prevents use of National Household Survey data at the sub-metropolitan scale. Comparison of the municipality of Rio and the surrounding counties has been based on either census information or independent surveys.

an average annual rate of just over 5 per cent. In the 1960s and early 1970s, the fastest rates of growth were recorded by cities with between 100,000 and 250,000 inhabitants. By the 1980s, although the economies of many of these secondary centres were continuing to prosper, their population growth rates slowed. The fastest urban growth rates were now to be found among the large metropolitan centres, particularly those in the north-east of the country.

Table 9.1 compares the rates of population growth in Rio and São Paulo between 1970 and 1991 with those in Brazil's other seven metropolitan areas.[2] It shows that the pace of population growth slowed markedly in the 1980s in all nine areas, partly the result of a slowing of natural increase in Brazil as a whole and partly the result of economic recession. However, the falls in the growth rates of Rio de

205

Table 9.2 **Metropolitan Rio de Janeiro: Migrants and natives, 1980**

	RJMA	Rio de Janeiro	Periphery Mean	Periphery Maximum	Periphery Minimum
Migrants/total population (%)	42.2	35.2	51.5	59.1	9.4
Recent migrants/total migrants (%)	14.8	10.0	21.0	31.1	10.6

Source: State of Rio de Janeiro Yearbook, 1988.

Janeiro and São Paulo were much more marked than those of the other cities. During the 1980s, Rio's population grew at 0.8 per cent per annum, São Paulo's at 1.7 per cent.

Table 9.1 also shows that the population of the central city has been expanding less quickly than the periphery in every metropolitan area of Brazil (see chapter 4). However, this process is much more advanced in Rio and São Paulo and is reflected in the large differential in those cities between the central and peripheral growth rates.

Over the years, migration has been a significant factor in Rio's growth and, in 1980, migrants made up more than 40 per cent of the total population. Research has shown that 70 per cent of migrants to metropolitan centres in Brazil originate from urban areas (Pastore and Haller, 1993; Tolosa, 1976). Most arrivals are first absorbed into either the construction industry or the service sector and eventually move to the suburbs. Table 9.2 shows the location of migrants to Rio de Janeiro in 1980. Most of these migrants were living in municipalities outside but relatively close to the central area: Nilópolis, São João de Meriti, Nova Iguaçu, São Gonçalo, and Caxias (figure 9.1). More distant towns, such as Petrópolis, with its pleasant site in the mountains more than 80 kilometres from downtown Rio, its economic base centred upon tourism and fairly sophisticated, clean industries, and its reliance on skilled labour, attracted fewer migrants. Among recent migrants there has been a stronger tendency to move into municipalities on the eastern banks of Guanabara Bay, notably Itaborai (31 per cent) and Magé (26 per cent).

During the 1980s, Rio's population growth slowed right down. The decline is explained by Brazil's economic recession and the slowing of metropolitan growth throughout the country. Fewer migrants moved to the major cities, a trend particularly marked in Rio owing to the latter's especially serious economic problems (see next section). But

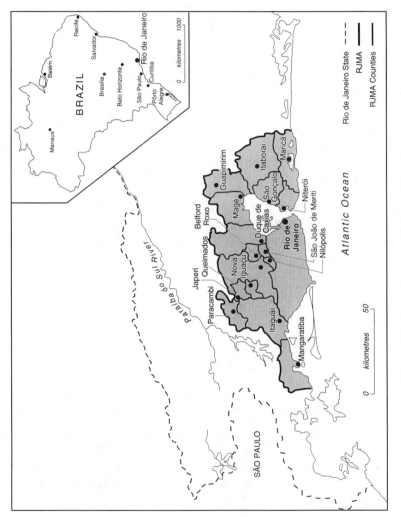

Figure 9.1 **Rio de Janeiro: Metropolitan area**

207

Table 9.3 **Metropolitan Rio de Janeiro: Major demographic characteristics, 1970–1988**

| Indicators | 1970 | | | 1980 | | | 1988 | |
	Rio de Janeiro	National	RJMA	Rio de Janeiro	National	RJMA	RJMA	National
Fertility	3.5	5.7	2.8	2.4	4.3	2.1		3.5
Infant mortality	–	117	77	68	88	36		63
Life expect-ancy	62.1	53.4	63.2	65.2	60.1	65.6		64.8
Household size	4.4	5.2	–	3.9	4.5	3.9		4.3

Sources: Demographic Census, 1970 and 1980; National Household Survey, 1988.

Notes: Fertility rate per 1000 women; infant mortality rate per 1000 live births; life expectancy rate in years; density in persons per square kilometre; household size = number of persons.

the slower pace of growth was also due to longer-term demographic trends. As table 9.3 shows, fertility rates plummeted in Rio between 1970 and 1988. And, while life expectancy increased, the rate of change was far less marked. As a result, there was a substantial fall in the rate of natural increase.

Employment

Between 1970 and 1988, employment in the Rio metropolitan area increased annually at 3.8 per cent. This was well above the 2.9 per cent annual growth in the economically-active age group (over 10 years old), so that participation rates rose markedly, from 45 per cent in 1970 to 52 per cent in 1988. Nevertheless, participation rates in Rio remain lower than the national urban average of 55 per cent because participation has been rising quickly in most metropolitan areas.

Despite the slackening pace of Rio's economic growth, the pace of employment growth hardly changed. Between 1970 and 1980, the latter grew annually at 4.0 per cent; between 1980 and 1988 by 3.9 per cent.

Table 9.4 shows most workers to be employed in the service sector and indicates how the dominance of this sector has increased during the years of decline. The national recession has brought a slight decline in employment in both construction and manufacturing.

The increase in service activity signifies a decline in the proportion

Table 9.4 **Rio de Janeiro: Economically active population by productive sector, 1982–1988 (percentage of population)**

Sector	1982	1985	1988
Industry	16.4	16.0	15.4
Construction	8.9	7.6	7.4
Services	67.5	70.0	75.0
Personal and domestic	(23.6)	(25.0)	(25.3)
Business services	(3.8)	(4.5)	(4.7)
Public administration	(11.5)	(11.4)	(12.5)
Other	7.2	6.4	2.2
Total	**100.0**	**100.0**	**100.0**

Source: National Household Survey, various years.

of the population with a formal contract. Few workers in personal or domestic services have social security coverage or, for that matter, any sort of legal protection or unemployment insurance. This group constitutes a substantial proportion of the "unprotected" segment of the metropolitan labour force. In 1988, about one-third of Rio's 3.5 million workers lacked a formal contract, with 800,000 lacking any kind of social security cover. These figures compare very unfavourably with the situation in São Paulo, where unprotected workers accounted for only 22 per cent of the labour force. Unprotected and self-employed workers have much lower average earnings than wage earners, the latter earning 4.5 times the minimum wage on average, unprotected workers only 1.7 times the minimum, and the self-employed 3.7 times the minimum.

During the 1970s, although the age of the average worker remained constant at around 35 years, the labour force recruited increasing numbers of people at both top and bottom of the age pyramid. First, more young workers entered the job market as large numbers of young in-migrants and baby-boomers looked for work. Second, with falling death rates, rising numbers of elderly people were also looking for employment. As education levels in Rio rose, however, the labour force became better educated, the average number of years of formal education rising from 5.9 in 1970 to 7.3 in 1988.

Perhaps the most dramatic change in Rio's labour force, however, has been its increasing feminization. The female participation rate rose from 27 per cent in 1970 to 38 per cent in 1988. The scattered empirical evidence suggests that female employment rose during the "miracle" years, as employers sought increasing numbers of cheap

Table 9.5 **Employment characteristics of the poor**^{*a*} **(percentages)**

	Informal labour		Under-employment		Open unem-ployment		Participation rates	
Indicators^{*b*}	1981	1985	1981	1985	1981	1985	1981	1985
Rio de Janeiro	46.5	54.3	20.6	18.6	16.9	9.2	41.2	48.6
São Paulo	39.8	46.2	14.4	14.7	19.5	14.0	44.1	48.6
Nine metropolitan areas	45.7	55.9	18.1	20.0	9.6	6.8	42.3	47.3

Sources: National Household Survey, various years; Rocha, 1990.
a. Refers to the population below the poverty line.
b. Informal labour includes those workers and wage earners not contributing to social security; underemployment is defined as those working less than 40 hours per week; open unemployment measures the proportion of poor workers looking for a job; and participation rates are calculated as a percentage of the poor population over 10 years of age.

workers, and continued during the recession of the 1980s, as women and children were called upon to offset reductions in family income due to unemployment and falling real wages.

Table 9.5 implicitly supports this interpretation by showing employment trends during the early 1980s among workers living below the poverty line. It reveals how unemployment fell during a period of rapidly rising labour participation in both Rio and São Paulo. Most of the rise in employment was absorbed by the informal sector.

The rise in both participation rates and the size of the informal labour force is a strong sign of deteriorating employment conditions. Combined with evidence of increasing levels of female and child labour, it is a clear sign of the terrible price paid by poor families during the economic crisis throughout metropolitan Brazil (table 9.5).

Poverty and the distribution of income

Both absolute and relative poverty got worse in Brazil during the 1980s as a result of the economic recession and the state's unsuccessful efforts to tackle inflation. Relative inequality improved slightly during the 1970s and deteriorated during the 1980s. Table 9.6 shows that inequality worsened during the 1980s in Brazil's three largest metropolitan areas. It also shows that inequality was greater in Rio than in either São Paulo or Belo Horizonte in both 1981 and 1989. Indeed, the situation in Rio has deteriorated faster than in any other metro-

Table 9.6 **Relative poverty in metropolitan areas of south-east Brazil, 1981 and 1989 (Gini coefficients)**

City	1981	1989
Rio de Janeiro	0.58	0.67
São Paulo	0.52	0.57
Belo Horizonte	0.57	0.62

Source: Rocha, 1991.

Note: The Gini coefficients were calculated on the basis of per capita family income.

Table 9.7 **Absolute poverty in metropolitan areas of south-east Brazil, 1981 and 1989**

Metropolitan Areas	Poverty lines (US$)		Poverty shares (%)	
	1981	1989	1981	1989
Rio de Janeiro	44.8	44.8	27.2	32.5
São Paulo	52.6	53.5	22.0	20.9
Belo Horizonte	40.7	38.8	31.1	27.2

Source: Rocha, 1991.

Notes: Per capita monthly family income converted into dollars using average annual exchange rate. The methodology employed in calculating the poverty lines is described fully in Rocha, 1988.

politan area. By 1989, Rio had the most unequal distribution of income of any metropolitan area in Brazil; during the 1980s it had displaced even the cities of the north-east from first place.[3]

Absolute poverty also increased dramatically during the 1980s and, in 1991, some 3.5 million people were living below the poverty line. According to table 9.7, however, the increase in poverty was reflected more in the rising proportion of poor families than in the level of immiseration. The average income of families living below the poverty line in Rio remained constant between 1981 and 1989. The pattern was very similar in São Paulo and Belo Horizonte. Like relative poverty, however, absolute poverty appears to be far worse in Rio than in the other two cities. São Paulo has a far lower share of its people living below the poverty line.[4] In fact, Rio had a higher proportion of its population living in absolute poverty than the Brazilian metropolitan average of 28.1 per cent.

Housing and infrastructure

Census information suggests that there was an overall improvement in housing conditions in Brazil during the 1970s. Rio was no exception to this trend, with the average dwelling improving in terms of both size and quality. Nevertheless, the city continued to face huge housing problems, particularly in the *favelas*. Referring to these self-help areas, the World Bank (1979: 22) noted that although

a large majority of families live in durable residential structures ... this minimum shelter standard fails to reflect the precarious location (on steep hillsides, in areas subject to periodic flooding or subject to hazardous environmental pollution) and overcrowding of many dwellings, as well as their lack of essential services. Given the modesty of this standard, those families living in structures which fail to classify as durable must make do with very inadequate living conditions.

Official government efforts have not managed to reduce this problem, indeed, the proportion of dwellings classified as slums or *favelas* appears to have increased through time.[5] The share of *favelas* rose from 9.8 per cent in 1970 to 12.4 per cent in 1991. This means that more than one million people in Rio are living in *favelas*. Table 9.8 shows the distribution of *favelas* in the metropolitan area relative to the total housing stock. Rather surprisingly, it shows that the municipality of Rio contains a higher proportion of *favelas* than more

Table 9.8 **Metropolitan Rio de Janeiro: Households living in *favelas*, 1991**

City	Total *favela* settlements	Total households (000s)	Total *favela* households (000s)	% *favelas*
Rio de Janeiro	394	1,627.8	203.2	12.4
Periphery (1)	158	839.3	31.9	3.8
Caxias	48	154.4	12.4	8.0
Niteroi	25	117.1	6.5	5.5
S.J. Meriti	18	100.4	3.2	3.2
Nova Iguaçu	57	315.6	8.6	2.7
Itaguaí	4	32.1	0.7	2.1
Other	6	125.2	0.6	0.0
RJMA (2)	552	2,467.1	235.2	9.5
(1)/(2) × 100	28.6	34.0	13.5	–

Source: IBGE, *Anuário Estatístico*, 1991, Rio de Janeiro.

Note: For statistical purposes, a dwelling is here understood as an independent living space having one or more rooms and a private entrance.

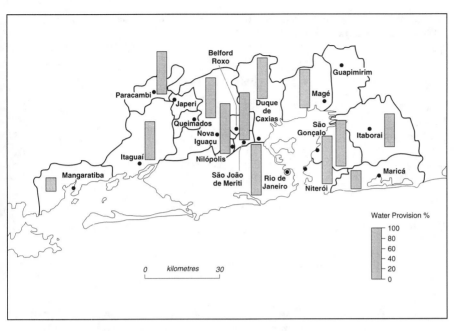

Figure 9.2 **Rio de Janeiro: Water provision per household by administrative area, 1988 (Source: Sydenstricker, 1993)**

peripheral neighbourhoods. Caxias has the second highest share, followed, at a considerable distance, by Niterói. The proportion of dwellings classified as *favelas* in the central area, however, has declined over time.[6]

In 1988, the metropolitan area of Rio contained over two million people living in dwellings lacking piped water. More homes lacked piped water than in most other metropolitan areas. As figure 9.2 demonstrates, the situation was particularly bad in the newer low-income areas. However, table 9.9 shows that levels of provision did improve between 1981 and 1988. The situation was somewhat better in terms of sewerage facilities, because many homes had a septic tank; again there was a dramatic improvement in the level of provision during the 1980s.

Table 9.9 shows that service and infrastructure provision for the poor is particularly bad. More than one-third of all homes lack water and fewer than one-half have their rubbish collected. The table also shows that conditions are hardly ideal even among the non-poor. The only consolation is that, despite the deteriorating economic conditions, the provision of piped water, sewerage, and rubbish collec-

213

Table 9.9 **Rio de Janeiro: Absence of infrastructure among the poor and non-poor, 1981–1988 (percentage without service)**

Facility	Poor			Non-poor		
	1981	1985	1988	1981	1985	1988
Piped water	51.2	35.6	35.6	18.7	8.2	12.9
Sewerage	53.1	27.0	31.8	22.6	8.1	9.7
Garbage collection	59.7	52.0	51.5	27.0	17.8	23.5
Basic education	17.2	15.7	17.1	6.6	3.2	5.1

Source: National Household Survey, various years.

tion improved during the 1980s, even if access to basic education did not.

Health and education

Health care in metropolitan areas is much better than in the country as a whole and Rio compares quite favourably to most other metropolitan areas. The ratio of doctors, nurses, and hospital beds to inhabitants is superior to that in most other metropolitan areas. And, in line with national trends, the per capita provision of services is improving through time.[7] In 1987, there was one hospital bed for every 170 inhabitants and one doctor for every 297 people.

What is disturbing is the unequal distribution of health care facilities within the city. Whereas there is one doctor for every 208 people in the municipality of Rio de Janeiro, the ratio is one to every 603 people in the rest of the city. There is also a major inequality between the provision of private and public health care. Public hospitals contained only one-third of all hospital beds in the municipality of Rio; in the periphery, the proportion was even lower, 14 per cent.

Between 1960 and 1980, the level of literacy in Rio improved from 53 per cent to 68 per cent; by 1988 it had apparently reached 88 per cent (Sydenstricker, 1993: 51). Again, however, there is a major difference between the central areas and the periphery of the city. In 1980, illiteracy in the municipality of Rio was 15 per cent compared to 22 per cent in the periphery.

Education provision seems also to have improved in recent decades. Certainly the numbers of teachers have increased greatly and student/teacher ratios have fallen as a result (table 9.10). The number

Table 9.10 **Rio de Janeiro: Education indicators, 1970–1988**

Education levels	1970	1980	1988
Primary[a,b]			
Number of schools	1,941	3,850	5,149
Enrolment (thousands)	592	1,698	1,850
Number of teachers	n.a.	67,984	88,055
Student/teacher ratio	n.a.	25	21
Secondary[a]			
Number of schools	692	577	754
Enrolment (thousands)	242	302	294
Number of teachers	16,940	21,139	24,019
Student/teacher ratio	14	14	12
Higher			
Number of institutions	209	241	n.a.
Enrolment (thousands)	55	77	n.a.
Number of teachers	7,340	14,690	n.a.
Student/teacher ratio	8	5	n.a.

Sources: Demographic Census, 1970 and 1980; National Household Survey, 1988; State of Rio de Janeiro Yearbook, various years.
a. Comprises public and private schools. In most cases, students attend school only in the morning or the afternoon.
b. Includes primary and pre-primary (or elementary) grades.
c. Refers to the number of available courses.

of students at school increased remarkably during the 1970s but slowed during the 1980s. Indeed, the number of secondary school students actually declined between 1980 and 1988 even though the population in the 14–19 age group increased by 23 per cent. This decline was an undoubted consequence of the recession.

Transport

Most journeys in Rio de Janeiro are made by bus. Indeed, at 62 per cent of all motorized trips, bus usage ranks very high by the standards of the world's largest metropolitan areas. It is certainly much higher than in other Latin American metropolises such as São Paulo (54 per cent), Mexico City (51 per cent), and Buenos Aires (45 per cent) (World Bank, 1986: 42–3). The car is the next most important transport mode, accounting for 24 per cent of trips, followed by the metro, with 11 per cent. Car use is much more limited in Rio than in São Paulo, reflecting the former's much lower rate of car ownership (one

Table 9.11 **Rio de Janeiro: Number of motor vehicles, 1978, 1982, and 1985**

Vehicles	Thousands			Growth rate	
	1978	1982	1985	1978–82	1982–85
Cars	721.2	1,018.9	1,058.0	14.2	3.8
Buses	8.9	15.3	13.1	47.1	−14.4
Commercial	29.5	39.8	42.0	18.6	5.5
Cargo	40.6	49.3	45.1	29.6	−8.5
Other	39.4	86.5	87.8	15.5	1.5
Total	**839.6**	**1,209.8**	**1,246.0**	**15.2**	**3.0**

Source: National Department of Roads Yearbook, various years.

car for every 9.6 people in 1980 compared to one car per 6.6 people in São Paulo).

There is a shortage of recent information on the vehicle fleet but data for the late 1970s and the early 1980s, show clearly the effects of the economic recession (see table 9.11). Between 1978 and 1982, there was a dramatic increase in most kinds of motor vehicle; from 1982 until 1985, however, the growth rate slowed and for some kinds of vehicles there was actually a decline. The impact of recession was clearly felt very strongly by the bus and cargo fleets.

Falling fuel consumption and tyre sales further demonstrate that the number of cars on the roads continued to grow very slowly after 1985. Gasohol consumption in the State of Rio de Janeiro reached a peak in 1988 and fell thereafter. What is perhaps more worrying are the figures for diesel-fuel consumption, a good proxy for bus and lorry trips. In a city so highly dependent on bus transport, the steady decline in 1989 and 1990 in diesel sales suggests that there are far fewer buses available. If this interpretation is correct, the poor have been hit particularly hard.

Under current economic conditions the transport situation in Rio is unlikely to change markedly in the near future. The current financial plight of the metro, which carried only 238,000 passengers a day in 1992, means that there is little chance of its being extended. In any case this would be a very expensive option given Rio's physical structure. Much more likely is the development of some kind of light rail solution employing trams or streetcars with dedicated traffic lanes. This would be both an equitable and an efficient approach to the traffic problem.[8]

Table 9.12 **Deaths from respiratory diseases associated with air pollution in major cities of south-east Brazil**

Year	City	Population (000s)	Deaths from respiratory diseases	Deaths associated with air pollution
1984	Rio de Janeiro	5,177	1,273	40
1988	Belo Horizonte	2,837	1,159	n.a.
1989	São Paulo	9,291	1,708	139

Source: Seroa da Motta and Fernandes Mendes, 1993.

Pollution and environmental policies

Rapid industrialization and metropolitan growth have led to a worsening of urban pollution. Deteriorating environmental conditions have been aggravated by the lack of integrated land-use policies and urban settlement controls. Air pollution unquestionably causes serious health problems and recent studies have tried to estimate the effect that it has on the incidence of respiratory diseases. Seroa da Motta and Fernandes Mendes (1993) show that the number of deaths from respiratory diseases in São Paulo is positively related to climatic conditions.

Table 9.12 presents the available data on deaths from respiratory diseases in Brazil's largest three cities and estimates the number of deaths caused by air pollution. As expected, São Paulo's higher level of industrialization and its much larger ratio of vehicles to inhabitants causes that city to record the highest proportion of deaths through air pollution. No doubt Rio's coastal location also helps to reduce levels of air pollution.

Whether its coastal location helps reduce water pollution is another question. Certainly, the fact that most of Rio's counties are located in a horseshoe around Guanabara Bay creates distinctive environmental problems. The Bay has an area of approximately 400 square kilometres and a perimeter of 131 kilometres and receives most of the city's domestic and industrial waste. Over 300 tons of organic sewage and seven tons of domestic solid waste flow directly into the bay every day. Food-processing, chemical, and petrochemical companies and a busy sea port with 16 oil terminals together discharge 80 tons of industrial waste, 4.7 tons of oil, and 0.4 tons of heavy metals every day (Dubeux, 1994).

Not surprisingly, there has been increasing concern about water pollution since the mid-1970s. Research conducted at local universities and technical agencies soon alerted the public to the seriousness of the issue. Such concern led to the initiation of a comprehensive water pollution control project by FEEMA (State Foundation for Environmental Engineering), the official agency in charge of environmental policies for the State of Rio de Janeiro (FEEMA, 1990).

A new strategy to fight water pollution in the Rio area is about to be implemented at a total cost of nearly US$800 million. The programme's major aims are to reduce the incidence of diseases caused by water pollution, to improve water quality conditions and to resuscitate the fishing industry. Major investments are planned in the area of water supply, sanitation, solid waste control, environmental monitoring, urban resettlement, and institutional support (FEEMA, 1993; JICA, 1993).

Crime

Recently, Rio has been subjected to major international press coverage of its crime problems. Articles and television programmes have appeared publicizing the rising crime rate, the drug problem, the activities of death squads, and the attacks being mounted on foreign tourists. An immediate result has been a spectacular fall in the number of tourists: a decline of 41 per cent between 1988 and 1989.[9]

Table 9.13 presents data on crime in the city from 1966 to 1986. These figures show that crimes against property, including larceny, robbery, extortion, housebreaking, and fraud, increased considerably,

Table 9.13 **Metropolitan Rio de Janeiro: Crime indicators, 1966, 1978, and 1986**

	RJMA		Rio de Janeiro		
Indicator[b]	1978	1986[a]	1966[a]	1978	1986
Crimes against property	n.a.	8.9	0.8	7.4	11.6
Crimes against persons	n.a.	3.2	14.7	5.3	3.4
Traffic accidents	28.2	14.8	40.3	23.4	12.3

Source: State of Rio de Janeiro Yearbook, various years.

a. The crime figures record crimes per thousand persons. The figure for 1966 is an average of those for 1965, 1966, and 1968 figures, and the figure for 1986 is an average of 1985, 1986, and 1987.

b. The number of traffic accidents involving death or injury was divided by the total number of motor vehicles in each administrative area.

but that crimes against the person, including murder and attempted murder, as well as abortions and certain minor offences, declined.

Of course, Brazilian crime statistics are unreliable because so few victims make reports to the police. Consequently, it is difficult to say whether the incidence of crime is higher or lower in Rio than in other major Brazilian cities. However, it is probably fair to say that serious crime is getting worse.

Growing crime rates in Rio de Janeiro are frequently attributed to growing poverty. They are perceived to form part of what Lewis (1968) called the "culture of poverty": "a way of life that develops among the poor, in a given social and historical context, characterized by lack of effective participation and integration in the major institutions of society." Drug dealing, prostitution, and organized crime are both a cause and a consequence of poverty. Unfortunately, the crime statistics in Rio are far too limited to investigate this point. What is clear is that crime has become a major political issue in the city.

Emerging issues for the coming decade

Unsuccessful attempts at stabilization in Brazil during the 1980s greatly aggravated the distributive problems caused by the earlier oil shocks and the debt crisis. They also made future recovery more difficult by cutting fixed capital formation as a percentage of the national product from 23 per cent in 1980 to 16 per cent in 1990. Certainly, the major metropolitan areas were badly affected by declines in manufacturing industry, manufacturing value added falling by 2.8 per cent during the 1980s. The vital machinery and metalworking sectors declined by 22 per cent and 4 per cent respectively during the same period. These economic changes have had a strong impact upon the urban system.

Since it is not clear how the national economy will develop in the next few years, it is difficult to predict what will happen to metropolitan growth. What is certain is that urbanization will continue in Brazil as a whole. Even if we assume a continuation of the 1980s trend of zero economic growth into the 1990s, the level of urbanization should still reach 80 per cent by the year 2000. If that mark should be reached, there will be 150 million urban dwellers in Brazil, almost half of whom will be living in the south-east of the country (Tolosa, 1992). Rio de Janeiro and São Paulo will have a combined population of nearly 37 million people. According to these estimates, Rio's population is expected to reach 14 million by the turn of the century.

What is more worrying is that with zero growth, it is likely to be a city with an even worse income distribution and a higher proportion of people living below the poverty line. Continued declines in investment in social infrastructure will have a further detrimental effect on living standards.

A second, more optimistic view of the national economy envisages an annual growth rate of between 4 and 5 per cent, still a little below the 1960–1990 average of 6 per cent. Such a recovery would be led by manufacturing, and most of the benefits would accrue to the major cities. Despite their problems, these centres still have better infrastructure than most other Brazilian cities. Rio and São Paulo are also located at the heart of the country's most prosperous region. This moderate growth scenario, therefore, foresees no real change in the urban growth pattern of the 1960s and 1970s.

Under either economic growth scenario, the population living in the major cities would grow. Rio will face an inevitable increase in the demand for social infrastructure. Urban services, such as water, sewerage, health, and education, will have to be improved, and one of the challenges facing the authorities is to provide the necessary finance to fund this investment. The new 1988 Brazilian Constitution is critical here in so far as it has modified the basis for public action. Essentially, it has encouraged fiscal decentralization, with more funds being transferred in increasing quantities from the federal government to the state and municipal authorities. In the process, the role of the municipality has become much more important. In future, municipal government will be responsible for public health and for primary education. It will also be required to organize and, if necessary, to provide public transport, to improve the efficiency of urban land use, and to protect the historical and cultural heritage.

If more responsibility has been given to municipal government, there has not been an equivalent transfer of resources. It is here that the Rio area faces a major challenge, since so much of current expenditure is concentrated in sectors such as health and primary education, where direct cost recovery is difficult. Since there is no practical way to bill the large proportion of poor people using those services, costs must be financed through general taxes and transfer revenues. Although cost recovery is possible in the case of services such as rubbish collection and public lighting, Rio's local authorities have a long way to travel in that direction. At present, charges for those two services cover less than one-quarter of their total cost.

Unfortunately, the local authorities have little or no control over the provision of major public services such as electricity, water, and sewerage. Services here are provided by federal agencies and uniform tariffs are applied across the nation. A progressive tariff structure exists in the electricity sector, but water and sewerage charges are based on a relatively high minimum tariff, which means that small consumers tend to pay more for the service than better-off households.

Whatever happens to urban policy under future governments, the future of Rio's people depends on the prospects for economic growth. Without growth there will be little opportunity to reduce poverty or to improve the quality of urban life. Even if growth occurs, adequate provision of basic services to the poor will depend on the efficiency and effectiveness of the local authorities. They need to show greater awareness of the needs of the poor and greater concern for the environment. It is by no means certain that the Rio authorities will be up to the task. If they are not, then social inequality in the metropolitan area is likely to worsen still further. So, too, will traffic congestion and the level of pollution.

Acknowledgements

The author wishes to thank Werner Baer, University of Illinois at Urbana-Champaign, and Ronaldo Seroa da Motta and Sonia Rocha, both from IPEA, Rio de Janeiro, for making comments on this paper.

Notes

1. Petrópolis county has recently decided to withdraw from the RJMA. Given the recent nature of the change, it has been retained as part of the metropolitan area in the discussion in this chapter.
2. In 1973, a federal law established the first group of eight metropolitan areas: São Paulo, Pôrto Alegre, Curitiba, Belo Horizonte, Salvador, Recife, Fortaleza, and Belém. One year later, the Rio de Janeiro Metropolitan Area (RJMA) was created. These nine cities together contained 42 million people in 1991.
3. In 1981, the three north-eastern cities of Recife, Fortaleza, and Salvador all had a Gini coefficient of 0.60.
4. Metropolitan poverty lines in Brazil are characterized by a large and increasing variance through time. Besides reflecting wide differences in relative prices between cities, they also reveal important differences in consumer habits and culture. In this respect, there is a major difference between Rio and São Paulo with its much more modern industrial structure and demand profile.
5. The National Housing Bank (BNH) was created in 1964 to finance housing, especially for the low-income urban population. In 1968 the Bank expanded in order to encompass other social infrastructure investments, in particular water supply and sewage disposal. In 1986, in a controversial political decision, the BNH was closed and most of its functions were trans-

ferred to the Federal Savings Bank (Caixa Económica Federal). In practical terms, however, this decision implied the virtual dismantling of the housing-finance system.

6. In 1970, the central area, known at the time as Guanabara State, contained 111,000 slum dwellings, with some 565,000 inhabitants, about 13.3 per cent of the population (State of Rio de Janeiro Yearbook, 1971: 27–8).

7. Overall, Brazil had 800 people per doctor in 1987 compared to 2,000 in 1970, although progress in terms of hospital bed provision showed a less marked improvement, from 263 people per bed in 1970 to 223 in 1987.

8. See also chapter 5, above, for a discussion of transport problems in Rio.

9. The annual number of visitors to Rio averaged 101,000 between 1967 and 1970, 286,000 between 1976 and 1978, and reached a peak in 1988, with 762,000 arrivals. The flow fell to 472,000 in 1989 and to 438,000 the year after.

References

Andrade, A., and R. Monte-Mor (1983) "Urbanização e custos numa economia em desenvolvimento." Mimeo, PNPE–IPEA.

Andrade, T., and R. Villela (1987) "Eficácia da institucionalização de regiões metropolitanas no Brasil: Análise da evolução dos serviços de saneamiento urbano." *Pesquisa e Planejamento Econômico* 17: 93–120.

Bhalla, A.S. (1971) "The role of services in employment expansion." In W. Galenson (ed.), *Essays on employment*, International Labour Office, 157–77.

—— (1973) "A disaggregative approach to employment in LDCs." *Journal of Development Studies* 10: 50–65.

Burle de Figueiredo, J.B. (1987) "Aspectos demográficos da política de desenvolvimento urbano, Rio de Janelro." Industrial Economics Institute.

Dubeux, C.B.S. (1994) "Pollution control program for Guanabara Bay." Mimeo, in *Proceedings of the Creeping Environmental Phenomena Workshop at the National Center of Atmospheric Research*, Boulder, Colorado, 7–9 February.

FEEMA [Fundação Estadual de Engenharia do Meio Ambiente] (1990) "Projeto de recuperação gradual do ecosistema da Baia da Guanabara, parte 1." Mimeo, Rio de Janeiro.

—— (1993) "Programa de saneamento básico da Baia da Guanabara. Análise ambiental." Rio de Janeiro.

JICA [Japan International Cooperation Agency] (1993) "Master plan of Guanabara Bay." Mimeo, Rio de Janeiro.

Lewis, O. (1968) "The culture of poverty." In D. Moynihan (ed.), *On understanding poverty*, Basic Books, 187–200.

Pastore, J., and A.O. Haller (1993) "O que está acontecendo com a mobilidade social no Brasil." In J.P. dos Reis Velloso and R. Cavalcanti de Albuquerque (eds.), *Pobreza e mobilidade social*, Livraria Nobel, São Paulo, 25–49.

Rizzieri, J., et al. (1979) "Costos comparativos de urbanização." Mimeo, FIPE-USP.

Rocha, S. (1988a) "Establecimento e comparação de linhas de pobreza para o Brasil." *IPEA Staff Papers* no. 153, Rio de Janeiro.

—— (1988b) "Linhas de pobreza as regiões metropolitanas na primeira metade da década de 80." *Proceedings of the National Association of Graduate Centres in Economics (ANPEC)* 4: 81–96.

—— (1990) "Caracterização da subpopulação pobre metropolitana nos anos 80." *Revista Brasileira de Economia* 44: 35–52.

—————— (1991) "Pobreza metropolitana e ciclos de curto prazo." *Boletim Conjuntural do IPEA* 12: 35–9.

Seroa da Motta, R., and A.P. Fernandes Mendes (1993) "Health costs associated with air pollution in Brazil." *IPEA Staff Papers* no. 332. Rio de Janeiro.

Sydenstricker, I. (ed.) (1993) *Guia sócio-econômico dos municípios do Estado do Rio de Janeiro*. Volume 1: *Região metropolitana*. Gráfica JB.

Tolosa, H.C. (1976) "Subutilização e mobilidade da mão de obra urbana." In J. Barat (ed.), *Política de desenvolvimento urbano*, IPEA–INPES, Rio de Janeiro, 23–78.

—————— (1978) "Causes of urban poverty in Brazil." *World Development* 6: 1087–1101.

—————— (1979) "Macroeconomics of Brazilian urbanization." *Brazilian Economic Studies* 1: 227–74.

—————— (1992) "Condicionantes da política urbana na década de 90." In *Perspectivas da Economia Brasileira 1992*, IPEA, 471–85.

World Bank (1979) *Brazil: Human Resources Special Report*. Washington DC.

—————— (1986) *Urban transport*. Washington DC.

10

São Paulo: A growth process full of contradictions

Milton Santos

The metropolitan region of São Paulo is a giant agglomeration consisting of 39 municipalities which together contain some 17 million people (figure 10.1). It is an economic powerhouse which contributes around 30 per cent of Brazil's gross national product. São Paulo's 2.1 million manufacturing workers make it the second largest industrial city in the world. They represent around one-third of the active population, a much higher proportion than that in any other large Brazilian city.[1]

Since the introduction of the motor car, urban expansion in São Paulo has followed a radial model. The radius of the built-up area did not exceed one kilometre until 1870; today, continuous urban development spreads 80 kilometres from east to west and 40 kilometres from north to south. Since 1980, the built-up area has been growing far more rapidly than the population (table 10.1). The city's land-use pattern has been strongly influenced by land speculation, which since the end of the last century, has ensured that the built-up area has expanded, leaving large areas of undeveloped space. This process has increased the price of serviced land and has helped accentuate social segregation.

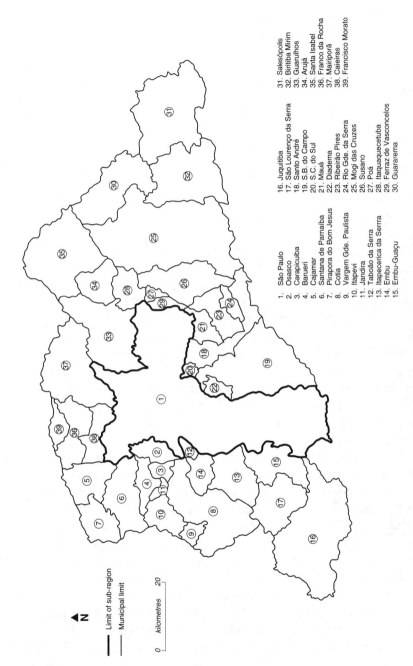

1. São Paulo
2. Osasco
3. Carapicuiba
4. Barueri
5. Cajamar
6. Santana de Parnaíba
7. Pirapora do Bom Jesus
8. Cotia
9. Vargem Gde. Paulista
10. Itapevi
11. Jandira
12. Taboão da Serra
13. Itapecerica da Serrra
14. Embu
15. Embu-Guaçu
16. Juquitiba
17. São Lourenço da Serra
18. Santo André
19. S.B. do Campo
20. S.C. do Sul
21. Mauá
22. Diadema
23. Ribeirão Pires
24. Rio Gde. da Serra
25. Mogi das Cruzes
26. Susano
27. Poá
28. Itaquaquecetuba
29. Ferraz de Vasconcelos
30. Guararema
31. Salesópolis
32. Biritiba Mirim
33. Guarulhos
34. Arujá
35. Santa Isabel
36. Franco da Rocha
37. Mairiporã
38. Caieiras
39. Francisco Morato

Limit of sub-region
Municipal limit

0   kilometres   20

Figure 10.1 **Metropolitan region of São Paulo: Administrative divisions**

225

Table 10.1 **Growth of metropolitan São Paulo**

Year	Population (million)	Growth rate (annual %)	Urban area (km^2)	Growth rate (annual %)
1930	1.0	–	130	–
1950	3.0	5.6	420	6.0
1965	6.5	5.3	550	1.8
1980	12.5	4.5	900	3.3
1987	14.2	1.8	1,523	7.8
1991	15.2	1.8	n.a.	n.a.
1994	16.0	1.8	n.a.	n.a.

Source: Santos, 1990.

Development of a metropolis

São Paulo began to grow rapidly during the last quarter of the nineteenth century. It developed on the basis of coffee production and the "Europeanization" of the urban hinterland. Modernization transformed the productive structure, the transport and communications systems, and the consumption structure of the region, changes reflected in the city's built environment. São Paulo and its region responded to every shift in material culture in the metropolitan countries, eagerly adopting every new innovation. Indeed, for a century, the adoption of one new invention after another was the basis of São Paulo's virtually uninterrupted economic growth. The process of modernization firmly entwined the fortunes of the city with those of its state.

Until the 1960s, Brazil lacked adequate modern transportation and there was no national market. São Paulo supplied the south and south-east, the only region of the country with a well-developed system of ports, railways, and roads. When the Brazilian "miracle," the construction of Brasília, and the opening of new roads into Amazonia finally unified the country, the São Paulo region benefited enormously. It became the undisputed economic centre of Brazil. Not only did its manufacturing and commercial activities thrive but it also developed into the country's main financial centre. Until 1960, finance had been mainly controlled from Rio de Janeiro, the headquarters of major public financial institutions such as the Central Bank and the National Bank for Economic Development. The transfer of these functions to Brasília and the integration of Brazil into a single market gave São Paulo the opportunity it needed to take over.

Between 1968 and 1984, São Paulo banks increased their share of the country's total bank deposits from 26 per cent to 42 per cent (Cordeiro, 1988: 158). By 1985, 33 per cent of Brazilian banks had their headquarters in the city. Many important banks moved their main offices from Rio de Janeiro to São Paulo; by 1989, 18 of the 23 foreign banks operating in Brazil had their principal Brazilian offices in the city, only five in Rio de Janeiro (Cordeiro, 1990). The growing financial clout of the city attracted other economic activities; for example, the headquarters of the FIAT holding company was located in São Paulo in 1990.

If Rio de Janeiro still maintains its superiority in the cultural world, with a major television complex and almost all cinema production, São Paulo increasingly controls the country's advertising business. In the early 1980s, its advertising billings were already higher than those of Rio, and by 1985 São Paulo companies controlled two-thirds of the billings. Today, São Paulo contains 60 per cent of the major agencies and nine of the eleven agencies with more than 250 employees. It is also now the country's major intellectual centre, with the largest university and research complex in Brazil and with a substantial proportion of the major scientific publishers.

Today, São Paulo is not only Brazil's dominant economic centre but has established itself as a major world city. In the process, it has begun to change its form. Without losing its industrial importance, it has become a centre of services and the indisputable hub of commercial decision-making. As industrial employment has begun to move out to nearby cities, São Paulo has been transforming itself into an informational complex. This is reflected in the growth of technical, scientific, and artistic employment in the city. From 205,000 workers in 1971, the total rose to 460,000 in 1981 and 760,000 in 1990 (National Household Survey, 1971, 1981, and 1990). Whereas the city's total workforce increased by 119 per cent between 1971 and 1990, the labour force in informational activities increased by 271 per cent; this sector's share of total employment expanded from 6.3 per cent to 10.4 per cent during the same period.

In the process, São Paulo's share of Brazil's gross national product has declined from 25 per cent in 1970 to 20 per cent in 1987. This decline is the result of its loss of manufacturing activity, which fell from 44 per cent in 1970 to 31 per cent in 1987 (table 10.2). Although total manufacturing employment has not actually fallen, employment in other parts of the State of São Paulo has been growing much more quickly (see next section).

227

Table 10.2 **Distribution of manufacturing industry in State of São Paulo, 1970–1987**

Area	1970	1975	1980	1987
Greater São Paulo	74.7	69.4	62.9	60.0
City of São Paulo	48.2	44.0	34.8	31.1
Other municipalities	26.5	25.4	28.1	28.9
Rest of state	25.3	30.6	37.1	40.0

Sources: Industrial censuses for 1970, 1975 and 1980; Fundação SEADE/Estado de São Paulo, 1992, vol. 3: 190.

São Paulo is now what Cordeiro (1988: 153) calls a "transitional metropolis," something completely different from an industrial city. Its functions and importance are no longer reflected in the mere flow of material goods, it now organizes those flows through its decision-making power and its control over information. São Paulo is therefore passing through its third phase of globalization. The first, based on commerce, began in the late nineteenth century and continued until the 1930s; the second, based on manufacturing, began in the 1930s and ended in the 1960s.

Metropolitan involution

During the 1980s, Brazil experienced an economic crisis. This crisis hit the large cities very hard but not all of the secondary cities. In the State of São Paulo, the smaller cities grew while the capital declined. This had a marked impact in terms of the spatial distribution of the state's gross internal product: in 1980 the São Paulo Metropolitan Area (SPMA) contributed 60 per cent of the state's income, while eight years later its share had fallen to 41 per cent (EMPLASA, 1980 and 1988).

Shifts in the location of industry were an important ingredient in this trend (table 10.2). Between 1980 and 1989, industrial employment grew by only 3 per cent in Greater São Paulo and by 18 per cent outside (Fundação SEADE/Governo do Estado de São Paulo, 1992: 103). Whereas value added in cities with less than 50,000 inhabitants grew by 2 per cent between 1980 and 1988, value added fell by 2 per cent in those with between 50,000 and 250,000 people, 11 per cent in those between 250,000 and one million, and 21 per cent in cities with over a million (*O Estado de São Paulo*, 28 January 1990). Average productivity and profitability were both lower in São Paulo than in many smaller cities (Azzoni, 1988). In 1980, profitability (measured in terms of value added minus labour costs) was higher in Baurú, Campinas, Vale do Paraíba, São José dos Campos, Taubaté, and Ribeirão Preto than in Greater São Paulo. Since value added per worker was much higher in the smaller cities, Greater São Paulo's share of industrial employment fell less rapidly. Between 1980 and 1988, the number of industrial workers in Greater São Paulo fell from 64 per cent to 62 per cent of the total workforce (*Folha de São Paulo*, 27 November 1989).

The locational shift from Greater São Paulo was not confined to industrial activity. Whereas total employment in the metropolitan area increased by 13 per cent between 1980 and 1989, in the interior it grew by 19 per cent. The numbers of public workers grew by 27 per cent in the metropolitan area and by 73 per cent outside it (Fundação SEADE/Governo de Estado do São Paulo, 1992: 103). Only employment in financial services and the communications sector continued to grow more rapidly in the state's major city (Dedecca and Montagner, 1992).

The changes in location were all part of the transformation of space and society in the State of São Paulo. Modernization and a shift to a more technically and scientifically based economy had both encouraged this change.

Quality of life in the State of São Paulo

Thanks to industrial deconcentration, rising public-sector employment, the modernization of agriculture, and the introduction of the Development Programme for Intermediate Cities, the quality of life improved markedly in the interior of the state. Rates of infant mortality fell, more and more households were linked to the water and electricity networks, and the provision of hospital beds in smaller cities improved.

Indeed, by the 1980s, several indicators showed that the quality of life in the metropolitan area was worse than in the intermediate cities. In 1985, life expectancy was one year lower in Greater São Paulo and there was a vast difference in infant mortality rates: 31 babies out of every thousand died in the intermediate cities compared to 54 in the metropolitan area (Carvalho Ferreira, 1989). Literacy rates also showed marked differences; whereas 16 per cent could not read or write in the intermediate cities in 1982, the proportion in Greater São Paulo was 20 per cent.

The empirical evidence suggests that a process of "metropolitan involution" was operating. So many poor people moved to São Paulo that the city could not provide for them. The labour market became segmented between highly skilled and well-paid jobs and large numbers of unskilled and poorly remunerated activities. This was not a process of "urban ruralization," because recent migrants from the countryside did not cling on to their rural values and in any case many of the poor migrants came from urban areas. It was a sign that so-called urban civilization was extending its tentacles throughout Brazilian society; the problem was that the great economic metropolis could not cope.

Metropolitan problems

In the late 1960s and throughout the 1970s, São Paulo benefited from the rapid expansion of the Brazilian economy. The city became enormously richer and the size of its middle class increased dramatically. At the same time, poverty and the numbers of people living in poverty worsened. In 1990, São Paulo contained 10 per cent of Brazil's population and 11 per cent of its labour force, but also 20 per cent of persons earning more than 10 times the minimum salary. But, although it had a higher proportion of high-income people than any other Brazilian city – 48,000 families were earning more than US$100,000 per annum – vast numbers earned very little. Indeed, in 1990, 850,000 people earned less than the minimum wage. Unfortunately, the living conditions of the very poor have not been improving. Rather, the 1980s and early 1990s saw a deterioration in conditions in the metropolitan area: employment, housing, transport, education, health, and crime all got worse.

Employment and unemployment

Trends in employment and unemployment in Greater São Paulo between 1985 and 1993 reflect those in Brazil as a whole (table 10.3). After the difficulties of the early 1980s, rates of unemployment had fallen by the end of the decade, only to rise rapidly during the 1990s. By 1992, there were more than 1.2 million unemployed people in the city, 16 per cent of the economically active population. In addition, there were strong signs of a growth in casual forms of employment. The proportion of the labour force that was self-employed rose from 16 per cent in 1986 to 21 per cent in 1993. The proportion that was working without a work permit (*carteira assinada*) rose from a mini-

Table 10.3 **Employment and unemployment in Greater São Paulo, 1985–1993**

Year	Economically active population (000s)	Unemployed (000s)	Unemployment rate (%)
1985	6,415	795	12.4
1986	6,665	647	9.7
1987	6,871	666	9.7
1988	6,933	652	9.4
1989	7,100	596	8.4
1990	7,285	809	11.1
1991	7,553	899	11.9
1992	7,784	1,253	16.1
1993[a]	7,948	1,224	15.4

Source: Fundação SEADE, 1993.
a. Estimate for July.

mum of 19 per cent in 1989 to 23 per cent in January 1993 (Fundação SEADE, 1991 and 1993). The employment situation in Greater São Paulo has undoubtedly deteriorated.

The unemployment problem is far worse in the periphery than in the municipality of São Paulo. The city's Blacks are also much more likely to be unemployed than other heads of household (Fundação SEADE, 1991 and 1993). Similarly, there are large numbers of young people engaged in casual forms of employment; in 1985, one in three workers under 18 years of age was employed without a work certificate. Nevertheless, it is not only the poor who are suffering; employment difficulties are also affecting skilled workers. For example, unemployment among workers with previous salaried work experience rose from 10 per cent in 1988 to 16 per cent in 1993 (Fundação SEADE, 1991).

Housing conditions

The housing situation is a visual reflection of what is happening in the rest of São Paulo society. Recent estimates refer to a housing deficit of more than one million units in a metropolitan area with 3.9 million homes. Ten thousand people live on the streets. In 1992, two-thirds of all homes fell into some category of low-quality shelter (*favela* houses built of flimsy materials, households living in overcrowded conditions, etc.). In 1991, 28 per cent of homes lacked a connection to the water system, and 50 per cent were not linked to the sewerage system (figure 10.2).

231

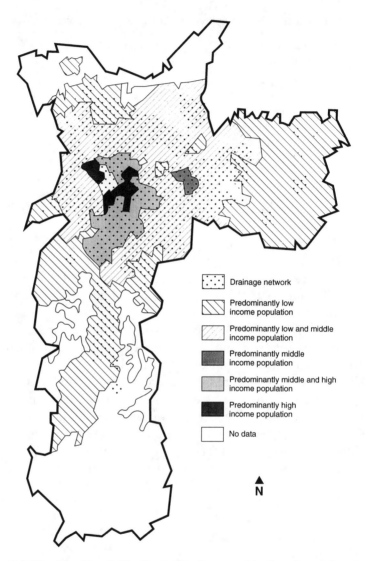

Figure 10.2 **Municipality of São Paulo: Drainage network and social segregation, 1987 (Source: PMSP, 1990)**

Around 70 per cent of all homes have been built through self-help methods and the proportion rises to 90 per cent in some peripheral municipalities (Santos, 1990: 43). A significant number of these homes offer their inhabitants very poor shelter. The proliferation of *favelas* is a comparatively new phenomenon in São Paulo: in 1973, there were only 73,000 *favelados*, today there are 1.1 million. In 1991, 11.3 per cent of the population lived in this form of housing, compared to only 1.1 per cent in 1973 (Veras and Taschner, 1992). There are now 1,600 *favelas* in the city, the largest, Héliopolis, accommodating some 50,000 people.

The pressure on some people to build their own home has led to a considerable shift in the tenure structure of the city. Whereas 41 per cent of families rented homes in 1972, the figure in 1990 was only 28 per cent. Nevertheless, the *cortiços* still represent a principal form of shelter available to the poor. Even if the proportion of families living in rental accommodation is in decline, the absolute numbers of tenants has been increasing rapidly, from 125,000 people in 1975 to 500,000 in 1982 and three million today. Many of the 88,000 *cortiços* in existence in 1987 were in a very bad state of repair (Pinheiro, 1992). In a survey in the municipality of São Paulo in 1986, only 19 per cent of homes had their own kitchen and fewer than 6 per cent their own tap. In four-fifths of the *cortiços* surveyed, an average of 2.6 people lived in every room, the rooms varying in size from 8 to 15 square metres.

The growth of rental accommodation in the central areas is due to the deteriorating employment situation and the growing importance of casual forms of work. Since the central areas contain the best locations for casual work and the real cost of transportation has been rising rapidly, many families have been forced into this kind of accommodation.

Transportation

Transportation is another serious problem in São Paulo. Its quality is poor, its services are not expanding sufficiently rapidly, and fares are rising faster than the incomes of the poor. One consequence is that the number of journeys per person has been diminishing over time. In 1987, every inhabitant made 1.15 journeys per day compared to 1.53 ten years earlier. The change has affected passengers whatever their income. Using education as an income indicator, the average daily journeys made by those with university education fell from 3.26 in 1977 to 2.81 in 1987; for those with primary education the average fell from 0.86 to 0.58. The greater percentage fall in average journeys for the latter group is symptomatic of the deterioration in public transport facilities. Indeed, the numbers of journeys on public transport diminished slightly between 1987 and 1991 despite the rise in the metropolitan region's total population. In the municipality of São

Paulo, the number of bus journeys fell by 4 per cent between 1992 and 1993, the number of buses in operation by 12 per cent.

Various efforts have been made in recent years to improve the service and the current municipal administration is planning to privatize public transport services in the next two years. The municipality will remain in charge of overall coordination and technological development.

Health

The quality of health care in the city is also deteriorating. Although the number of doctors has been increasing, the urban population has been growing faster. This does not just represent a failure to keep up with population increase, for the numbers of hospital beds and of hospital ancillary staff fell absolutely between 1977 and 1987 (Santos, 1992: 33). Hospital-bed occupancy rates have fallen to only 73 per cent, and many hospitals have been closing wards. No doubt the occupancy problem is accentuated by the distribution of hospital facilities: two-thirds of all hospitals are located in the central areas and 40 of the 54 public hospitals are found in middle-class neighbourhoods (Fundação SEADE, 1993).

Education

The educational system is also in dire straits. In the lower grades, the number of students is growing so quickly that the system cannot cope. Matriculation into primary schools rose annually by 3.5 per cent in eleven years after 1980; a total of 3.1 million children registered in 1991 (Fundação SEADE, 1993). At the primary level, the number of private pupils is expanding fast, although at present that is not true of secondary education. The problems of secondary education are perhaps best reflected in the fact that 11 per cent of 17-year-olds are neither in work nor in education.

Pollution

Water pollution is getting worse despite official efforts to protect the city's water sources. Recent legislation, intended to limit urban growth in the areas near the reservoirs, has failed (figure 10.3). Indeed, a significant share of urban expansion has occurred precisely in those areas, invasion settlements and illegal subdivisions having

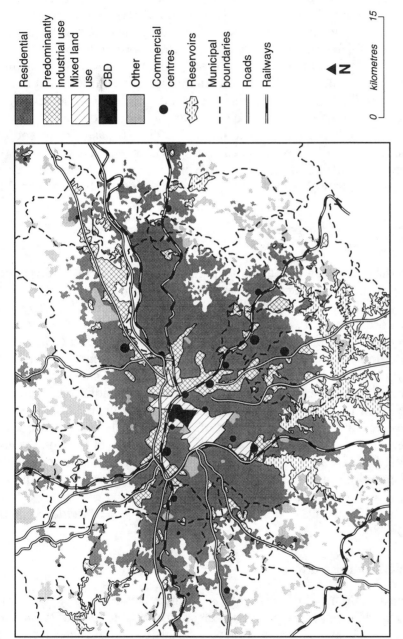

Figure 10.3 **Metropolitan São Paulo: Land use and major sub-centres, 1993 (Source: EMPLASA, 1993)**

Residential

Predominantly industrial use

Mixed land use

CBD

Other

● Commercial centres

Reservoirs

Municipal boundaries

Roads

Railways

N

0   *kilometres*   15

occupied large areas of protected land. Rising levels of pollution in the reservoirs have posed major problems for the Environmental Technology and Sanitation Company (CETESB).

At least, some success has been achieved against the major air polluters, CETESB having convinced the 162 major polluters (responsible for 96 per cent of particulate emissions) to follow their recommended procedures. Even so, recommended air pollution levels are being exceeded in terms of suspended dust and smoke levels. Prescribed maxima for levels of ozone, carbon monoxide, and sulphur dioxide are also regularly exceeded and CETESB has been forced to introduce special measures during the winter, when the effects of temperature inversions are at their worst. The city's 4.5 million cars are a particular problem with respect to air pollution, especially in the central areas.

Crime

There has been a sharp and worrying rise in the crime rate. Recorded crimes against the person increased annually by 7 per cent over a twenty-year period, from 41,000 in 1973 to 162,000 in 1991. Property crime rose even more quickly, with an annual increase of 9.3 per cent during the same period (Pastore et al., 1991: 69; Fundação SEADE/Estado de São Paulo, 1992).[2] Crime has been increasing in all parts of the city but especially in the central area. The likely causes are rising unemployment, increasing levels of drug use, deterioration in family values, and the rising numbers of children living in the street (often themselves the victims of crimes of violence). The perpetrators of crime are certainly not confined to the lower ranks of society: during the last three years between 5 and 10 per cent of recorded criminals came from the middle class. The police themselves are also committing more crimes: deaths at the hands of the police rose from 165 in 1983 to 1,350 in 1992 (Pinheiro, 1991: 95; *Folha de São Paulo*, 31 May 1993).

Public administration

As the problems of the metropolis are increasing, the local authorities are facing greater problems in confronting them. In 1974, the federal government created new administrative agencies for the country's nine metropolitan areas. It was hoped that these new agencies would be much less bureaucratic than the existing local government structures. The new agency for São Paulo, EMPLASA (the Metropolitan Agency for Greater São Paulo), was effective but it took over responsibility only for transportation and for management of the region's water resources. This left the municipalities to address all the other serious problems, with only limited help from the state and federal governments.

The 39 municipalities which make up the metropolitan region receive half of their revenues from higher levels of government (in 1990, 5.6 per cent from the federal government and 45.1 per cent from the state government) and generate the rest themselves. The municipal financial situation has deteriorated recently, owing to the economic recession and the increasing numbers of under- and unemployed workers. The federal government transfers part of its income tax and industrial value-added taxes into a Participation Fund. This fund, which accounts for 17 per cent of federal revenues, is divided between the municipalities on a per capita basis. The smaller municipalities gain most of their revenues from this source; larger authorities are better able to supplement this source of income from their own tax base. The State of São Paulo transfers funds to the municipalities from its taxes on commerce, services, and vehicle ownership. The municipalities' own revenues are derived from taxes on land and property, property transactions, sales of petroleum and other lubricants, and professional services. In 1990, the tax on services (ISS) generated 60 per cent of the municipal tax revenue in the metropolitan region; the taxes on land and property a further 19 per cent (EMPLASA, 1992). The other significant source of revenue in the past has been foreign loans, a fact reflected in the current cost of interest payments, which absorbed 6 per cent of the budget in 1990 (EMPLASA, 1992).

Municipal expenditures have been growing fast in the area of public works and falling in the social sectors. This has been particularly marked since the beginning of *abertura*, when political attention focused on transport subsidies and on the maintainance and renovation of roads. Whereas the budget for education, health, and housing fell by US$600 million between 1993 and 1994, the cost of building a tunnel under the River Pinheiros raised the road budget by 185 millions. The latter project is likely to cost the municipality of São Paulo US$3 billion over the next few years and a major question must be asked about the social benefits to be derived from this scheme.

The future

Between 1970 and 1980, 4.6 million people were added to the metropolitan population, 2.3 million of them as migrants. During the same period, the population of Rio de Janeiro increased by "only" 2.1 million people and the number of migrants into the whole of Amazonia totalled only 2 million. Seventeen per cent of all migrants in the country – 40 per cent of all the migrants who moved to the nine metropolitan regions – moved to São Paulo.

Fortunately, the pace of growth slowed during the 1980s and the forecast of 19 million inhabitants by 1990 was well wide of the mark. A halving of the annual growth rate of some 250,000 people per annum meant that the city had only 15.2 million inhabitants in 1991. Annual growth in the 1980s had averaged 1.9 per cent compared to 4.5 per cent in the 1970s.

One reason for this slowing in growth is the dramatic fall in fertility in the country. In the early 1950s, the average woman bore 6.2 children in her lifetime, in the early 1980s only 3.5. Brazil's population growth rate fell from 3.7 per cent per annum in the 1970s to 1.9 per cent during the 1980s. A further reason for the marked slowing in São Paulo's population increase is the changing pattern of migration. During the 1980s, there was an important reversal in the long-term trend, the metropolitan area suffering a net loss in the numbers of people moving into and out of the city (Perillo and Aranha, 1992). In the 1970s, the metropolitan area gained 2.3 million people through migration; between 1980 and 1991, it lost 430,000.[3] By contrast, net migration to the rest of the state increased by 838,000 in the 1980s compared to 751,000 in the 1970s. People have turned their backs on the city of São Paulo.

The change can be explained by the decentralization of manufacturing and service activity to areas beyond the metropolitan region. This trend is very worrying at a time of increasing social needs, because it promises to cut the tax revenues of the city authorities. Local government can no longer rely on the federal budget, which is likely to decline in real terms, nor on foreign loans. The difficulties of providing infrastructure in the 1970s were addressed with the help of loans from the World Bank and the Inter-American Bank, but this option is much less open to the authorities today. A critical issue today, therefore, is how to provide infrastructure and services to satisfy the ever-increasing demands of both industrial and residential users in an environment of declining resources. The prospects for social spending do not look good.

Even if the authorities are helped by the slower rate of demographic growth, the city's population will continue to grow. It will take an enormous effort to address the needs of these additional people as well as those of the people who were neglected during the lost decade of the 1980s. Such an effort will be helped if the economy begins to grow once again, but, even if it does, one major policy change is vital: more tax resources must be shifted from the State of São Paulo and from the nation to the municipal authorities. Without larger fiscal transfers the prospects for the city look bleak.

Notes

1. Pôrto Alegre has 26 per cent of its labour force in manufacturing and Curitiba 18 per cent; in other major Brazilian cities the percentage is rather less.
2. Crime rates are under-recorded because not every victim reports a crime, nor do the police bother recording every crime that is reported to them.
3. Not surprisingly, there was a large net outflow of people from the municipality of São Paulo. Whereas it gained 1.14 million people in the 1970s, it lost 900,000 during the 1980s.

References

Azzoni, C.A. (1988) "Rentabilidade da indústria no interior de São Paulo." *Folha de São Paulo*, 21 March.

Carvalho Ferreira, C.E. (1989) "Mortalidade infantil: a manifestação mais cruel das desigualdades sociais." *São Paulo em Perspectiva* 3: 24–9.

Cordeiro, H.K. (1988) "Os principais pontos de contrôle da economia transnacional no espaço brasileiro." *Boletim de Geografia Teorética* 16–17: 153–96.

Cordeiro, H.K., and D.A. Bovo (1990) "A modernidade do espaço brasileiro através da rede nacional do telex." *Revista Brasileira de Geografia* 52: 107–55.

Dedecca, C.S., and P. Montagner (1992) "Crise econômica e desempenho do terciário." *São Paulo em Perspectiva* 6: 2–15.

EMPLASA [Empresa Metropolitana de Planejamento da Grande São Paulo] (1980) *Sumario de dados da Grande São Paulo*. São Paulo.

—— (1988) *Sumario de dados da Grande São Paulo*. São Paulo.

—— (1992) *Sumario de dados da Grande São Paulo*. São Paulo.

Ferreira, C.E.C. (1990) "Uma comparação entre a Grande São Paulo e o Interior do Estado." *Conjuntura Demográfica* 9.

Fundação SEADE (1991) *Anuário Estatístico do Estado de São Paulo 1991*. São Paulo.

—— (1993) *Anuário Estatístico do Estado de São Paulo 1993*. São Paulo.

Fundação SEADE/Governo do Estado de São Paulo (1992) *São Paulo no limiar do século XXI*. São Paulo.

Pastore, J., et al. (1991) *Crime e violência urbana*. Instituto de Pesquisas Econômicas, Universidade de São Paulo.

Perillo, S.R., and V.J. Aranha (1992) "Tendências recentes na migraçao." *São Paulo en perspectiva* 6: 109–15.

Pinheiro, P.S. (1991) "Violencia fatal: Conflitos policiais em São Paulo." *Revista da Universidade de São Paulo*.

—— (1992) *São Paulo: People on the margin and civil society*. Paper given at the Conference on the City and the Law, New York City University, 10–11 September.

PMSP [Prefeitura do Municipio de São Paulo] (1990) *São Paulo crise e mundança*. São Paulo: Editora Brasiliense (second edition).

Santos, M. (1990) *São Paulo. Metrópole corporativa fragmentada*. Editora Nobel.

Santos, G.F. dos (1992) "A capacidade productiva da rede de assistência médica." *São Paulo em perspectiva* 6: 29–37.

Veras, M., and S.P. Taschner (1992) "Evolução e mudanças nas favelas paulistanas." Mimeo, São Paulo.

11

Santa Fé de Bogotá: A Latin American special case?

Alan Gilbert

Introduction

Bogotá[1] is a very unusual Latin American capital. First, it is not a primate city; it does not dominate Colombia in the way that Buenos Aires overshadows Argentina or Lima controls Peru. Second, during the 1980s, Bogotá's population continued to grow rapidly. Third, Bogotá suffered little from the economic recession and debt crisis of the 1980s. Good national management kept the level of external debt down, and the discovery of new export resources, such as coal and petroleum, attracted foreign capital to Colombia and helped to maintain a thoroughly respectable rate of economic growth.[2] Fourth, Bogotá's economy does not seem to have suffered from the government's policy since 1986 of opening up the national economy to foreign competition. Even if Bogotá is not a major export centre, it has lost few jobs because of trade liberalization; its experience is very different from that of, say, Mexico City. Finally, Bogotá is atypical of metropolitan Latin America in so far as most *bogotanos* seem to have improved the quality of their lives in recent decades. The numbers of people living in poverty has declined relatively, the result of a buoyant national economy and Bogotá's central role in Colombian economic life.

At the same time, Bogotá also suffers from many problems similar to those faced in other Latin American cities. Providing jobs for a rapidly expanding labour force is a critical issue, even if the level of unemployment is currently very low. Although personal incomes are not actually falling, far too many *bogotanos* live in poverty. Malnutrition and poor health are rife and too many families live in overcrowded conditions or in homes lacking adequate services. Bogotá suffers badly from traffic congestion, a situation aggravated by a poor public transport system. Environmental problems are also serious and most forms of pollution are getting worse.

Population and demographic structure

Bogotá was founded by the Spanish in 1538. They chose a good spot to found a city, in a rich agricultural area with plenty of water and space in which to expand. Of course, its elevated location far from the Caribbean and Pacific coasts, together with the mountainous terrain of western Colombia, impeded efforts to control the national territory. Bogotá long remained a *primus inter pares*, never becoming a "primate" city (Gilbert, 1994; Jaramillo and Cuervo, 1987).

Bogotá has become a large city only in the last fifty years; in 1938, it had only 300,000 or so inhabitants. It began to expand rapidly when falling rural death rates and increasing levels of rural violence, superimposed on an inequitable distribution of land, encouraged cityward migration. With economic growth creating jobs in Bogotá, migrants began to arrive in large numbers. During the 1940s and 1950s, the city was growing annually at over 5 per cent; in the 1960s and 1970s, at almost 7 per cent (table 11.1). During the 1980s, the pace of growth slowed, but, unlike most of metropolitan Latin America (see chapter 2), the city continued to grow relatively quickly.

Migration was the key element in urban growth from the 1930s until the late 1960s. Migrants arrived from all over Colombia, but principally from the neighbouring departments of Cundinamarca, Boyacá, and Tolima (Gilbert and Ward, 1986; Castañeda, 1993). More women moved to the city than men: in 1951, Bogotá had 100 women to every 77 men in the 20–24 year age group (Alcaldía Mayor de Bogotá and CCB, 1987: 49).[3]

In recent years, natural increase has contributed more to Bogotá's

Table 11.1 **Bogotá: Population growth**

Year	Population (000s)	Annual growth (%)	Bogota/next three largest cities[b]
1905	100		0.80
1918	144	2.8	0.76
1938	356	4.6	0.84
1951	715	5.5	0.65
1964	1,697[a]	6.9	0.74
1973	2,855[a]	7.6	0.89
1985	4,268[a]	3.4	0.96
1993[c]	6,498[a]	5.4	1.27
1993	5,898[a]	4.1	1.16

Sources: Gilbert, 1978; population censuses.

a. Including Soacha.

b. Medellín (including Bello, Envigado, and Itagüí), Cali (including Yumbo), and Barranquilla (including Soledad).

c. The National Planning Department has decided that the population of Bogotá was probably overestimated in the 1993 census and has reduced it by 600,000. The census results are currently being recalculated. Both figures have been included in the table.

growth than migration. In the first half of the 1970s, migration generated approximately half of Bogotá's growth, but, by the first half of the 1990s, only 22 per cent (Yepes and Bosoni, 1993: 52).[4] This change was not due to any slowing in the number of migrants coming to the city: 74,000 arrived in 1992 compared to 57,000 in 1982. It was mainly a consequence of the age structure of Bogotá: despite a rapid decline in age-specific fertility rates, there were more young adults to bear children.

Bogotá's population also expanded because life expectancy rose significantly. In the early 1970s, the average *bogotano* lived for 66 years, by the early 1990s for 71 years. Greater longevity was helped by a spectacular fall in infant mortality, from 50 per 1,000 live births in the first half of the 1970s to 23 in the the early 1990s.

Declining fertility and increased life expectancy has had a marked effect on the city's age structure. The population under 15 fell from 42 per cent of the total in 1964 to 31 per cent in 1985 (table 11.2). While the relative decline in the number of children has reduced demands on the education system, it has increased the demand for jobs. If Bogotá's population is getting older, there are still very few people over 60 years of age; that is a difficulty to be faced in the future.

Table 11.2 **Bogotá: Age structure, 1951–1995**

Year	0–14 years	15–44 years	45–64 years	65+ years
1951	34.8	52.3	10.5	2.4
1964	42.1	46.1	9.6	2.2
1973	38.5	49.4	9.7	2.4
1985	31.3	54.0	11.5	3.3
1995	30.1	———— 65.9 ————		4.1

Sources: Alcaldía Mayor de Bogotá and Cámara de Comercio de Bogotá, 1987: 47; for 1995, Yepes and Bosoni, 1993: 53.

Table 11.3 **Manufacturing employment in Colombia's major cities, 1945–1992 (thousands of jobs)**

City	1945	1958	1980	1992
Bogotá	22.6	60.1	148.1	193.3
Medellín	30.4	52.0	122.9	116.6
Cali	10.0	26.2	61.1	69.8
Barranquilla	14.3	23.2	40.0	29.4

Sources: Jaramillo and Cuervo, 1987: 53; ANDI, 1994.

Bogotá's national role

Bogotá has never managed to dominate the Colombian economy, always fighting for supremacy against powerful regional rivals. The history of industrial development in Colombia reflects this rivalry clearly. At the turn of the century, Medellín was the country's largest manufacturing centre. It still retained that position in 1945, when it had one-third more industrial jobs than Bogotá (table 11.3). It was only when import substitution became national policy in the 1950s that Bogotá managed to overtake its great rival. Thenceforth, the capital's larger market and its privileged access to government and political decision-making began to count in its favour (Gilbert, 1975). By 1958, Bogotá had more manufacturing jobs than Medellín and its dominance continued to increase over the years. Even so, Colombia's industry is still highly regionalized (table 11.3).

In recent years, Colombia's economy has become more centralized. Between 1960 and 1985, Bogotá increased its share of the gross domestic product from 15 to 25 per cent. In 1993, the head offices of 26 major banks were located in Bogotá, compared with only five in other Colombian cities (*Revista del Banco de la República*, June 1993).

Table 11.4 **Bogotá's gross regional product, 1989**

Sector	Percentage
Agriculture	0.3
Mining	0.2
Manufacturing	24.9
Electricity, gas, and water	0.9
Construction	4.2
Commerce	9.6
Transport and communications	10.2
Banks, insurance, and productive services	12.8
Rents	12.3
Personal services	10.2
Government services	15.1
Domestic services	0.5
Total	**101.2**[a]

Source: DANE, 1992.

a. Does not sum to 100 per cent because imputed bank services and taxes on imports have not been included.

In 1992, it provided work for 34 per cent of the country's manufacturing employees; in 1988, 43 per cent of all students in higher education were studying in Bogotá. In 1993, Bogotá's population at last exceeded the sum of the populations of the next three cities (table 11.1).

The economy

Manufacturing generates around one-quarter of Bogotá's gross urban product (table 11.4). The city has fewer manufacturing workers per capita than Medellín but a better balanced industrial sector. Its strength lies in the printing, metals, transport, chemicals, and plastics sectors (ANDI, 1994). Most production is for the domestic market; manufacturing in Bogotá has never generated much in the way of industrial exports.

Government is a vital component in the Bogotá economy, contributing 15 per cent of the gross domestic product in 1989. Some 34,000 government employees worked in the city in 1987, almost one-third of the national total (López, 1990: 37). Financial services constitute the city's third most important generator of value added and, along with construction, constituted one of the most dynamic elements in Bogotá's growth during the 1980s.

245

Bogotá's economic future is uncertain but hardly problematic. The city's economy was built, of course, during a period when the trade regime was highly protective. Since 1986, the government has been gradually opening up the national economy, a process that was accelerated in 1990 (DNP, 1991). The question is whether Bogotá can cope with freer trade and with newly competitive labour and financial markets. As the head of the Chamber of Commerce recently put it: "Bogotá, the capital of protectionism, now has to overcome various difficulties if it wants to become the capital of the opening" (Fernández de Soto, 1994: 44).

The major worry for Bogotá is that it currently generates very little in the way of exports. In 1991, the city produced only US$188 of exports per capita.[5] To judge from the sales of the city's 100 largest exporters in 1992, Bogotá's major exports are flowers (41 per cent), emeralds (29 per cent), agricultural products (12 per cent), leather goods (7 per cent), and clothing (5 per cent) (Pineda et al., 1993). Bogotá clearly has problems in exporting manufactures because of its location. The only foreign market that can be reached easily by road is that of Venezuela. Between 1990 and 1994, trade liberalization trebled Colombia's trade with its neighbour but further expansion will be hindered by the current plight of the Venezuelan economy. Since most of Bogotá's exports go by air, its international competitiveness is not helped by the limited size of its airport; El Dorado desperately needs a second runway.

Of course, optimism about Bogotá's economic future is greatly helped by the healthy state of the Colombian economy. During the early 1990s, *apertura* led to the repatriation of large sums of Colombian capital, and the discovery of new mineral resources is attracting large amounts of foreign investment. Bogotá's strengths in producer services, higher education, research, and commerce mean that it is bound to benefit from any growth in the national economy. Reforms are needed if the city is to maintain its current pace of economic growth, but it hardly faces an insurmountable challenge.

Employment

Where Bogotá does face a serious problem is in providing work for its rapidly growing labour force. The working-age population grew from 2.4 million in 1976 to 4.8 million in 1995 and the economically active population more than doubled from 1.2 million to 3.0 million. The latter grew so quickly because of a substantial rise in the labour

Table 11.5 **Employment and unemployment, 1981–1995**

Year[a]	Global participation rate	Gross participation rate	Unemployment
1981	38.5	52.2	5.8
1982	40.1	54.3	8.4
1983	40.2	54.1	7.9
1984	42.9	57.7	12.6
1985	44.5	59.6	13.4
1986	45.1	60.0	14.3
1987	46.4	61.1	13.0
1988	45.9	60.7	12.1
1989	45.4	59.6	9.7
1990	44.1	59.7	7.9
1991	46.5	61.8	9.2
1992	47.0	60.9[b]	8.4
1993	46.6	61.9[b]	7.3
1994	47.5	n.a.	8.1
1995	47.3	62.5	6.5

Sources: DANE, 1991; *Boletín de Estadística* 491 (1994); *Revista del Banco de la República*, October 1995.
a. March of each year.
b. Annual averages.

participation rate (table 11.5). Labour participation rates rose across all age groups with the gross participation rate (economically active population as a proportion of working-age population) rising from 51 per cent in 1976 to 62 per cent in 1993 (DANE, 1991). But the really significant change was among women. Their participation rate rose from 36 per cent in 1976 to 50 per cent in 1995 compared with a relatively small rise in the male rate, from 69 to 77 per cent (Gómez and Pérez, n.d.: 11). In 1995, women made up 42 per cent of Bogotá's work force.

Despite such rapid growth, the quality of the labour force improved. In 1976, only 14 per cent of the labour force had received any university education; fifteen years later the proportion had risen to 22 per cent. The proportion of workers with only primary-school education fell from 47 per cent of the total to 29 per cent during the same period.

Unemployment, which has never been as severe as in Medellín or in the major Caribbean cities, actually fell during the 1990s.[6] In 1995, 7.0 per cent were out of work compared with an average of 11.5 per cent during the 1980s.[7] The reason why unemployment has remained low is that increasing numbers of workers have been employed in

247

Table 11.6 **Bogotá: Formal and informal employment by sector, 1990**

Sector	Informal workers[a]		Formal workers	
	Number	%	Number	%
Agriculture	10,678	1.3	15,144	1.7
Mining	1,382	0.2	10,317	1.1
Manufacturing	174,725	20.8	238,015	26.1
Electricity, gas, and water	232	0.0	7,428	0.8
Construction	70,140	8.3	47,721	5.2
Commerce	266,081	31.9	140,886	15.5
Transport and communications	49,036	5.8	58,392	6.4
Banks, insurance, and productive services	30,916	3.7	130,606	14.3
Services	236,482	28.1	263,069	28.9
Total	**841,672**	**100.0**	**911,578**	**100.0**

Source: Gómez and Pérez, n.d.: 160.

a. Informal-sector workers include those employed in domestic service, family employment, self-employed who are neither professionals nor technicians, and employees in companies with less than 10 workers.

poorly remunerated work. Much of this work is in the so-called informal sector, mainly concentrated in commerce, construction, services, and manufacturing; indeed, employment in the commerce and construction sectors is dominated by informal workers (table 11.6). Between 1976 and 1990, the proportion of workers earning less than twice the minimum salary rose from 50 to 58 per cent (Gómez and Pérez, n.d.: 81). Even if the number of domestic servants decreased as a proportion of the Bogotá workforce from 10 per cent in 1976 to 5 per cent in 1991, signifying some improvement in the employment situation, the so-called informal sector was growing: it expanded from 48 per cent to 52 per cent between 1990 and 1992 alone (ibid.: 161).

Poverty and social indicators

Over the last two or three decades, the quality of life in Bogotá has undoubtedly improved. Life expectancy rose by five years between the early 1970s and the early 1990s and the infant mortality rate fell from 50 per thousand live births in 1971 to 22 in 1993 (Rinaudo et al., 1994: 28). The proportion of homes built out of flimsy materials fell from 7 per cent in 1973 to 3 per cent in 1993. Per capita incomes have been rising, and between 1971 and 1993 the city's gross domestic product rose at an annual rate of 2.2 per cent. Poverty has also been falling, with the proportion of *bogotanos* living in poverty declining from 57 per cent in 1973 to 17 per cent in 1991, and of those living in extreme need from 26 to 4 per cent (Londoño de la Cuesta, 1992: 15).

Bogotá has much less poverty than most other Colombian cities. In 1984–85, household expenditure showed that while 18 per cent of *bogotanos* were living below the poverty line, the equivalent figures for 13 other major cities ranged from a low of 22 per cent in Bucaramanga to 40 per cent in Montería (Muñoz, 1991: 286). Since 1980, most *bogotanos* have fared much better than the inhabitants of Lima, Mexico City, or Rio de Janeiro. Nevertheless, far too many people live in poverty. Some 800,000 people lack basic needs and 200,000 live in misery (Londoño de la Cuesta, 1992: 15).[8] Bogotá is also a very unequal city; in 1985, the poorest quintile received only 4 per cent of the city's income, the top decile 37 per cent (López, 1990: 41). There is little sign that the distribution of income has improved over time. Escobar (n.d.) was unable to show whether the distribution of income in the city had improved or deteriorated between 1985 and 1991, a disturbing finding in a city which has a higher level of inequality than that found in the country's other major cities.

The shape of the city

Bogotá's physical area increased from 900 hectares in 1900 to more than 30,000 hectares today (Gilbert, 1978; Pineda and Jiménez, 1990). The pace of urban growth accelerated with the development of motorized transport and particularly when private car ownership exploded in the 1970s. Gradually, the urban area spilled across Bogotá's administrative boundaries. In 1954, the difficulty this posed for good management was resolved when six municipalities – Bosa, Engativa, Fontibón, Suba, Usaquén, and Usme – were absorbed into the Special District. Since then, the city has again spread beyond its boundaries (figure 11.1). It began to encroach into Soacha in the 1960s and is now absorbing substantial parts of Cajicá, Chía, Cota, and Mosquera (Forero et al., 1995).

The organization of space within the city has changed markedly. Employment has become much more decentralized and many professionals have moved their offices north from the traditional city centre. Major newspapers, such as *El Tiempo* and *El Espectador*, have moved their printing facilities to more peripheral sites. As a result, employment in the central area has been increasing much

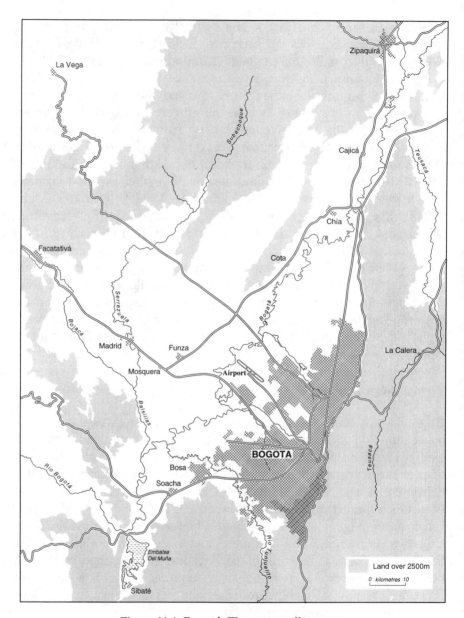

Figure 11.1 **Bogotá: The metropolitan area**

more slowly than in the city as a whole (Pineda and Jiménez, 1990). New sub-centres have also emerged, many located around shopping malls, such as Unicentro and Búlevar Niza, others connected with office developments, such as the National Administrative Centre

(CAN), new transport termini, such as the Terminal de Buses, and new wholesale market centres, such as Corabastos. During the past twenty or thirty years, the central area's dominance has declined sharply.

The city's residential structure has also changed. In the 1930s, the rich lived in the north of the city and the poor in the south (Amato, 1969). Figure 11.2 shows that today the social geography of the city is less easy to describe. Two main factors explain this shift (see chapter 4). First, high-income residential areas have expanded outwards until they have reached older low-income areas. Second, the rising price of land has forced the expanding middle class to occupy land in areas that would earlier have been regarded as beyond the social pale. During the 1970s, several large construction companies developed middle-class suburbs on land in the west and south-west (Gilbert and Ward, 1985: 116).

Mohan (1994: 93) claims that in the 1970s, "the spatial separation of rich and poor appears to have increased ... The spatial separation is more pronounced by radial sectors than by distance from the city center, the norm in cities in developed countries." Certainly there is little sign that the level of segregation has declined since 1980. Recent changes have made no difference to the huge social divide between *barrios* in Bogotá; most suburbs are socially homogeneous and are clearly recognizable as the territory of a particular income group. Vast tracts of land are occupied by low-income groups while other areas have few poor people. In 1985, for example, the Ciudad Bolívar district had 29 per cent of its population living in miserable housing conditions and 41 per cent living in overcrowded shelter; by contrast, Chapinero, Antonio Nariño, and Teusaquillo had very few families living in such conditions (Molina et al., 1993: 45).

Housing

There is a lot of good housing in Bogotá. Vast areas in the north and west of the city provide good accommodation for the extensive middle class, and much of the working class lives in well-consolidated self-help housing. Judged by the standards of most third world cities, and even those of other Colombian cities, most families have decent shelter. Equally encouraging is that the general standard of Bogotá's housing improved between 1951 and 1985 (table 11.7). At the same time, the city has a serious housing problem and far too many families live in bad accommodation. In 1985, 13 per cent of Bogotá's homes

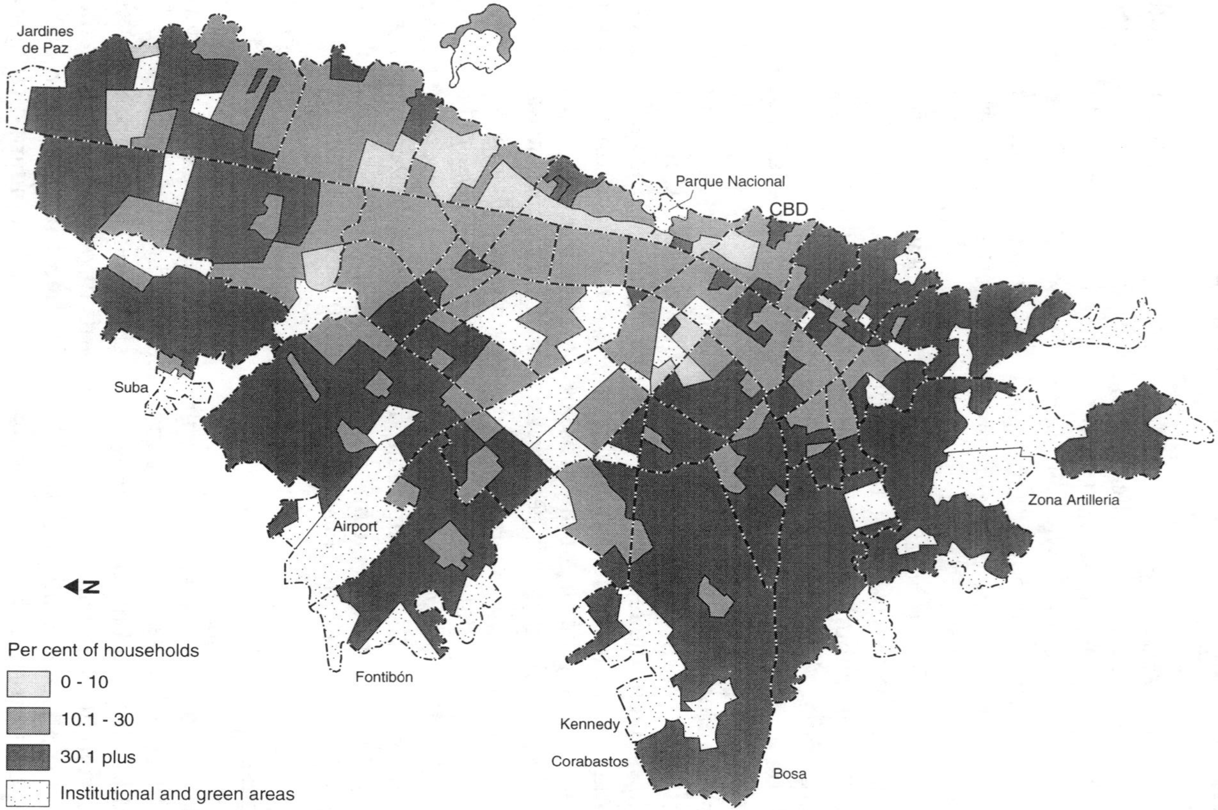
Jardines de Paz
Parque Nacional
CBD
Suba
Airport
Fontibón
Kennedy
Corabastos
Bosa
Zona Artilleria
N
Per cent of households
0 - 10
10.1 - 30
30.1 plus
Institutional and green areas

Figure 11.2 **Bogotá: Homes with miserable living conditions, 1985**

Table 11.7 **Bogotá: Housing indicators, 1951–1993 (percentages)**

Service	1951	1964	1973	1985	1993
Water	85.8	89.5	91.8	95.9	88.3
Electricity	81.9	88.1	95.3	98.4	90.0
Drainage	80.0	87.6	91.7	95.6	86.3
All three services	n.a.	n.a.	87.1	93.5	n.a.
Without any service	n.a.	2.7	2.4	0.7	1.0
Ownership	42.7	46.2	41.9	57.1	n.a.
Population living 4 persons to a room	7.6	18.5	23.0	14.9	n.a.
Homes built of flimsy materials	9.5	7.6	7.0	3.2	3.2

Sources: Jaramillo, 1990; *El Tiempo*, 3 August 1994.

were overcrowded and 4 per cent of families lived in miserable housing conditions. Table 11.7 shows that conditions for many households deteriorated between 1985 and 1993. Critically, the service agencies seem to have lost their earlier ability to supply the expanding city.

A high proportion of Bogotá's population lives in self-help housing. This does not constitute a problem in itself because such housing often produces perfectly satisfactory accommodation. However, in Bogotá too much self-help housing is built on land which lacks services and where it is difficult to provide infrastructure cheaply. A lot of this housing lies below the level of the River Bogotá or on hillsides where it is expensive to provide water. Many of the difficulties are caused by the way that land is urbanized: most low-income settlements are developed through illegal processes.[9] Between 1935 and 1985, 31 per cent of all housing was built on land that was developed illegally. Admittedly, the proportion of homes built in such areas appears to be declining through time: 55 per cent of all homes were built in illegal subdivisions in the 1940s compared to "only" 29 per cent between 1973 and 1985 (Molina et al., 1993: 53). Nevertheless, despite regular government efforts to tackle the problem of "pirate" urbanization, it refuses to disappear.[10] Between 1987 and 1991, 127 hectares a year were developed in this manner, 42 per cent of the city's total new housing land (ibid.).

A further problem for housing in Bogotá is that the cost of land appears to be rising over time. FEDELONJAS (1988) claim that real land prices increased roughly sixfold between 1959 and 1988, and Villamizar (1982) calculates that they increased annually by 4 per cent per annum between 1955 and 1978. Prices in pirate settlements have risen as quickly as those in legal developments; according to Molina et al. (1993: 124), prices of plots have risen by annual rates of between 9 and 20 per cent in five peripheral districts of the city (Suba, Kennedy, Usme, San Cristóbal, and Usaquén). Although there are considerable doubts about the reliability of such data (see chapter 4), the real cost of land does seem to be rising over time. The rising price of land is cutting the size of the average plot. Between 1968 and 1973, the typical self-help plot was almost 200 square metres in area; between 1983 and 1985 the average had fallen to only 78 square metres (Molina, 1990: 305).[11] Too much self-help housing is now being built on tiny parcels of land. Many new developments in the south of the city are selling lots as small as 36 square metres. Unlike the better-off, who can compensate for higher land prices by building up, the poor "substitute land by crowding" (Mohan, 1994: 70).

Irrespective of the level of income, the size of the average new home in Bogotá is falling. In 1974, the average new home contained 191 square metres of floor space; by 1985 the mean had declined to 70 square metres. Homes for the rich declined from 245 square metres in 1974 to 112 square metres in 1985 (Molina et al., 1993: table 2.7). Of course, the tendency for more families to live in high-rise apartments explains part of this change, but the principal cause is higher prices.

Rising house prices are making it difficult for young middle-class families to buy their first home. The cost of one square metre of housing space rose 41 per cent faster than incomes between November 1981 and September 1990 (Soler, 1991). The construction boom of 1992–95 was also associated with a major rise in prices. At the very least, many young families are having to buy worse accommodation than in the past.

Public services

By the standards of most Latin American cities, the provision of public services in Bogotá is quite good. During the 1960s and 1970s, the authorities did an excellent job in providing the city with electricity, water, and telephones. The public transport system was never good, but Bogotá always had a relatively well-developed road network. The services and infrastructure required by commerce and industry were supplied through major investment projects, many financed by large loans from the multinational development banks.

Unfortunately, all is not well with the service agencies (see below) and fewer homes are being supplied with electricity, water, and drainage. Between 1985 and 1993, census data reveal that the proportion of homes with electricity fell from 98 per cent to 90 per cent and those with water from 96 per cent to 88 per cent.

Electricity

Bogotá is supplied by a decentralized local government agency. For years, the company was very successful in expanding capacity: between 1960 and 1980, electricity generation increased annually by 8.3 per cent (Otero and Avella, 1995). Unfortunately, demand was increasing even more quickly, and rationing was forced on the city in 1984 and again in 1992. On both occasions the situation was made worse by dry climatic conditions; a major problem since Colombia is almost entirely dependent on hydro-electric power. In 1992, indeed, the rationing was nationwide. The supply shortages were aggravated by the failure to complete major dam projects on time; Chingaza in the early 1980s, and Guavio in the late 1980s and early 1990s.

The electricity company currently faces a severe financial crisis and has an enormous debt. In 1990, it owed US$1,281 million abroad and US$228 million at home. Most of its financial problems are linked to the development of the Guavio generating complex. Begun in 1981, the first stage of the project should have been completed in 1987, but the scheme was not inaugurated until 1992, with the last of the five generating units not operating until June 1993.[12] The project was also plagued by vast cost overruns; it was estimated that costs in 1991 were 53 per cent higher than forecast (Otero and Avella, 1995: 85). The project has been managed very poorly, some would even say corruptly. The financial difficulties of the company were aggravated by devaluation in the middle 1980s, which greatly increased its foreign interest repayments, and by electricity rationing in 1992, which cut its revenues substantially. The loss of one-quarter of the electricity supplied to the city has not helped the financial situation (Otero and Avella, 1995).

The company's principal response to its financial crisis has been to raise prices. Residential tariffs rose 80 per cent between 1980 and 1992 and charges to commercial users by 150 per cent. The Chamber of Commerce complains that charges to industry are higher than those in any other city in the country and are probably higher than those anywhere in the Andean Pact (Fernández, 1994: 45). Prices will continue to rise over the next few years as the company seeks to improve its financial situation. Fortunately, the worst of the company's problems are probably behind it.

The interesting question is how the company got itself into such a mess. In the 1970s, it was one of Bogotá's most efficient state agencies and under close scrutiny from the World Bank. Some blame the politicization of the board of directors after 1970, something that has been modified by the Reform Statute of 1993. Others blame loose supervision over the Guavio project. Whatever the cause, the electricity company changed from being one of Bogotá's strengths to being its Achilles' heel.

Water and sanitation

Water and sanitation are provided by a decentralized agency of the city government. For many years the company managed to expand capacity; between 1971 and 1991, it supplied three million additional people (Yepes, 1993: 76). While the agency's ability to provide sewerage was less impressive, and its failure to treat waste was lamentable (see below), its general performance was not unimpressive (Gilbert and Ward, 1985). During the 1980s, however, service provision failed to keep up with the growth of the city. By the late 1980s, although sufficient water was available, the company lacked the means to distribute it (Díaz Arbeláez, 1988: 269). The company was also facing a worsening financial situation. It failed to charge most customers the full economic cost of the service, a situation aggravated by the loss of a great deal of water. In 1991, the company could not account for 44 per cent of its water (Yepes, 1993: 78).

Telephones

Telephones in the city are also operated by a decentralized agency of the Bogotá government. During the 1980s, the number of lines rose annually by 8 per cent (CCB, 1991: 180), and in 1990 there were more than one million subscribers. The major difficulties facing the company are the lack of lines in the poorer areas of the city, particularly in Bosa, Ciudad Bolívar, San Cristóbal, and Usme, and a shortage of public telephones. It is also claimed that the company is run rather inefficiently; it has too large a staff and has been improving their working conditions at the expense of the company (Pachón and Associates, 1992: 276).

Health

Health care in Bogotá is provided by the private sector, the social security system, and public hospitals and clinics. In theory, the first deals with the better-off, the second with formal-sector workers, and the third with those not covered by the first two systems. Until 1995, the social security system provided only limited cover for workers' families and its coverage was therefore very patchy. In 1986, 72 per cent of salaried workers were eligible for care but only 33 per cent of non-salaried workers, 44 per cent of the economically inactive, and 47 per cent of children under five (Yepes and Bosoni, 1993: 62). The pattern of use in the different health sectors cannot easily be generalized, because it varies greatly according to the kind of treatment required. Consultations with private doctors are common among all income groups, but few hospital patients are treated privately: in 1986, 65 per cent of cases were treated in public hospitals, 16 per cent in social security clinics, and 18 per cent in private hospitals (Yepes and Bosoni, 1993: 63).

At its best, private health care is excellent; at its worst, it is both expensive and of poor quality. Even more questions have to be asked about the effectiveness of the official health systems. First, although the population of Bogotá is increasing rapidly, the number of hospital beds is falling. In 1970, the city had 9,378 beds, but by 1990 the total had fallen to 8,425. There is a grave shortage of emergency beds: in 1986, there were 17.5 emergency beds per 100,000 people in the private and social security sectors but only 4.3 beds per 100,000 in the public system.

Second, the quality of treatment leaves a great deal to be desired. One recent account of the health system (Caro, 1990: 93) began with the following comment:

For the user of the state's health services, speaking of medical attention is immediately associated with long queues (due both to the number of patients and non-attendance by the doctor); impolite or inconsiderate treatment; the need to pay for critical elements of treatment; the poor location of the health-care facilities; hospital hours that do not meet the needs of the patients; and so on.

Third, the social security and government systems are badly managed. Many beds are underutilized while some specialized hospitals deal with many cases that ought to be treated in lower-grade units. Such inefficiency is a result of inadequate budgets and overcentralization; in turn, both are an outcome of too much political interference in the management of the sector.

It is a sad fact that although infant mortality and general death rates have fallen dramatically in Bogotá, the public health system has contributed little to the improvement. Better health is a consequence of rising living standards; the public health system continues to be a disgrace.

Education

Most primary school education is provided by the public sector (62 per cent of students in 1988), although most students at the secondary and tertiary levels study in private institutions (60 per cent and 79 per cent of students respectively) (Rodríguez, 1990: 236–8). At all levels of education, the poorer the family the more likely the children are to depend on the public sector. Unfortunately, even if education standards in the public sector are better in Bogotá than in the rest of Colombia, the quality is still rather low. Large numbers of students drop out and many others are forced to repeat years. Student–staff ratios are also rather high; in 1988, there were 34 students per teacher in public primary schools and 24 in secondary schools.

Despite these problems, levels of education in Bogotá have improved over time. Literacy rose from 85 per cent in 1971 to 96 per cent in 1993, and primary and secondary school recruitment increased from 74 per cent to 83 per cent over the same period (Rinaudo et al., 1994: 28).

Public transport

Bogotá's transport system is now run wholly by the private sector. The national railway company operates inter-city services but runs no commuter trains. Although numerous plans have been developed to construct some kind of metro (see below), nothing has so far been built. As a result, Bogotá's population is wholly dependent on road transport.

For many years a public bus company operated in a small-scale and very inefficient way. The government compensated for the failures of its own company by subsidizing private bus services. However, as the cost of the subsidy rose, cuts were required. Today, subsidies are limited and bus fares are increasing in real terms. A further problem is that many companies have chosen to operate smaller buses, which has contributed to the level of traffic congestion (Acevedo, 1990). Congestion is aggravated by the fact that most buses follow similar routes to the city centre. Traffic conditions are hardly helped by the way that both buses and passengers ignore the bus stops. Buses swerve dangerously across the traffic lanes when they spot a potential passenger.

What many *bogotanos* want is a metro system (see below). The problem here is simple; neither the national nor the city government wants to pay for it. Clearly, any metro system will not be finished for many years.

The city's principal problems

In addition to the long-standing challenges facing the city in terms of employment, housing, health, education, public transport, and economic growth, there are four current issues which are exciting considerable discussion in Bogotá: the high rate of crime, the deteriorating urban environment, traffic congestion, and the quality of the city's government.

Crime

Colombia has a reputation as a violent country and the country's major cities have long suffered from high crime rates. In 1993, there were 58 murders for every 100,000 inhabitants in Bogotá, placing it among the world's most violent cities.[13] The rate is also increasing: in 1971 there were "only" 23 murders per 100,000 people.

It is uncertain whether the murder rate is increasing faster than crime generally, and there has long been a justified concern about the high incidence of burglary. Private security firms are benefiting greatly from the booming demand for their services: currently the city has three times more people working for private security firms than for the police (Londoño de la Cuesta, 1992: 22). Fear of crime has also affected lifestyles; many upper-middle-class families have forsaken their detached houses for the relative security of high-rise flats and few housing estates are built without elaborate security devices.

Environment

The city dumps most of its waste directly into the River Bogotá and the amount of sewage has now overwhelmed the river. It is estimated that the inflow of sewage is roughly equal to the amount of water carried by the river at Cota (*Coyuntura Social*, 1990: 50). Human waste, industrial effluent, motor oil, and fertilizer all go straight into the river.

The level of pollution affects the health of communities living close to the river and its tributaries. Sanitary conditions close to the Tunjuelito river in the south of the city are particularly bad. Since the polluted water is also used for irrigation, all of Bogotá's people are at risk when they consume milk and vegetables produced near to the city.

Air pollution is also getting worse. Pollution levels are particularly high along the major bus routes, in the industrial zone and in the poor south (*Coyuntura Social*, 1990). In 1990, suspended air particles reached 567 microgrammes per cubic metre in the south, sulphur dioxide levels peaked at 95 particles per billion, and nitrogen oxide at 278 particles per billion. The air quality is certainly not helped by temperature inversions and by the amount of traffic.

Noise pollution is also reaching dangerous levels. Along the main roads in the central area, noise levels regularly exceed the 80 decibel maximum recommended by the health authorities (Londoño de la Cuesta, 1992: 28).

Traffic congestion

Congestion is becoming a really serious issue in the city. Along the two major bus routes into the centre, Avenida Caracas and Carrera Décima, average speeds are often as low as 15 kilometres per hour (*Coyuntura Social*, 1991: 40). The major cause of congestion is the huge expansion in private car ownership. Between 1977 and 1985, the number of road vehicles registered in Bogotá and ten nearby municipalities increased annually by 8 per cent (Acevedo, 1990: 92). In 1993, 460,000 vehicles were registered in Bogotá. But, if vehicles registered in the neighbouring muncipalities are included, the number of vehicles regularly using Bogotá's streets rose from 232,000 in 1977 to 825,000 in 1993.

For many, the only answer to the traffic problem is to build a metro. For years *bogotanos* have been demanding such a "solution" and, in 1989, Congress established the ground rules for metro construction (Acevedo, 1990: 106). The key issues are now its cost, the kind of system to use, and who will pay for it. It seems unlikely that

Bogotá will ever build an underground system because that would be far too expensive. The most probable answer is a mass-transit system that will use the existing rail tracks. This leaves the problem of who will pay for it. Congress has decreed that the national government should contribute no more than one-fifth of the investment cost, Bogotá covering the rest as well as the full cost of running the system. The mayor of Bogotá is currently involved in a public debate with the National Planning Department about the level of the city's contribution. Clearly, nothing will happen for many years; until then, journey times will continue to lengthen.

The quality of government

Bogotanos have long thought that their city was badly governed. By the end of the 1980s, when the local authority owed some US$2 billion dollars, they knew it was poorly managed.

The state of the public service agencies certainly leaves a great deal to be desired. First, their total debt currently makes up 90 per cent of that of the city (Castro, 1994: 38). Second, they are failing to keep up with the demand for their services: water, electricity, and sewerage coverage all declined during the 1990s. Third, they are being managed very badly: they have too many workers, there is too much corruption, and there is excessive political interference in the companies' day-to-day activities (Yepes, 1993; Díaz Arbeláez, 1988; Gilbert, 1990). Finally, most companies charge less than the cost of the service and, in the process of trying to help the poor, they often subsidize higher income groups.

The government of Bogotá's image is also not helped by the fact that one million people are living in poverty, traffic is almost at a standstill, and the public health system is in chaos. The public's view was echoed recently by the president of the local chamber of commerce:

It is an open secret that Bogotá has become the most difficult city in the country to manage. The lack of any community identity, the lack of any kind of systematic or integrated planning, the long-standing institutional limbo that has slowed its administrative development, and the increasingly suffocating financial constraints which prevent it from satisfying the needs of its inhabitants, have led everyone to think that Bogotá is an ungovernable city. (Férnandez de Soto, 1994)

Administration of the city

In an attempt to improve the quality of Bogotá's administration, a new statute was approved in 1993. Bogotá was made into a Capital District and relations between the mayor and the council were altered substantially. The decree also sought to improve the city's financial situation, to reduce the possibilities for fraud and corruption, to improve the management of its decentralized service agencies, and to increase the opportunities for public participation. How effective are the changes likely to be in improving management of the city?

The creation of a Capital District

Bogotá is geographically part of the surrounding Department of Cundinamarca. For years the city was a municipality within the department. The city always wanted independence; the department long feared for its financial health if its major source of income were removed. This conflict of interest resulted in the administrative status of the city changing several times during the century (Vidal-Perdomo, 1994). In 1905 Bogotá was elevated to a Capital District, but in 1909 it was returned to the department. The 1945 Constitution stipulated that Bogotá could withdraw from Cundinamarca, and in 1954 Bogotá became a Special District. In 1991, the national constitution again established Bogotá as a Capital District.

In becoming a Capital District, Bogotá has achieved three new rights. First, it has become a separate electoral area, sending its own representatives to the national Congress. Second, it has obtained administrative autonomy from the Department of Cundinamarca. Finally, it has obtained more control over its own budget. Seemingly, Bogotá could have won these additional rights while remaining a Special District; according to Vidal-Perdomo (1994: 54) not a great deal has changed.

The mayor and the council

Bogotá's mayor used to be appointed by the national president and the first election for mayor did not take place until March 1988. The first three incumbents were members of one of the country's two major parties but the current mayor, Antanas Mockus, was elected largely because he represented no party at all.[14]

The relationship between the mayor and the council has always been different from that in most other Latin American cities (see chapter 3). The mayor has never been an appointee of the council nor a member of it. Today, he is elected independently (Vidal-Perdomo, 1994: 56). One result of the mayor's independence is that relations between the mayor and the council have always been difficult. Their relationship has not been eased by the overlapping responsibilities of the two. The 1993 reforms tried to remedy that situation. They made the council responsible for legislation and for overseeing the actions of the executive and made the mayor responsible for administering the city. In practice, the change seems to have given more powers to the mayor and less to the council.

So far, the new division of responsibilities does not seem to have helped reduce conflict. Relations between Mayor Mockus and the council have been troublesome. The problems may reflect the independent political status of the mayor. If not, they are an in-built feature of the new arrangements.

Improving the city's finances

During the 1980s, Bogotá's spending soared but its tax revenues did not (Pachón and Associates, 1992: 274). The government relied on credit to balance the books and took on new loans to soften its debt payments. Even though their incomes rose, *bogotanos* were paying the same amount in taxes in 1993 as they had in 1961 (Castro, 1994; Fernández de Soto, 1994). Taxes per capita were well below those in Medellín (Montenegro, 1992) and, in 1992, taxes amounted to only 2.4 per cent of the city's gross regional product (Orozco and Pardo, 1992: 315).

The recent reforms aim to rectify this situation. They have created new sources of income, increasing the sums likely to be generated by the general valorization tax, improving the procedure for assessing property values and allowing the mayor to apply a levy on the price of gasoline. Although the statute did not provide the authorities with any additional taxes, it does allow tolls to be charged on new roads, thereby encouraging the construction of privately run freeways (Castro, 1994: 38).

What the statute fails to do is to increase the amount of money that the city receives from the national government. Although Bogotá generates a large share of the country's tax revenues, it receives a relatively small proportion of the money that the national government allocates to local government.[15] As a result, although the

263

financial health of Bogotá has improved, the future continues to look uncertain.

The public service agencies

The large public service agencies are all decentralized institutes of the Bogotá government. They have long had independent boards of directors. For many years a majority of directors were representatives of major financial institutions (Gilbert and Ward, 1985) but, gradually, more and more directors were political appointees. The latter have been blamed for many of the failings of the agencies and the 1993 reforms have changed the appointment process. Councillors can no longer act as directors, nor can they appoint their own representatives. Two-thirds of the members of the boards will be named by the mayor and the remaining one-third will be delegates of users, civic organizations, trades unions, or the community. The powers of the directors have also been reduced and full responsibility for negotiating contracts has been given to the chief executive. The agencies have also been turned into industrial and commercial companies which, it is hoped, will improve their accounting and management systems and will encourage them to collaborate more with the private sector (Cárdenas and Olaya, 1994).

Moralization

An effort has also been made to reduce the opportunities for corruption (Castro, 1994). A public "observer" has been appointed to oversee the efficiency and honesty of government. In addition, the mayor and his appointees now have total responsibility for negotiating contracts. It is hoped that the transparency of the new arrangements will increase accountability.

The future

Undoubtedly, Bogotá faces a series of major challenges. It has to compete in an increasingly competitive international market, even if it is not well positioned to do so. It has to create up to one million jobs in the next decade (Fernández de Soto, 1994: 45). It has to resolve the serious problem of its traffic congestion. It has to improve the quality of its administration and put its service agencies back on track. It has to overcome the government's debt problem while also facing up to the possible costs of building a new metro system. It also has to tackle the rising crime wave.

In overcoming these challenges, Bogotá has a significant advantage. Unlike most of its Latin American neighbours, the Colombian economy experienced few problems during the 1980s and can look forward to rapid growth in the future. The discovery of vast new reserves of petroleum and minerals should at least maintain the current rate of economic growth. Bogotá will find it easier to improve living conditions if the economy continues to grow at around 5 per cent per annum.

Bogotá also has the advantage that it has not accumulated a "social debt"; few of its social problems actually got worse during the 1980s. During the last three decades, poverty declined and the quality of housing and service provision improved.

But there is no room for complacency. Crime, pollution, and traffic congestion are getting worse. And, in so far as the ordinary *bogotano* is living in better accommodation and owns more consumer durables than ever before, it has not been due to any improvement in the distribution of income or the quality of public administration. If family incomes have risen, it is because more people are working; salaries for most ordinary workers have hardly changed. If most households now have a television set, it is because more family members are employed. Whether this has improved the quality of life is debatable, although it would certainly be deemed to be progress by the poor of Buenos Aires, Lima, Mexico City, and Rio de Janeiro. In this sense, Bogotá is very much a special case among the mega-cities of Latin America. In comparison with the region's other metropolitan areas, its future is generally very promising.

Notes

1. Bogotá was renamed Santa Fé de Bogotá in 1993, when the national government issued a decree laying down the political, administrative, and fiscal responsibilities of the new Capital District. I shall continue to refer to the city by its earlier name, the one still used by the majority of its people.
2. Colombia's economy grew annually at 4.7 per cent between 1981 and 1994. Its economy never actually declined in any year during that period.
3. This tendency has continued to this day. Of the 70,000 migrants who arrived in the city between September 1991 and August 1992, 65 per cent were women (Castañeda, 1993: 122).
4. Migration was increasing Bogotá's population annually by 2 per cent during the early 1970s; in the early 1990s, by 1.5 per cent (Castañeda, 1993: 123). This calculation was based on a 1992 population of 4.9 millions. If in fact it was 6.3 millions the rate was only 1.2 per cent.

5. This figure compares with $667 in the case of Santiago de Chile, $723 in São Paulo, and $813 in Mexico City (Pineda et al., 1993: 33).
6. Those who are out of work tend to be less well-qualified. Workers with a secondary education are almost twice as likely to be unemployed as university graduates. In terms of age, 20–29 year olds are three times as likely to be unemployed as 30–59 year olds. Women are more than twice as likely to be unemployed as men.
7. Rates for March each year. There have been major variations in the level of unemployment since 1980. The peak of 14.3 per cent was reached in 1986, the low of 5.8 per cent in 1981 (DANE, 1991).
8. The unsatisfied basic needs index was developed by the United Nations. It measures the quality of housing construction, the level of household services, the extent of overcrowding, and the numbers of young children not attending primary school. It is intended as a measure of structural poverty. Short-term poverty is measured in terms of the ability of families to buy a basket of essential goods.
9. Land is rarely invaded in Bogotá. Most is subdivided illegally by the owner. Full descriptions of this process in Bogotá are included in Doebele (1975), Vernez (1993), Cardona (1969), Carroll (1980), and Gilbert (1981).
10. The authorities have tried to prohibit "pirate" urbanization, have arrested the developers, have tried to launch official sites and services programmes, have legalized and serviced illegal developments, and have eased the planning requirements on such developments, all without success. For many years, the public sector also built homes for the poor (Gutiérrez Cuevas, 1989; Jaramillo, 1982 and 1990; Laun, 1976; Ortiz, 1995; Robledo, 1985). Between 1973 and 1985, the state built 29 per cent of all the homes constructed legally in the city, even if its annual output varied dramatically. For example, state housing accounted for 51 per cent of all construction in 1973 and 46 per cent in 1980, but only 18 per cent in 1974 and 15 per cent in 1983 (Molina et al., 1993: 58).
11. In the 1970s, lot sizes in new self-help settlements in Bogotá were already smaller than in Mexico City and in Valencia, Venezuela (Gilbert and Ward, 1985).
12. Located 120 kilometres by road to the east of the city, the project's first stage was planned to add 1,000 megawatts of capacity and the second stage a further 600 megawatts. Total effective capacity of the whole Bogotá generating system at the end of 1987 was 1,259 megawatts (Díaz Arbeláez, 1988: 278).
13. According to Camp (1994: 78) the most violent place among the 100 largest cities in the world was Cape Town, with 65 murders per 100,000 inhabitants. The only consolation is that Bogotá's rate is well below the average for the country as a whole: 82 murders per 100,000 people (Rinaudo et al., 1994: 29).
14. The following mayors have been democratically elected: Andrés Pastrana (1988–89), from the Conservative Party; Juan Manuel Caicedo Ferrer (1990–91), representing the Liberal Party; Jaime Castro (1992–94), from the Liberal Party; and Antanas Mockus (1995–date), representing an independent alliance. The city has traditionally had a large Liberal majority: Andrés Pastrana won in March 1988 because the Liberal Party put up two candidates. Recently, local electorates in Colombia have frequently been returning "non-political" candidates to mayoral office; Antanas Mockus was one such candidate.
15. Fernández (1994: 43) claims that although Bogotá has 15 per cent of Colombia's people it receives only 9.3 per cent of the *situado fiscal* and 7.4 per cent of the municipal transfers.

References

Acevedo, J. (1990) "El transporte en Bogotá." In López et al. (eds.), 89–114.
Alcaldía Mayor de Bogotá and Cámara de Comercio de Bogotá (1987) *Bogotá para todos 1987–1990.* Bogotá.

Amato, P. (1969) "Environmental quality and locational behaviour in a Latin American city." *Urban Affairs Quarterly* 11: 83–101.

ANDI [Asociación National de Industriales] (1994) *Industria manufacturera colombiana 1983–1992.* Bogotá.

Camp, S. (1994) "Condiciones de vida en las 100 áreas metropolitanas más grandes del mundo." *Revista Camacol* 59, 74–82.

Cárdenas, M., and J. Olaya (1994) "Empresas de servicios públicos: Una administración ágil y eficiente." *Revista de la Cámara de Comercio de Bogotá* 89: 57–64.

Cardona, R. (1969) *Las invasiones de terrenos urbanos.* Tercer Mundo.

Caro, B.L. (1990) "La administración de salud pública en Bogotá: Una prioridad y un reto por resolver." *Coyuntura Social* 3: 93–116.

Carreiro, Y.P. (1992) "El sector de energía eléctrica." In DNP (ed.), 103–114.

Carroll, A. (1980) "Pirate urbanizations and the market for residential lots." In *Bogotá*, City Study Project no. 7. World Bank.

Castañeda, W. (1993) "Patrones de migración hacia Bogotá, Medellín, Cali y Barranquilla. Un estudio comparativo." *Coyuntura Social* 9, 121–35.

Castro, J. (1994) "Herramientas contra la corrupción y la deshonestad." *Revista de la Cámara de Comercio de Bogotá* 89: 35–8.

CCB [Cámara de Comercio de Bogotá] (1991) *Bogotá en la década de los 80: Indicadores para la toma de decisiones en la década del noventa.* Bogotá.

DANE [Departamento Nacional de Estadística] (1991) *20 años de la encuesta de hogares en Colombia.* Bogotá.

———— (1992) *Cuentas departamentales de Colombia 1980–1989.* Bogotá.

Díaz Arbeláez, J. (1988) "Los servicios públicos en el Distrito Especial de Bogotá." In P. Santana et al. (eds.), *Bogotá 450 años: Retos y realidades*, Ediciones Foro Nacional, 247–313.

DNP [Departamento Nacional de Planeación] (1991) *La Revolución Pacífica.* Santafé de Bogotá.

———— (1995) *El salto social: Plan National de Desarrollo: Ley de inversiones 1994–1998.* Santafé de Bogotá.

DNP (ed.) (1992) *Bogotá: Problemas y soluciones.* Bogotá.

Doebele, W. (1975) "The private market and low-income urbanization in developing countries: The 'pirate' subdivision of Bogotá." Harvard University, Department of City and Regional Planning Discussion Paper D75–11.

Escobar, D. (no date) *El futuro de la capital: Pobreza y distribución del ingreso.* Misión Bogotá Siglo XXI.

FEDELONJAS Federación Colombiana de Lonjas de Propiedad Raíz] (1988) *El valor del suelo urbano en Bogotá, 1959–1988.* Bogotá.

Fernández de Soto, G. (1994) "Bogotá: Crisis es oportunidad." *Revista de la Cámara de Comercio de Bogotá* 89: 39–46.

Forero, C. (1995) "Participación participativa: Una primera evaluación." *Revista Foro* 26: 25–30.

Forero, E., et al. (1995) *Estudio prospectivo de las relaciones de Santafé de Bogotá con Cundinamarca.* Misión Siglo XXI.

Gilbert, A.G. (1975) "Urban and regional development programs in Colombia since 1951." In W. Cornelius and F. Trueblood (eds.), *Latin American urban research* 5, Sage, 241–75.

—— (1978) "Bogotá: Politics, planning, and the crisis of lost opportunities." In W. Cornelius and R.V. Kemper (eds.), *Latin American urban research* 6, Sage, 87–126.

—— (1981) "Pirates and invaders: Land acquisition in urban Colombia and Venezuela." *World Development* 9: 657–78.

—— (1990) "The provision of public services and the debt crisis in Latin America: The case of Bogotá." *Economic Geography* 66: 349–61.

—— (1994) *The Latin American city.* Latin America Bureau.

Gilbert, A.G., and P.M. Ward (1985) *Housing, the state and the poor: Policy and practice in three Latin American cities.* Cambridge University Press. Published in Spanish in 1987 as: *Asentamientos populares versus el poder del estado*, Gustavo Gili, Mexico City.

—— (1986) "Latin American migrants: A tale of three cities." In F. Slater (ed.), *Peoples and environments: Issues and enquiries*, Collins Educational, 24–42.

Gómez, A., and M.A. Pérez (no date) *El futuro de la capital: El mercado laboral.* Misión Bogotá Siglo XXI.

Gutiérrez Cuevas, C. (1989) "ICT: 50 años cumpliendo con Colombia." *Revista Camacol* 39: 10–22.

Jaramillo, S. (1982) "La política de vivienda en Colombia ¿hacia una redefinición de sus objetivos?" *Desarrollo y Sociedad Cuaderno* 4: 11–26.

—— (1990) "La estructura urbana y la vivienda en Bogotá." In López et al. (eds.), 51–88.

Jaramillo, S., and L.M. Cuervo (1987) *La configuración del espacio regional en Colombia.* CEDE Serie Estudios 1, Universidad de los Andes.

Laun, J.I. (1976) "El estado y la vivienda en Colombia: Análisis de urbanizaciones del Instituto de Crédito Territorial en Bogotá." In C. Castillo, (ed.), *Vida urbana y urbanismo*, Instituto Colombiano de Cultura, 295–334.

Londoño de la Cuesta, J.L. (1992) "Problemas, instituciones y finanzas para el desarrollo de Bogotá: Algunos interrogantes." In DNP (ed.), 13–38.

López, J.F. (1990) "Características económicas de Bogotá." In López et al. (eds.), 21–50.

López, J.F., et al. (eds.) (1990) *Vivir en Bogotá.* Ediciones Foro Nacional por Colombia.

Mohan, R. (1994) *Understanding the developing metropolis: Lessons from the City Study of Bogotá and Cali, Colombia.* Oxford University Press.

Molina, H. (1990) "Bogotá: competition and substitution between urban land markets." In P. Baross and J. van der Linden (eds.), *The transformation of land supply systems in third world cities*, Avebury, 295–308.

Molina, I., et al. (1993) *El futuro de la capital: Estudio prospectivo de vivienda.* Misión Bogotá Siglo XXI.

Montenegro, A. (1992) "Palabras." In DNP (ed.), 451–63.

Muñoz, M. (1991) "La pobreza en 13 ciudades según líneas de pobreza e indigencia 1985." In Fresneda, O. et al. (eds.), *Pobreza, violencia y desigualdad: Retos para la nueva Colombia*, UNDP, 273–92.

Orozco, A.L., and S. Pardo (1992) "Comentarios." In DNP (ed.), 315–34.

Ortiz, C. (1995) "The impact of current global housing strategies on the development of the housing sector in Colombia." *DPU Working Paper* no. 71, University College London.

Otero, D., and L. Avella (1995) *Estudio prospectivo de energía eléctrica.* Misión Bogotá Siglo XXI.

Pachón, A., and Associates (1992) "Las finanzas del Distrito Capital: Visión retrospectiva, estado actual y perspectivas." In DNP (ed.), 121–308.

Pineda, J.F., and L.C. Jiménez (1990) "Consideraciones sobre el crecimiento físico de Bogotá D.E." Mimeo, Misión Bogotá Siglo XXI.

Pineda, S., A. Trejos, and E. Gerlein (1993) "Las empresas más exportadoras de Bogotá." *Revista de la Cámara de Comercio de Bogotá* 86: 26–30.

Rinaudo, U., C.G., Molina, M. Alviar, and D. Salazar (1994) *El futuro de la capital: Estudio prospectivo del desarrollo social y humano.* Misión Bogotá Siglo XXI.

Robledo, J. (1985) *El drama de la vivienda en Colombia y la política del "si se puede".* El Ancora Editores.

Rodríguez, A. (1990) "La educación en Bogotá." In López et al. (eds.), 209–77.

Salazar, S.E. (1994) "Vivienda social." *Revista Camacol* 61: 28–32.

Soler, Y. (1991) "La vivienda y el ingreso familiar en los años ochenta." Mimeo, Departamento Administrativo de Planeación Distrital, Bogotá.

Vernez, G. (1993) "Bogotá's pirate settlements: An opportunity for metropolitan development." Doctoral dissertation, University of California at Berkeley.

Vidal-Perdomo, J. (1994) "De Distrito Especial a Distrito Capital." *Revista de la Cámara de Comercio de Bogotá* 89: 47–56.

Villamizar, R. (1982) "Land prices in Bogotá between 1955 and 1978: A descriptive analysis." In J.V. Henderson (ed.), *Research in urban economics*, vol. 2. Jai Press.

Yepes, G. (1993) "La situación de la EAAB desde una perspectiva internacional." *Revista Camacol* 55: 76–82.

Yepes, F.J., and M. Bosoni (1993) *Estudio prospectivo de la salud.* Misión Bogotá Siglo XXI.

Contributors

Luís Ainstein Instituto Superior de Urbanismo, Facultad de Arquitectura, Diseño y Urbanismo, University of Buenos Aires, Argentina.

Oscar Figueroa Monsalve Instituto de Estudios Urbanos, Universidad Católica de Chile, Santiago, Chile.

Alan Gilbert Department of Geography, University College London, United Kingdom.

Peter Gordon School of Urban and Regional Planning, University of Southern California, Los Angeles, California, USA.

Gustavo Riofrío Centro de Estudios y Promoción del Desarrollo (DESCO), Lima, Peru.

Jorge Rodríguez Centro Latinoamericano de Demografía (CELADE), Santiago, Chile.

Allison Rowland School of Urban and Regional Planning, University of Southern California, Los Angeles, California, USA.

Milton Santos Facultade de Filosofia, Letras e Ciências Humanas, Universidade de São Paulo, Brazil.

Hamilton Tolosa Directoria de Projetos Especiais, Conjunto Universitario Candido Mendes, Rio de Janeiro, Brazil.

Miguel Villa Centro Latinoamericano de Demografía (CELADE), Santiago, Chile.

Peter Ward Lyndon B. Johnson School of Public Affairs, University of Texas at Austin, USA.

270

Index